# The Art and Craft of Political Theory

*The Art and Craft of Political Theory* provides a critical overview of the discipline's core concepts and concerns and highlights its development of critical thinking and practical judgment. The field's interdisciplinary strengths are deployed to grapple with emerging issues and engage afresh enduring ideals and quandaries. While conventional definitions of key concepts are provided, original and controversial perspectives are also explored, revealing continuity in a tradition of thought while emphasizing its diversity and innovations. *The Art and Craft of Political Theory* illustrates the analytic and interpretive skills, the moral and philosophic discernment, and the historical knowledge needed to appreciate a tradition of thought, to contest its claims, and to make good use of its insights.

Topics include:

- science, ideology and normative theory
- biology, culture, human nature, power and violence
- ancient, modern and postmodern political thought
- liberty, equality, justice, reason and democracy
- racial, religious, gender and economic identities
- liberalism, socialism, capitalism, communism, anarchism, feminism and environmentalism
- social media, automation, artificial intelligence and other emerging technologies.

This concise, lively and accessibly written book is essential reading for all students of political theory.

**Leslie Paul Thiele** is Distinguished Professor of Political Science at the University of Florida and Director of the Center for Adaptive Innovation, Resilience, Ethics and Science. His teaching and interdisciplinary research focuses on political thought, sustainability, emerging technologies and the intersection of political philosophy and the natural sciences. His central concerns are the responsibilities of citizenship and opportunities for leadership in a world of rapid technological, social and ecological change.

"Theory is essential, in navigating politics no less than elsewhere. If you want to know how to read, interpret, assess and craft political theory, this is the book for you. Leslie Thiele is a splendid guide to the world of political theory."

—*John S. Dryzek, Centre for Deliberative Democracy and*
*Global Governance, University of Canberra*

"I can think of no one better qualified to write the story of political theory than Leslie Paul Thiele. A long-time practitioner of the art and craft himself, Thiele brings erudition, rigor, clarity and fondness to this comprehensive study of the core and periphery of the field of political theory."

—*Simone Chambers, University of California, Irvine*

"To many 'political theory' sounds like an oxymoron; equated with the brute struggle for power, politics seems far removed from theory or reflection. As is evident from his earlier book *Thinking Politics*, Thiele has never subscribed to this view. Steeped in an older legacy, he has always celebrated politics as a thoughtful civic praxis, linked with prudence, foresight and moral responsibility. His new book *The Art and Craft of Political Theory* elaborates on the many implications of such praxis. May it serve as an antidote and bulwark against the thoughtless 'will to power' devotees in our time."

—*Fred Dallmayr, University of Notre Dame*

# THE ART AND CRAFT OF POLITICAL THEORY

## Leslie Paul Thiele

Routledge
Taylor & Francis Group

NEW YORK AND LONDON

First published 2019
by Routledge
711 Third Avenue, New York, NY 10017

and by Routledge
2 Park Square, Milton Park, Abingdon, Oxon, OX14 4RN

*Routledge is an imprint of the Taylor & Francis Group, an informa business*

*Library of Congress Cataloging-in-Publication Data*
Names: Thiele, Leslie Paul, author.
Title: The art and craft of political theory / Leslie Paul Thiele.
Description: New York, NY : Routledge, 2019. | Includes index.
Identifiers: LCCN 2018018580| ISBN 9781138616776 (hardback) | ISBN 9781138616790 (paperback) |
    ISBN 9780429461859 (Master) | ISBN 9780429867965 (WebPDF) | ISBN 9780429867958 (epub) | ISBN
    9780429867941 (mobipocket/kindle)
Subjects: LCSH: Political science—Philosophy.
Classification: LCC JA71 .T5195 2019 | DDC 320.01—dc23
LC record available at https://lccn.loc.gov/2018018580

ISBN: 978-1-138-61677-6 (hbk)
ISBN: 978-1-138-61679-0 (pbk)
ISBN: 978-0-429-46185-9 (ebk)

Typeset in ITC Legacy Serif
by Apex CoVantage, LLC

Printed and bound in Great Britain by
TJ International Ltd, Padstow, Cornwall

# CONTENTS

Introduction    1

1. Theory, Ideology and Irony    3

2. Human Nature, Power and Politics    37

3. Ancient, Modern and Postmodern Political Thought    71

4. The Politics of Identity and Difference    105

5. Enduring Challenges in a Changing World    140

6. Technology and the Human Prospect    174

*Index*    211

# DETAILED CONTENTS

| | |
|---|---|
| **Introduction** | **1** |
| 1. **Theory, Ideology and Irony** | **3** |
| Setting Our Sights | 3 |
| Parsimony, Accuracy and Significance | 5 |
| Scientific Theory and Social Science | 7 |
| The Interpretive Nature of Political Theory | 11 |
| Intersubjective Understanding | 13 |
| The Normative Nature of Theory | 16 |
| Conceptual and Historical Analysis | 20 |
| Ideology | 23 |
| Irony | 28 |
| Between Ideology and Irony | 30 |
| | |
| 2. **Human Nature, Power and Politics** | **37** |
| Political Animals | 37 |
| The Significance of Human Nature | 39 |
| Nature and Nurture | 44 |
| Genes and Mores | 46 |
| Biological and Cultural Reproduction | 49 |
| The Public Good and the Private Realm | 52 |
| Power, Force and Violence | 55 |
| Rule and Resistance | 60 |
| Equality and Elites | 64 |
| | |
| 3. **Ancient, Modern and Postmodern Political Thought** | **71** |
| Statecraft and Soulcraft in Ancient Greece | 71 |
| Ordering the Soul and State | 73 |
| Modern Political Thought | 78 |
| Individualist Theories of Politics | 82 |
| Structuralist Theories of Politics | 84 |
| Postmodern Thought | 88 |

Identity and the Exercise of Power                                93
Social Control and Individual Freedom                             97
Theorizing at the Edge of Modernity                              101

**4. The Politics of Identity and Difference**                  **105**
We Hold These Truths...                                          105
Race, Religion and Otherness                                     108
   *The Other in America*                          110
   *Identity and Difference*                       113
Gender and Identity                                              116
   *Feminism and Gender Justice*                   117
   *Equality and Difference*                       121
   *Liberalism, Patriarchy and Power Feminism*     124
The Politics of Class                                            127
   *Alienation and Revolution*                     128
   *Materialism and Idealism*                      130
   *Communism versus Socialism*                    134

**5. Enduring Challenges in a Changing World**                  **140**
The Life of Liberty                                              140
   *Positive and Negative Liberty*                 142
   *Forced to be Free*                             146
   *Freedom in the Balance*                        148
Rule within Reason                                               150
   *Economic Reason*                               151
   *Political Reason*                              154
   *Ecological Reason*                             157
The Scales of Justice                                            159
   *The Primacy of Justice*                        160
   *Equity and Practical Judgment*                 162
   *Giving to Each What is Due*                    165

**6. Technology and the Human Prospect**                        **174**
Promethean Origins                                               174
The Machinery of Government and Symbolic Tools                   176
Becoming the Tools of Our Tools                                  178
The Midas Touch                                                  181
Theories of Technology                                           185
The Politics of Information Technology                           190

Automation and Artificial Intelligence   197
The Technology of Theory   202
Conclusion   205

*Index*   211

# INTRODUCTION

This book introduces and illustrates the art and craft of political theory. Its aim is to foster a sensibility to the ways in which the domain of politics may be intellectually and ethically engaged. The art and craft of political theory is less the invocation of principles or application of techniques than an exercise in critical thinking and practical judgment. To learn political theory is to discover and develop the analytic and interpretive skills, the moral and philosophic discernment, and the social and historical knowledge needed to employ and advance the insights of a tradition of thought and contest its claims.

The study of political theory is often circumscribed within a canon of thinkers that originates in antiquity and proceeds through medieval and modern periods to contemporary times. Yet the canon is largely a retrospective construction. Most of its representative figures did not identify themselves as contributors to a single tradition. Nonetheless, the voices that animate the history of political thought have produced a sustained, if unruly, conversation over the ages. It is a conversation well worth entering.

References to canonical figures in these pages are meant less to invoke authorities than to stimulate and guide thinking about politics. While standard definitions of key political concepts are provided, they are also frequently challenged. In turn, original and controversial perspectives are explored. The point is to illustrate what it means to think theoretically about politics, acknowledging continuity in a tradition of thought without losing sense of its diversity and innovations.

Much of the diversity and innovation within political theory arises from its interdisciplinary nature. Political theory crossed paths with philosophy since ancient times, and is often called political philosophy. Today, the discipline intersects with many fields of study, including anthropology, ecology, economics, evolutionary biology, history, literary criticism, neuroscience, psychology, sociology and technological studies. *The Art and Craft of Political Theory* makes use of these kindred disciplines to grapple with emerging issues and engage afresh enduring concepts, ideals, and quandaries.

1

Some sections of my book *Thinking Politics* (2003) have been utilized here in a revised form. Much of what follows is wholly new, including the final chapter. There I tie the knot in a unifying thread running through these pages, and provide an original reframing of the mission of political theory. Like the tradition of thought it examines and appraises, this book demonstrates continuity and innovation in its voices. My hope is that the reader finds the conversation more sustained than unruly, and well worth entering.

## CHAPTER 1

# THEORY, IDEOLOGY AND IRONY

Political theory is an art and craft that cultivates and employs critical thinking and practical judgment. The chapter distinguishes political theory from scientific theory while underlining their shared concern for parsimony, accuracy and significance. The discipline's interpretive, intersubjective, normative, conceptual and historical nature is explored, as well as its fraught relationship with ideology. In turn, the chapter introduces the notion of irony, a kind of skeptical reserve that serves political theorists as a countervailing force to ideology.

## SETTING OUR SIGHTS

We all have lenses in our eyes that focus light on our retinas. Many people also wear optical lenses made of glass or plastic to correct poor vision. In turn, microscopes and telescopes have magnifying lenses that bend light in specific ways, allowing one to see very small or very distant objects. Lenses focus light to produce clear images.

Theories are best understood as conceptual lenses. Theories help us put the world in focus. What optical lenses do for our vision, theories do for our understanding. Whereas optical lenses improve our sight, theories improve our insight. Theories help us produce clear mental images.

Most of us can see quite well without artificial lenses. Our unaided vision suffices. Likewise, most of us can get along quite well without engaging in formal theorizing. Our unaided intellect, common sense, and traditional cultural viewpoints prove adequate. Nevertheless, like the lenses we make out of glass or plastic to see more clearly, the theories we fashion out of concepts allow us to understand the world more thoroughly and profoundly. They provide magnified views of various features of the world that otherwise would go unnoticed. By allowing us greater insight, theories take us beyond superficial overviews. They enable *radical* insight. The word "radical" derives from the Latin word for "root." Theories help us dig beneath the surface, getting to the roots of things.

We could certainly survive without theories. But science would end, as would philosophy, and cultural life would become greatly impoverished. Many practical affairs, such as agriculture and education would revert to quite primitive levels. A world without theory would be very different from the world we now inhabit.

Theory stands in contrast to practice, and that distinction is often employed to undercut the status of the former. "Principles are one thing, politics another, and even our best efforts to 'live up' to our ideals typically founder on the gap between theory and practice," Michael Sandel acknowledges. Still, theory and practice are engaged in a cyclical rather than hierarchical relationship. There is much more to theory than meets the eye, and much more theory behind practices than we might realize. As Sandel adds, "our practices and institutions are embodiments of theory. To engage in a political practice is already to stand in relation to theory. For all our uncertainties about ultimate questions of political philosophy—of justice and value and the nature of the good life—the one thing we know is that we live *some* answer all the time."[1] Theory, in one form or other, undergirds our practices, channeling and enabling perceptions, attitudes, opinions, values, judgments and actions.

The French thinker Auguste Comte (1798-1857) was perhaps the first modern social scientist to insist that "no real observation of any kind of phenomenon is possible, except in as far as it is first directed, and finally interpreted, by some theory."[2] To say that our most basic perceptions are directed and interpreted by theory is not to suggest that there is no reality out there apart from our theoretical musings about it. Indeed, the problem theorists face is not an absence of facts but an overabundance of them. Theories are the conceptual lenses that allow us to sort through a plethora of data and distill it into something useful. Theories organize the innumerable features and facets of reality. Without theories, we would not be able to tell which bits of reality are most relevant, and how they might be put into order.

As anyone who has worked with optical lenses knows, bringing specific things into clear view means that other things, which lie closer or further away, necessarily remain out of focus. The same principle holds for the lenses in our eyes. After gazing for a time upon some distant object, quickly glance back at the pages of this book. A moment of blurry vision occurs. Muscles in your eyes then rapidly alter the shape of your lens to adjust its focal distance, making the written words legible. Lenses allow us to focus on specific things. The rest of the world remains a blur.

Theories likewise focus our attention on specific clumps of reality, causing us to lose sight of other things that lie nearer or farther away. An economic theory that seeks to explain present levels of unemployment may focus expansively on the history of industrial cycles over large time scales. To do so, however, it would have to forego an in-depth psychological investigation of whether there has been a breakdown of the work ethic in recent generations. Likewise, a biological theory might suggest the inevitability of war based on an analysis of human hormones that induce aggression. In doing so, it might ignore evidence that collective violence may be decreased if not eliminated through the creation of political institutions. By organizing ideas, principles, and facts in specific ways, theories give us insight into parts of the world that otherwise would remain too complex and too chaotic to comprehend. In producing such focused images, however, theories necessarily leave a good deal out of the picture.

Lenses bend light to create focused images. But not all available light is used. The apertures of cameras and the irises perforated by the pupils in our eyes restrict the amount of light that passes through the lens. Too much light leads to overexposure, with much detail lost in the glare. Too little light leads to underexposure, with much detail lost in the gloom. As anyone knows who has walked into a dark theater from a well-lit lobby or out of a matinee performance into the brilliant afternoon sunshine, one can be blinded not only by darkness but by light.

Theories have analogous characteristics. They effectively regulate the amount of information we receive and the conceptual networks we form. Too little data or a dearth of conceptual linkages lead to dim, underexposed and impoverished images of the world. Yet too much data and a glut of conceptual linkages are no better. They produce overexposed images, a confusing hodgepodge of phenomena that is difficult to decipher. To produce a clear image, shadows are as necessary as well-lit surfaces.

Theories, like optical lenses, also direct our vision. They determine not only *how* we perceive but *where* we look. Those armed with telescopes do not point their lenses at bacteria, just as those equipped with microscopes do not chart planetary motion. Our conceptual lenses likewise influence what parts of the world we engage. Theories not only focus vision, they determine its direction.

Like photographers, theorists choose different lenses to do different jobs. In turn, they select the correct aperture, avoiding both underexposed and overexposed images. And the themes and topics they explore are largely products of the sorts of lenses theorists have at hand. Like optical lenses, theories are tools that help us better perceive and navigate the world. To best refract light and produce clear images, optical lenses must be carefully designed and manufactured to minimize distortions or aberrations. Likewise, to develop a good theory, three qualities must be in evidence.

## PARSIMONY, ACCURACY AND SIGNIFICANCE

There are no hard and fast rules for what makes a good theory. Still, three qualities are widely recognized to be crucial. The first is *parsimony*. To be parsimonious is to be sparing or frugal. To be theoretically parsimonious is to forgo all unnecessary speculation and detail. A good theory is thrifty: its descriptions, interpretations, explanations, and predictions are not cluttered with unnecessary facts or assumptions.

Theorizing, in this sense, is like mapmaking. Maps offer us outlines. The more details included in these outlines, the better they represent the actual geography. But too much detail is a problem. Lewis Carroll, the whimsical author of *Alice in Wonderland*, once told of a map of the German countryside that had a scale of one to one. It was, of course, a wonderfully detailed representation. But it could not be used because when unfolded it covered all the crops.

The pursuit of parsimony goes too far if it makes a theory not only simple but simplistic. If the map we create is simplified to the point where crucial details are lost, it will not help us find our way about. A map that reveals mountain ranges and major bodies of water but leaves out all highways and thoroughfares might be wonderfully simple and compact, but it will not help us travel from city to city. Accordingly, the second quality that makes for a good theory is *accuracy*. An accurate theory reveals those parts of the world it is targeting with precision and without distortion. Theories should be sufficiently accurate to allow for fine-grained analysis.

If a theory is both parsimonious and accurate, it is deemed elegant. An elegant theory concisely and precisely interprets, describes, explains, or predicts. It simplifies reality enough to make it comprehensible but remains detailed enough to avoid ambiguity.

The third quality for which theorists strive is *significance*. Significant theories illuminate an important part of the world. If we create maps of places no one ever visits, wants to visit, or ever will visit, we theorize in vain. If we do not point our conceptual lenses at interesting and important things, there is not much point in looking through them. However parsimonious and accurate they might be, if our theories fail to offer significant insights, they fail as theories.

There are two key threats to significance. The first is tautology. To say that all bachelors are unmarried is to speak tautologically. It is simply to utter a definition. A theory becomes tautological when it offers nothing more than a reiteration of accepted terms. The important work of reasoning is foregone. A theory that predicts that all political science majors will, at some point during their college careers, enroll in political science courses is tautological. By "political science major" we mean a student taking courses in political science. This theory does not interpret, describe, explain, or predict. It simply (re)defines.

Tautological theories cannot be falsified. No evidence could be presented that would repudiate their claims. No gathering of new facts, no elucidation of principles or ideas, and no subsequent reasoning could undermine it. A tautological theory may provide a set of useful definitions that simply and accurately label features of the world. But its definitions do not challenge or reorganize our common understandings or illuminate the world in an original way.

To avoid tautology, a set of propositions must make itself vulnerable to refutation or falsification. Good theories are open to challenge, either from argument or evidence. One should be able to construct or at least imagine a set of reasons or an empirical test that would disconfirm it. Far from constituting a shortcoming, being susceptible to refutation or falsification is a prerequisite for good theory. If a set of propositions is not open to contestation by reasoned argument or gathered evidence then it is not a theory but a dogma, which is to say, an article of faith wrapped up in a circular series of definitions.

The second threat to significance occurs if our theories become trite. Something is trite when it is commonplace or self-evident. Trite propositions or theories affirm the obvious. To suggest that every student of political theory, regardless of race, gender or class, will take a breath at least once every five minutes is to say something trite. Because the statement could be falsified by a very determined student with excellent lung capacity, it is not a tautology. But we do not need a sophisticated theory to make such a banal statement. Simple observation and common sense tells us as much. To avoid triteness, theories must help us better understand a complex world. They must be insightful.

## SCIENTIFIC THEORY AND SOCIAL SCIENCE

Parsimony, accuracy and significance are qualities of any good theory. But they are typically identified as qualities of scientific theories. Scientific theories expound the laws or regularities that describe the behavior of things. Originally, the word *science*, from the Latin *scientia*, simply meant knowledge. Eventually, science came to mean knowledge of a certain sort, namely, a body of related physical laws combined with trusted methods for obtaining and testing such laws. These laws pertain to the regular, recurrent, and ideally invariant associations between and among events and things within the natural world.

A scientific theory is a set of hypotheses with robust explanatory force. It elucidates the way things behave with such parsimony and accuracy that a thorough explanation of the past and prediction of the future becomes possible. Still, scientific theories are never proven true. Their explanations and predictions might always be falsified based on further evidence or experimentation. While a scientific theory is never proven, it can be validated. Indeed, it is validated every time it survives an attempt to refute it. After many such validations, a scientific theory comes to be accepted as provisionally confirmed.

The typical method of confirmation in the natural sciences is the methodologically rigorous replication of the experimental process. This entails very precise forms of measurement. To the extent that human beings may be studied as mechanical objects or biological organisms, they are subject to scientific theorizing, rigorous experimentation, and the precise measurement this entails. Much modern medical research, for example, proceeds under these conditions. After all, the laws of physics, chemistry and biology apply to human beings no less than to rocks, trees, and other animals. Nevertheless, the farther one moves from the purely physical aspects of human life, the more difficult it becomes to study it scientifically.

Employing physiological and evolutionary theories, one may with great accuracy explain why and predict how a person will cry out and pull away suddenly if jabbed with a sharp pencil. With somewhat less accuracy, employing economic theories and accounting for cultural traits, one may be able to explain why and predict how a person will react if offered $1,000 to break a pencil in two. In this case, the laws of physiology find an approximate analog in the demands of economic life that stimulate people to act in the light of perceived costs and benefits. While economic incentives do not produce as predictable a reaction as acute physical pain, certain regularities are nonetheless observable. But science cannot accurately predict how a person will react when given a pencil and paper and asked to respond to the question "How should liberty in a political community be balanced with the pursuit of justice?" Investigating the differences between political theory and scientific theory helps us understand why.

Certain social sciences (also known as behavioral sciences), including some forms of political science, strive to duplicate in the study of culture what has been achieved in the study of nature. Behavioral social sciences often employ statistical methods of analysis to quantitatively measure the attitudes and actions of individuals and social groups. Their theories attempt to explain and predict human behavior based on the statistical regularities observed. These empirical theories are testable through repeated observation and precise measurement, if not repeated experimentation.

The term *social science* first came into use during the French Revolution, as intellectuals attempted to ground the political changes sweeping France on scientific principles. One of the most prominent advocates of a science of politics was the French philosopher Claude Henri de Saint-Simon (1760–1825). Saint-Simon wrote:

> Hitherto, the method of the sciences of observation has not been introduced into political questions; every man has imported his point of view, method of reasoning and judging, and hence there is not yet any precision in the answers, or universality in the results. The time has come when this infancy of the science should cease, and certainly it is desirable it should cease, for the troubles of the social order arise from the obscurities in political theory.[3]

Likewise, the English political theorist and philosopher John Stuart Mill (1806–73) wrote in his *System of Logic* that "the backward state of the moral sciences can only be remedied by applying to them the methods of physical science, duly extended and generalized."[4] Saint-Simon's and Mill's vision is shared by certain social scientists today who believe that "we are in the political sciences where the natural sciences were two hundred years ago." The task at hand is to "apply scientific methods to the management of society as we have been learning to apply them in the natural world."[5] Most social scientists acknowledge that they will never attain the explanatory or predictive power currently enjoyed by natural scientists. Nonetheless, many social scientists approximate the methods of natural science as closely as possible.

Will social science eventually produce laws that are as robust as those of physics or chemistry? Efforts have certainly been made. These attempts have all fallen short of the mark, but their achievements have not been negligible. The political sociologist Robert Michels (1876–1936), for instance, developed the famous "iron law of oligarchy" after studying political parties in Europe at the turn of the century. Oligarchy means rule by the few. The iron law of oligarchy states that an essential characteristic of all human groups is a hierarchical structure wherein a minority exercises most of the power and effectively rules over a majority.

Michels writes: "It is organization which gives birth to the dominion of the elected over the electors, of the mandataries over the mandators, of the delegates over the delegators. Who says organization, says oligarchy."[6] Michels' law, like scientific law, is predictive and testable. Given an organization (and particularly a political party), one may predict its rule by an oligarchy. Like most "laws" of social science, however, the iron law of oligarchy is not very precise. The law supplies us with no way of knowing, or even guessing, how soon an oligarchy will form, how strong an oligarchy will become once it forms, how long it will last, or how and why it will decrease in strength, dissipate, or change form. Unlike Isaac Newton's law of physics, which stipulates that force is equal to mass multiplied by acceleration ($F = ma$), the iron law of oligarchy is not a precise equation. Unlike Newton's law, which makes for quite exact measurements, calculations, and predictions, Michels' law allows only very general statements about the social world. Moreover, Michels' law does not apply equally to all organizations. Small organizations whose members have close, friendly relations are frequent exceptions.

One reason why social science falls short of achieving the parsimony, accuracy and predictive power of natural science is that the methods of scientific theory are not easily adapted to social and political concerns. Outside the laboratory, too many uncontrolled and unforeseen forces affect social and political life to allow for precise measurement. And the study of political life cannot be carried out in controlled laboratory conditions. In the social sciences, experimentation, let alone repeated experimentation, is very difficult if not impossible to arrange. Often experimentation would be morally repugnant if it could be arranged. One might adequately observe the reaction of a democratic people to a coup d'état, for example, and subsequently develop a theory to account for such behavior. Yet it would be ethically unacceptable to stage a second coup d'état under similar circumstances to verify the results.

Social and political practices are seldom if ever replicable. Comparative studies of different people, organizations, or countries, or the same people, organizations or countries at different times, can be very informative. But they cannot duplicate the precise experimental conditions of the natural sciences. Humans learn from history and from each other. Repeated observations of social phenomena, therefore, are not observations of the same phenomena. The actors involved have thought about themselves and their world in the meantime and, in all likelihood, have changed their conditions and behavior as a result.

Experimental observation allows for the construction of scientific theory because the objects of study operate in relatively fixed patterns and display regularities that accord with ascertainable physical laws. For the political scientist, in contrast, the objects of study are thinking human beings whose behavior is far more irregular and unpredictable than that of other species or of inorganic forms of matter. While social scientific theories may systematically chart human behavior, they seldom, if ever, fully explain or predict it. Their subject matter is simply too complex and variable.

Given these challenges, the German economist and sociologist Max Weber (1864–1920) argued that social scientists should not search for laws that fully explain and predict human behavior. Rather, they should insightfully describe historical correlations and tendencies. Weber held that the mandate of social science was to understand human behavior profoundly not to predict it precisely.[7]

Despite his reluctance to mimic the natural sciences, Weber was opposed to any historical description of events that made no systematic attempt at explanation. He suggested that explanatory theories be developed and actively employed in the social sciences. These social scientific theories would be based on the observed correlations of human events, institutions, attitudes and values.

Weber called these correlations "ideal types." An ideal type is not a moral category but a conceptual construct that accentuates specific features of social phenomena to explain them efficiently and elegantly. One might, for instance, accentuate the role played by the president or prime minister of a country to make sense of that country's foreign policy. Perhaps a strong correlation can be found between foreign policy and the top executive's psychological type, personal history, or ideological orientation. This conceptual framework may allow one to explain foreign policy neatly without muddying the waters with complicated analyses of the role played by advisers, bureaucracies, the economic climate, election cycles, or international institutions.

Ideal types put historical events, institutions, or (sets of) attitudes and values into their "most consistent and logical forms."[8] Achieving this consistency and logic, Weber admitted, entails doing a certain amount of "violence to historical reality."[9] Ideal types are "one-sided." Without ideal types to simplify matters, however, the social scientist could not understand or portray the complex interplay of cultural and material forces that produce human history. The task at hand, according to Weber, was to do as little violence as possible to a complex reality while still illuminating it by way of a theory.

Many social scientists adopt a Weberian approach in their efforts to understand and explain political phenomena. Others mingle elements of Weber's insights with methods more prominent in the natural sciences. The discipline of political science is varied in its methodologies. Nonetheless, each of its traditional fields (such as comparative politics, international relations, and public policy), aims to develop good theories that are confirmed by reliable data. Their practitioners, regardless of methodological approach, strive to construct theories that produce parsimonious, accurate and significant accounts of political reality. In turn, they empirically investigate the political world to confirm, or disconfirm, their theories.

## THE INTERPRETIVE NATURE OF POLITICAL THEORY

Political theory stands out among the traditional fields of political science by focusing less on prediction and more on interpretation, less on the collection of empirical data and more on the conceptual and historical analysis of texts, less on the precise measurement of political phenomena and more on their normative assessment.

Human beings consciously distinguish themselves from their environment, think about themselves and others, and often organize and distill these thoughts into concepts and theories. This spiral of self-reflective thought, and the behavior it stimulates, has no foreseeable pathway or conclusion. Accordingly, the political theorist generally does not aim at prediction. Rather, the political theorist *interprets* human thought and action in ways that are illuminating and promote understanding.

This brings us to a major difference between scientific theory and political theory. Scientific theory strives for objectivity. The scientist is an impartial observer whose personal predilections are best left outside the laboratory. She employs tools of analysis and measurement that anyone with similar skills could employ. Only in this way can repeated experimentation confirm theory, since any other scientist, employing the same procedures under the same conditions, should arrive at the same results.

For theorists of social and political life, in contrast, the ability to feel and think in ways similar to the object of study is a crucial component of their work. The analysis of responses to the question about the appropriate balance between liberty and justice, for example, is necessarily grounded in the theorist's own reflective experiences of the challenges and compromises associated with political life. Without such resonance between the theorist and the theorized, little of interest can be said. To make sense of a form of behavior, one needs to understand the motivations that underlie it. Humans, unlike plants and rocks, interpret themselves and take actions based on their interpretations. To understand a self-interpreting being, one has to be a self-interpreting being.[10]

A central task of political theory is to understand how humans understand themselves and their world. The theorist is concerned with meaning, with what matters. The value of a political theory, therefore, is not primarily based on its generation of verifiable predictions. Its value is found in its capacity to interrogate, inform, illuminate and inspire political life. For these reasons, political theory is an art or craft more than a science. Political theories are not so much confirmed or disconfirmed as they are shown to be helpful or unhelpful in understanding and navigating political life, a phenomenon rife with meaning but short on truth.

This is not to say that political theorists need not worry about truth. All too often, political theorists get historical, demographic or scientific facts wrong, make faulty arguments, and neglect evidence. Their theories suffer as a result. Even absent these unfortunate mistakes, however, the task remains fundamentally interpretive. To this end, political theory entails the exercise of practical judgment.

Sheldon Wolin observes that "a political theory is, among many other things, a sum of judgments, shaped by the theorist's notion of what matters, and embodying a series of discriminations about where one province begins and another leaves off."[11] Likewise, Philip Pettit writes: "The aim of political theory is to find a yardstick for political institutions . . . an ideal that proves, on reflection and perhaps after revision . . . to equilibriate with our judgements ...and to help in the extrapolation of those judgments to new cases."[12] The theorist's capacity for good judgment develops by way of worldly experience, as she interpretively navigates political life. It also develops by way of what might be called second-hand experience, as the theorist learns how other citizens and statespeople, either historically or more recently, have navigated political life. Any fool can learn from his mistakes, the adage goes, but it takes a wise person to learn from the mistakes of others. Practical judgment requires learning from one's own and others' mistakes—and successes—in the world of politics.[13] This learning is a reflective, interpretive endeavor.

Political theorists vary in the degree to which they tend toward the interpretive or scientific end of the social science spectrum. Some, like Weber, try to steer a middle course, taking what they can from science and balancing it with interpretive insight. Strict social scientists are often critical of interpretive theorists for producing ambiguous descriptions and lofty concepts with little empirical application. The charge is that the interpretive approach is too speculative and too subjective to aid us in explaining, predicting, or controlling concrete reality. For their part, interpretive political theorists are often critical of their social scientific colleagues for misunderstanding the nature of political life and the task of those who study it. They claim that social scientists too often view citizens as objects to be measured and efficiently managed instead of subjects to be critically understood and morally engaged.

Often it is appropriate to measure and manage people. Measuring the habits of automobile drivers and controlling their behavior is crucial to avoiding accidents and congestion. But measuring and managing commuters does not unduly detract from, and generally enhances, the experience of driving. Measuring and managing citizens may not always be so benign. For example, ever-increasing data is gathered about citizens through governmental offices, commercial internet sites and social media platforms. Much of this data is gathered without the knowledge or consent of the subjects, and is employed for purposes they may not endorse. As we will see in Chapter 6, the mining and analytics of "big data" have a significant impact on social and political life.

The ancient Greek philosopher Aristotle (384–322 B.C.) suggests that politics is a realm of freedom in which citizens mutually coordinate their activities in pursuit of the good life. If this is true, then a crucial characteristic of citizens, namely, their autonomy and moral purpose, is not susceptible to precise measurement and may be threatened by too efficient control. For these reasons, political theorists approach political events and actors more like works of art inviting interpretation than chemical reactions subject to explanation, prediction and control.

Interpretive theory, like scientific theory, attempts parsimoniously, accurately, and significantly to account for worldly phenomena. Yet it does so without making precise, law-like pronouncements that are subject to experimental confirmation. Instead, it develops historical, conceptual and normative insights grounded upon intersubjective understanding.

## INTERSUBJECTIVE UNDERSTANDING

The word "theory" comes from the Greek word *theoros*. The *theoros* was originally an emissary sent on behalf of the state to consult an oracle (something like a fortune-teller) or to perform a religious rite. Later, the *theoros* took on the role of an envoy or spectator of foreign religious and cultural events who would report back to his native city. In time, *theoria*, the activity of the *theoros*, came to mean a form of contemplation, a kind of internal spectating. The terms *theoria* and *theoros* stem from *thea*, which means to look upon or view. The fundamental relationship between theory and mental vision was already established in ancient Greece, where Western political theory began.

How do you suppose the early Greek *theoros* reported on his voyages? How would he describe and explain to his compatriots the religious and cultural spectacles witnessed in other lands? Very likely, the *theoros* would make sense of these events, and make them understood to others, by producing meaningful comparisons. For example, he might inform his audience that in the splendid Egyptian festival of the goddesses, the worship of Isis resembled the worship of the goddess Demeter in Greece. Drawing on the similarities between these two agricultural deities, the *theoros* would then be able to highlight some differences between the two festivals and perhaps speculate on their origins and purposes.

The chemist does not have to know what molecular bonding "feels like" to explain chemical reactions. To comprehend the concerns and passions that underlie a foreign religious practice, in contrast, the *theoros* would have to have experienced similar concerns and passions. When one is studying a network of self-reflective motivations, attitudes and actions, comprehension demands common experiences. Interpretive theory, it follows, aims less at an objective explanation than intersubjective understanding. The map of the world that interpretive theory produces is necessarily grounded in shared experiences of this world.

This is not to say that one cannot theorize about events without having participated in these same events or that one cannot understand someone's beliefs, feelings, or behavior without having identical beliefs and feelings or without having engaged in the same behavior. Often, because distance allows broader insight or because emotions do not cloud vision, a detached observer might understand a person's motivations or attitudes better than that person herself. The detached observer could not do so, however, if she had never experienced similar motivations or attitudes. One can understand a child's fervent belief in Santa Claus without currently believing, or ever having believed, in jolly old Saint Nick and his magic sleigh. But one cannot well understand the nature of the child's experience without ever having held a belief grounded in hope or hearsay.

Intersubjective understanding is as important to the theorist as the faculty of sight is to someone trying to describe the experience of seeing a mountain panorama or the faculty of hearing is to someone trying to describe the experience of listening to one of Beethoven's symphonies. The theoretical task of understanding the relationship of justice to liberty is only possible for those who have intersubjectively experienced these features of political life, however attenuated or restricted their experiences may have been.

The interpretive theorist seeks to understand other human beings as the thinking, feeling and socially integrated beings they are. The theorist would be at a severe disadvantage were she somehow to discard all her own values and commitments to approach this task as a wholly detached observer. Without a palette of shared experiences to draw on, the theorist could not paint pictures of political reality that others could appreciate. While drawing upon her own experiences, however, the theorist ought not paint pictures that always and only display her favorite colors. She should guard against prejudices and predilections that weaken or distort intersubjective understanding.

In this regard, political theory is often considered a hermeneutic exercise. Hermeneuts were people employed by the early Christian church to interpret the religious service and scripture to worshippers who spoke a different language. (The word *hermeneut* derives from the name of the Greek god Hermes, who was the patron deity of speech and writing.) In the nineteenth century, hermeneutics developed as a method of interpreting biblical texts and, later, other legal and literary documents. The German philosopher Wilhelm Dilthey (1833–1911) further expanded hermeneutics to encompass the interpretation of human experience in general, the historical text of human life.

Dilthey, who influenced Max Weber, argued that nature provided a field for explanation but that humanity provided a field for *understanding*, in German, *Verstehen*. Explanation is based on external observation. Understanding is based on what Dilthey called "lived experience." Dilthey wrote that "understanding of other people and their expressions is developed on the basis of experience and self-understanding and the constant interaction between them."[14] We understand other's thoughts, speech and actions because we share the experience of exercising these capacities.

Like the biblical hermeneuts who interpreted religious services and scripture for fellow believers, political theorists share certain attitudes and experiences with their audience. Not all attitudes and experiences are held in common, however. If they were, there would be little for the theorist to communicate and nothing for her to argue about.

Political theories build bridges of understanding between diverse perspectives using the foundations of shared experience.

Much political theory today consists of hermeneutic analysis and critique of the great texts of political thought. Plato's *Republic*, Aristotle's *Politics*, Augustine's *City of God*, Niccolò Machiavelli's *The Prince*, Thomas Hobbes' *Leviathan*, John Locke's *Second Treatise of Government*, Jean-Jacques Rousseau's *The Social Contract*, John Stuart Mill's *On Liberty* and John Rawls' *Theory of Justice*, among many others, have each been subject to thousands of interpretive analyses. Here interpretation may clarify or criticize a text's arguments, establish its practical import, or infer the assumptions or intent of its author. Political theory may also focus on active life rather than formal writing. Political attitudes, beliefs and practices may be viewed as kinds of texts in need of close and critical reading.

Whether making its appearance on paper or on the stage of life, politics presents theorists with the challenge of interpretation grounded in intersubjective experience. Intersubjective experience is a mix of emotions, desires, motivations, beliefs, attitudes, dispositions, values, judgments and behaviors. Theorists employ such experience to gain interpretive traction.

Hans-Georg Gadamer, who is well known for his hermeneutic analyses, observes that whenever we attempt to understand a text we always "project" our own "fore-conceptions" and "fore-meanings" on it. "To interpret," Gadamer writes, "means precisely to use one's own preconceptions so that the meaning of the text can really be made to speak for us."[15] A fore-conception is less a distortion that mars the purity of understanding than the condition under which understanding becomes possible. Fore-conceptions, Gadamer writes, "constitute the initial directedness of our whole ability to experience. . . . They are simply conditions whereby we experience something—whereby what we encounter says something to us."[16] Fore-conceptions make for friction between the theorist and the text. They cause the theorist to move slowly and pay attention. But friction also makes movement possible. If one tries to run on sheer ice with flat shoes, forward motion is very difficult. There is nothing against which one can push off, nothing that allows one to get started. Trying to theorize in the absence of fore-conceptions is like attempting to move in the absence of friction. Fore-conceptions provide traction.

The point is not blindly or uncritically to promote one's biases. Their retention is certainly not the goal. One's own attitudes, beliefs and values simply provide a starting point. "The important thing," Gadamer writes, "is to be aware of one's own bias, so that the text may present itself in all its newness and thus be able to assert its own truth against one's own fore-meanings."[17] Good interpretation constantly seeks to replace initial biases with more suitable beliefs as the reading of the text progresses. The first step for the theorist, however, is to "abandon the prejudice of imagining that one can abandon all prejudice."[18]

Biases are not limited to personal beliefs and values. Empirical studies document the sorts of biases that are endemic to almost all human interpretation and decision making.[19] Some of these biases, known as heuristics, amount to useful, shorthand ways of making quick decisions. "Look before you leap" is a good example. But natural biases can also lead to systematic errors that have significant political consequences. Most everyone displays a bias towards conformity, for instance. People amend their judgments and actions to accord with the orientations of those around them.[20] Theorists are as prone to this as everyone else. In turn, most people evidence an overconfidence bias, which prompts them to unduly estimate their own merits and powers, including their capacity for good judgment. People, including experts, are often wrong but seldom in doubt.[21] The confirmation bias is also widespread. People perceive and seek supporting evidence for their beliefs and values and ignore or avoid disconfirming evidence. The confirmation bias, which we address further in Chapter 6, has significant political impacts.

Knowing oneself—including all the common and idiosyncratic biases to which one is prone—is a condition of knowing and interpreting others. The obverse relation is also true. Knowing and interpreting others is a condition of knowing oneself. The task of interpretation demands that the theorist become porous, capable of absorbing and integrating unfamiliar perceptions and insights. Gadamer calls this a "fusion of horizons."[22] To fuse horizons is not to agree with everything another person thinks, believes, or feels. Rather, it entails the development, from initially divergent positions, of a sufficient level of intersubjective understanding such that meaningful conversation can take place. A meaningful conversation does not necessarily produce agreement. But it does require a shared belief in the importance of the questions being asked and the merit of pursuing the conversation as a means of addressing them.

Making oneself porous in the pursuit of intersubjective understanding leaves one vulnerable but also poised for growth. As Gadamer writes:

> Understanding is an adventure and, like any other adventure, is dangerous. . . . Hermeneutical experience has a far less degree of certainty than that attained by the methods of the natural sciences. But when one realizes that understanding is an adventure, this implies that it affords unique opportunities as well. It is capable of contributing in a special way to the broadening of our human experiences, our self-knowledge, and our horizon.[23]

To do political theory is not to confirm one's prejudices but critically and constructively to engage them. To this end, one must first acknowledge them. Then one must become open to horizon-broadening encounters with other texts and other people.

## THE NORMATIVE NATURE OF THEORY

Political theory is inherently critical. To criticize means to judge, and to judge is to measure something against a standard. The inherently critical nature of political theory derives from its concern for norms. For this reason, interpretive political theory is often called normative theory. A norm is an authoritative rule or standard. The word "norm" derives from *norma*, which is the Latin word for a carpenter's square. Normative theory is concerned with the way things measure up. It seeks to understand not only the way things *are* but also the way things *ought to be*.

If the theorist primarily focuses on the way people ought to act or behave, then she is concerned with the realm of ethics. Normative political theory, in this sense, is a form of ethical or moral theory. According to Aristotle, the theorist concerned with ethics not only aims to discover what the good is; she attempts to become good herself, to exemplify her normative standards.[24] Theorists do not necessarily view themselves as (the best) practitioners of what they preach. Nonetheless, the normative theorist concerns herself with moral principles and advocates specific standards for political life. She might, for instance, propose a standard of distributive justice that stipulates how individuals within a political community ought to allocate benefits and share burdens. Alternatively, she might propose a standard of civil rights that stipulates the extent to which the basic liberties of citizens ought to be protected from incursion by society or the state.

The normative theorist may be less interested in the way people act or behave and more concerned with the way people think, learn, or form beliefs. Such a theorist would be primarily interested in epistemology, that is, in the study of the foundations of knowledge. The norms studied by epistemologically oriented theorists are the rules or standards that determine when and how something gains the status of knowledge or truth. Certain feminist theorists, for instance, argue that women have different standards for (acquiring or generating) knowledge than men and that these standards should not be judged inadequate simply because they are unlike those upheld by their male counterparts. Similar arguments have been made regarding the epistemological standards of different cultures. We investigate these claims further in Chapter 4.

Since words and deeds, thinking and acting generally go together, political theorists are interested in both epistemology and ethics. Indeed, the distinction between epistemology and ethics is often rather tenuous. People typically act on the basis of their beliefs and understandings and these beliefs and understandings develop out of their active engagements and experiences. In supplying better ways of understanding political life, political theorists are suggesting that there are better ways of participating in political life based on these improved understandings. To supply a better way of knowing is to imply a better way of acting. To analyze or formulate the norms that regulate political life is to enter the overlapping fields of epistemology and ethics.

For many political theorists, making normative judgments about the political world is an essential part of their enterprise. Leo Strauss (1899–1973) writes:

> It is impossible to study social phenomena, i.e., all important social phenomena, without making value judgments. A man who sees no reason for not despising people whose horizon

is limited to their consumption of food and their digestion may be a tolerable econometrist; he cannot say anything relevant about the character of human society. A man who refuses to distinguish between great statesmen, mediocrities, and insane impostors may be a good biographer; he cannot say anything relevant about politics and political history. . . . Generally speaking, it is impossible to understand thought or action or work without evaluating it. If we are unable to evaluate adequately, as we very frequently are, we have not yet succeeded in understanding adequately.[25]

To be a good political theorist, Strauss is saying, one must be concerned with the standards of political life.

This is not to say that political theorists ought to impose their beliefs and values upon others. Indeed, the norms the theorist studies and advocates—particularly if they are oriented to democracy, diversity, fairness, tolerance, and individual liberties and rights—may strongly militate against the imposition of personal moral standards on others. Nonetheless, the defense of ideals, including that of respect for others' moral autonomy, remains a normative enterprise. "I know of no safe depository of the ultimate powers of the society but the people themselves," Thomas Jefferson (1743–1826) wrote, "and if we think them not enlightened enough to exercise their control with a wholesome discretion, the remedy is not to take it from them, but to inform their discretion."[26] To inform people's discretion is to adopt and inculcate specific standards. Yet this eminently normative enterprise is grounded in democratic beliefs about the moral autonomy and political equality of fellow citizens.

Some normative theorists argue for very specific beliefs or values. Others avoid explicitly advocating a moral position. They remain more broadly concerned with understanding the means and processes by which diverse attitudes and interests become articulated and integrated into political life. Nonetheless, every political theory facilitates the development of some but not all beliefs, attitudes, interests and values and the pursuit of some but not all courses of action. Political theories prompt us to accept certain features of our world and to change others that are judged to be deficient. All good theories, moreover, demonstrate the quality of significance—and we have no alternative but to rely on judgments of value (what we, or a community of scholars, find interesting and important) to determine whether a theory is significant.

In turn, the methods employed by the theorist have normative implications. To employ statistical analysis is to imply the importance of aggregated opinions and behaviors and their capacity to inform understanding of the body politic. To employ in-depth psychological analysis, in contrast, is to imply the importance of individual desires or unconscious drives. Methodologies are ways of "shaping the mind."[27] When we select our methodologies, we are implicitly if not explicitly suggesting which things are worthwhile objects of study. Methodologies are epistemological norms. And as we have seen, epistemology and ethics are inextricably related. To endorse a specific way of knowing is to imply a proper way of acting.

The *Republic*, written by the ancient Greek philosopher Plato (c. 427–347 B.C.), is a case in point. The *Republic* is widely recognized as the first major work of political theory. It remains to this day, by many estimates, the most important. The *Republic* examines the concept of justice by way of an extended discussion between Socrates (469–399 B.C.), Plato's teacher, and other Athenians, mostly young men. Here Socrates argues that *to know* the just is also *to be* just. Knowledge is virtue. One can only act viciously out of ignorance. Epistemology and ethics not only go hand in hand, they march in lockstep. Sustained philosophical analysis carried out earnestly in the pursuit of truth, Plato suggests, is the only route to creating adequate political norms and securing the good life.

On the portals of Plato's school, called the Academy, were inscribed the words: "Let no one unacquainted with geometry enter here." Plato's students were trained in geometry because the study of mathematical axioms was believed to be the proper preparation for the discovery of moral and political truths. One might read Plato to say that moral and political knowledge, like mathematical formula, are eternal and unchanging. The ideals that the political realm should embody are already to be found—enduring and invariable—in the heavens.

Plato insists these ideals can be apprehended by humans, but only through the intellect rather than the senses. Sensory experience is suspect because it cannot lead to knowledge of unchanging truth, which Plato called the Forms. Through our senses we never experience true circles, for instance, but only approximations of them. Only an abstract, intellectual understanding of a circle—as a plane figure whose curved boundary (circumference) consists of points equidistant from a fixed point within the curve—allows this geometric entity to be truly known. Likewise, Plato suggests that political concepts such as justice can never be adequately grasped by our senses. They are apprehended only through intellection and are as inflexible and immutable as the principles of geometry. Plato's proposal for the authoritarian rule of philosopher kings over a caste society reflects this geometric invariance. If we read the *Republic* literally (rather than as a work of irony), Plato's rigid theoretical lenses produce an equally rigid form of political life.

Plato's famous student, Aristotle, contested his teacher's claim that knowledge constitutes virtue. One might know what justice demands, Aristotle observes, but not act justly. Aristotle also criticizes Plato for reducing the diverse, evolving political community to an unchanging, unitary state. Geometric principles, Aristotle argues, are not the sort of standards by which human affairs can or should be measured. The mark of a good education, Aristotle held, is knowing which fields of study allow for certainty and exactitude and which do not. Politics, he observes, is not an exact science. Its study depends less on precise measurement than on contextual understanding grounded in shared experience.

In his *Nichomachean Ethics*, Aristotle states that we should not attempt to fashion political norms with the precision of the carpenter's square. He aptly observes that when measuring things political, it is best to use a ruler that is flexible, like the measuring rod made of soft lead that was developed in his time by the architects and masons on the island of Lesbos. Politics is a variable affair. The methodological exactness we pursue in assessing it should not exceed that allowed by the subject matter.

A leaden rule can measure things of various shapes better than a rigid square because it can bend to conform to these shapes. Likewise, the norms appropriate for assessing the world of politics need to be flexible. To buttress his point, Aristotle records the varieties of political life encountered in other lands and in other times. He demonstrates that comparative investigations, by broadening our perspective, may give us the theoretical flexibility appropriate to the study of politics. In turn, Aristotle emphasizes the importance of worldly (sensory) experience for the development of practical judgment, and the importance of practical judgment for understanding and navigating political life. Pure intellection is insufficient. As such, Aristotle has a higher opinion of citizens' practical capacity to govern themselves than does Plato.

## CONCEPTUAL AND HISTORICAL ANALYSIS

Political theorizing is inherently a normative enterprise. But it is not an exercise in preaching or proselytization. Rather, the theorist pursues better and deeper ways of understanding political life, including its ideals and standards. The primary means employed by the theorist to study political life are *conceptual analysis* and *historical analysis*.

To analyze is to divide a whole into its constituent parts. Conceptual analysis takes a complex concept or system of ideas and examines its components to determine the relationships they form with each other, and whether they constitute a coherent whole. For instance, one might analyze the concept of the nation-state by first dividing it into its constituent parts of geographic territory, a sovereign government that administers this territory, and a citizenry over which the government rules. Sovereign government, in turn, may be defined as the set of formal institutions through which binding decisions are made for a citizenry. Governments are formed by election or appointment (the gaining of political power), and engage in lawmaking (the legislative exercise of political power) and administration (the executive exercise of political power). Each of these elements of government might become the object of further analysis. Engaging in conceptual analysis is like using a microscopic lens to investigate the inner workings of things.

Historical analysis employs a telescopic lens to see objects at a temporal distance in the context of what precedes and follows them. The objects of historical analysis may be the political events or institutions of previous times. Alternatively, the objects of historical study may be the political writings of theorists from earlier eras. In both cases, the theorist seeks not only to understand the past but to gain insight to contemporary phenomena by viewing them afresh through historical lenses.

Effective political action entails historical understanding. "Those who cannot remember the past," George Santayana (1863–1952) famously said, "are condemned to repeat it." Understanding how things came to be is a precondition for understanding how they might be changed. Understanding how things came to be also informs our understanding of how they ought to change. In this respect, as Judith Shklar observes, "Political theory . . . lives in the territory between history and ethics."[28] Only in the context of their historical development can we well understand current opportunities and obligations.

Much historically oriented political theory effectively constitutes a history of the present. It demonstrates that many features of contemporary political life are taken for granted, developed at particular times for particular purposes, often as a product of struggle and strife. The nation-state, for instance, is less than 400 years old. It developed in the 1600s, largely as a means of alleviating the bloody religious conflicts that afflicted Europe at the time. Previously, the chief political units were empires, kingdoms and principalities, with the Catholic Church in Rome highly involved in governmental affairs throughout Europe. The sovereign nation-state rose to prominence with the Peace of Westphalia in 1648, at the end of the Thirty Years War. Princes rather than popes now determined the laws of the land as well as its creed. Historical analysis demonstrates that the nation-state is not an indelible feature of political life and may not be the chief political unit in the future. The nation-state is a historical artifact.

For Quentin Skinner, studying the history of political thought demonstrates

> the extent to which those features of our own arrangements which we may be disposed to accept as traditional or even "timeless" truths may in fact be the merest contingencies of our particular history and social structure. . . . Our society places unrecognizable constraints upon our imaginations. . . . The historical study of the ideas of other societies should be undertaken as an indispensable and irreplaceable means of placing limits on these constraints. . . . To learn from the past—and we cannot otherwise learn it at all—the distinction between what is necessary and what is the product merely of our own contingent arrangements, is to learn the key to self-awareness itself.[29]

Political theory entails both thinking *about* politics and thinking *through* politics. That is to say, its historical orientation encourages self-awareness: the understanding that the theorist's own attitudes, beliefs, and values are themselves products of the historical development of political life.

The cultivation of such self-awareness among contemporary political theorists is often abetted by investigating how predecessors thought through politics. Richard Ashcraft observes that we should view the political theorists of yesteryear as "deeply immersed in their times, political battles, and ideological struggles." These theorists were people with stakes in the political games being played out around them. They were "interested parties" in specific political struggles, even if they observed these struggles from the intellectual sidelines. With this in mind, Ashcraft states, "if political theory is not seen in its historical dimensions, neither is it viewed as being political."[30] Political theories are, inevitably, politicized theories. The theorist not only thinks about the politics of her day, she thinks through the politics of her day. The historical study of political theory enables one to appreciate the politics inherent in theory.

The "hypothesis that theories of politics are themselves a part of politics," George Sabine argues, should inform both the historical study of political theory and our contemporary efforts.[31] This brings us back to the status of conceptual analysis. William Connolly writes that "the language of politics is not a neutral medium that conveys ideas independently formed; it is an institutionalized structure of meanings that channels political thought and action in certain directions." Connolly adjusts the optical metaphor introduced at the beginning of this chapter, observing that "the concepts of politics do not simply provide a lens through which to observe a process that is independent of them. As we have seen, they are themselves part of that political life—they help to constitute it."[32] The conceptual lenses we employ to understand politics are products of political life. In turn, they shape political life. By conceptually structuring the language of politics, political theorists effectively channel thought and action. Their efforts influence not only political discourse but also political practice.

Given the stakes in the game, it should be no surprise that the terms of political discourse are, to employ the phrase of W.B. Gallie, "essentially contested concepts." The meanings of these concepts never get resolved once and for all. They are subject to ongoing contestation, as are the values and interests they represent and promote. The words and concepts traditionally employed to interpret, describe, or explain political life act like gatekeepers. They regulate how we understand things and events and influence our judgments, beliefs, and actions. So the language of politics will always be subject to heated debate, the fragile and temporary outcome of which will likely serve some people's interests, bolster some people's beliefs and values, and reaffirm some people's identities, more than others.

How, then, can one argue for the legitimacy of a political theory when the very vocabulary employed to construct it is entangled in and a product of political life? What does it mean to persuade others to accept an idea or moral position that one cannot ground in a firm, uncontroversial, neutral set of concepts? It means that one is taking on the challenge of living as a political animal.

Connolly writes that "there is no contradiction in first affirming the essential contestability of a concept and then making the strongest case available for one of the positions within that range. That's politics."[33] The terms and concepts political theorists employ always exist in tension with a network of competing terms and concepts. And that is a good thing. The end of contestation could only occur with an end to politics. It might happen in places such as Aldous Huxley's *Brave New World*, where genetic engineering and mind-altering drugs rob inhabitants of individuality; or in George Orwell's dystopic novel, *Nineteen Eighty-four*, where the language of Newspeak stultifies originality and imagination and "thought police" enforce mental paralysis.[34] In these worlds, the very opportunity for political life has been erased.

George Orwell observed that "in our time, political speech and writing are largely the defense of the indefensible."[35] Orwell exaggerates the venality of his times to underscore the frequent corruption of public life. Nonetheless, political speech and writing are always defending or promoting something. Oftentimes, as Marshall McLuhan stated, "the medium is the message." What is being defended or promoted are specific words and concepts. The defense and promotion of one's vocabulary, in other words, is an intrinsic part of politics. So is the criticism of competing vocabularies. For those who wish to participate in political life, or in the life of political theory, there is no alternative to engaging in the politics of language.

## IDEOLOGY

At the onset of modernity, Francis Bacon (1561–1626), an English philosopher, attempted to furnish humankind with a new, scientific route to knowledge. It entailed expunging all biases, mistaken premises, and false methodologies that had accumulated in human learning over thousands of years. "I have purged and swept and leveled the floor of the mind," Bacon wrote.[36] This is precisely what the scientific elite who rule the technocratic utopia described in Bacon's novel *The New Atlantis* set out to do. On this pristine foundation, a sturdy edifice of knowledge is built using only the tools of reason and the methods of science.

Key among the prejudices that Bacon hoped to expunge were what he called the "idols of the marketplace." These were mistaken beliefs that "crept into the understanding through the alliances of words and names," the kinds of misunderstandings that grow whenever people congregate and exchange stories. Putting the wrong labels on things, or making the wrong connections between these labels, led to bad thinking and faulty beliefs. To get one's language straight was the first and most important step toward straightening out one's mind. The straightening of minds, Bacon held, was the only way to put the world right.

Two hundred years after Bacon wrote about the idols of the marketplace, a French scholar and former nobleman, Antoine Destutt de Tracy (1754–1836), coined the word *ideology*. De Tracy worked at the prestigious Institute de France. In 1796, during the French Directory and after the revolutionary Reign of Terror, he developed his theory of ideology as a "science of ideas." An ideological science, de Tracy believed, would allow for a full knowledge of human nature through the empirical analysis of individual sensations and perceptions. De Tracy and other "Ideologues" gained seats in the French senate and attempted to reform the nation's educational system, which was left in disarray after the revolution had disenfranchised the church. The strategy was to focus on the use of language among children. Following the tradition of Francis Bacon (and the path of other empiricist thinkers), de Tracy attempted to ground all human thought and action in reason and to ground reason in the precise use of language.

Employing a notion developed by the British philosopher John Locke (1632–1704), de Tracy maintained that the mind of the child at birth was a *tabula rasa*, a blank slate on which perceptions and ideas become engraved over time. De Tracy hoped that clear concepts, correct ideas, proper beliefs, and good behavior could be developed by strictly supervising the use of language by children, whose mental slates had yet to be marred by inappropriately cataloged experiences and the idols of the marketplace.

Initially, de Tracy's ideological science enjoyed official support and a certain measure of success. Napoleon Bonaparte (1769–1821), who had recently come to power, favored the "science of ideas" and venerated the work of de Tracy's Institute. The work of the Ideologues was widely promulgated in France and abroad. Thomas Jefferson and John Quincy Adams read and heartily approved of de Tracy's writings. In time, however, Jefferson and Adams abandoned the science of ideas. After the failures of his military campaign in Russia, Napoleon also lost interest. He became less enamored with lofty ideas and more concerned with the grisly task of holding on to power. He also found it increasingly necessary to court the favors of the Catholic church, which was reestablishing its traditional authority and was antagonistic to progressive science.

Eventually, Napoleon became harshly critical of the Ideologues, dismissing them as "windbags" and charging them with impracticality and idealism. Ideology, Napoleon charged, had become a "sinister metaphysics."[37] The French emperor lambasted the Ideologues for the same reason that Bacon had earlier criticized the scholastics. These were people who made "imaginary laws for imaginary commonwealths." The problem, Bacon charged, was that "their discourses are as the stars, which give little light because they are so high."[38] Though intended to illuminate the minds and direct the behavior of an entire people, de Tracy's science of ideas fell into disfavor owing to its abstractness and failure to achieve practical results.

Under Napoleon, ideology eventually became a pejorative term, denoting an unrealistic set of beliefs that was practically useless if not socially pernicious. This pejorative connotation was taken up by Karl Marx (1818–83), a German thinker who had studied de Tracy's works. De Tracy believed that the troubles of the social order arose from obscurities in theory and that the practical world could be straightened out if theorists would simply tidy up the conceptual world. For Marx, concepts are merely the "efflux" of material circumstances. Ideas and ideologies are the effect, not the cause, of social conditions. Marx criticized de Tracy, as he had the philosopher G.W.F. Hegel and other German idealists, for inverting reality.

Marx employed the term ideology to describe the false beliefs and values that legitimize the power of the ruling class. Ideology, he held, produces a distorted or false consciousness that serves the economic interests of the bourgeoisie. Marx recognized, however, that if thought is the product of material conditions, then even inverted, ideological thoughts must have material origins. He wrote: "The phantoms formed in the human brain are also, necessarily, sublimates of their material life-process, which is empirically verifiable and bound to material premises. Morality, religion, metaphysics, all the rest of ideology and their corresponding forms of consciousness, thus no longer retain the semblance of independence."[39] That is to say, ideology is a system of false beliefs used to legitimate social and economic relations that serve the interests of the class in power. Bad ideas are generated by a bad social system, as a means of propping up that system. Marx speculates that the abolition of classes by way of a proletarian revolution would also abolish ideology.

Over the century and a half since Marx wrote his major works, the term ideology has retained its pejorative connotation. It is often used to describe a system of beliefs that distorts reality to justify or rationalize class interests. Marx's frequent co-author, Friedrich Engels, claimed that Marxist thought escaped all ideology because it constituted a "scientific socialism." Conservative critics claim that Marxism is a highly ideological enterprise precisely because it abandons pragmatic thought for revolutionary ideals. Ideology is used as a term of opprobrium by both sides of the political spectrum.

Some forms of ideology are considered useful and good—even by Marxists. Vladimir Lenin (1870–1924), the Russian revolutionary and theorist, is largely responsible for this modification. In support of a communist revolution in Russia, Lenin argued that ideology could be either good or bad, depending on the social class with which it was aligned. There are, however, only two choices: a proletarian (socialist) ideology and a bourgeois (capitalist) ideology. The latter, Lenin insists, distorts consciousness by upholding and justifying property rights. The former signifies a true consciousness that stimulates the revolutionary overthrow of the capitalist system.

Socialist ideology is necessary, Lenin argues, to combat bourgeois ideology. Creating and propagating socialist ideology becomes the job of revolutionary intelligentsia or "socialist theoreticians."[40] Lenin understands ideology to constitute an important intellectual force. Indeed, he suggests that ideology may at times become the primary force fostering revolutionary change. This stands in marked contrast to Marx's claim that ideology is only the efflux of material conditions.

Ideology is most often employed as a negative epithet implying that an individual's or group's beliefs and values constitute rationalizations of its social power or class privilege. But it is also used as a relatively neutral term to denote any system of belief about society or politics, especially if has practical implications. College courses on political ideologies typically focus on a wide range of the "isms" that compose the traditional political spectrum—anarchism, communism, socialism, liberalism, conservatism, and fascism—alongside an assortment of other "isms," including nationalism, feminism, environmentalism, populism and (religious) fundamentalism.

In the years following World War II, many intellectuals (such as Edward Shils, Raymond Aron, Seymour Lipset, and most notably Daniel Bell) spoke about the "end of ideology." They believed that a consensus had arisen, at least in the Western world, about the bankruptcy of communism and the immorality of unconstrained capitalism. Free enterprise and liberal democracy, in tandem with a welfare system that served as an adequate safety net for the less fortunate, was deemed too good and too stable a system to require revolutionary change or even significant reform. Consequently, it was believed that pragmatic politics aimed at incremental, technical solutions of complex social problems would replace the simplified worldviews, apocalyptic visions, and strident claims to world-historic truths promulgated by ideologists of the past.

A few decades later, and with a Hegelian slant, Francis Fukuyama pursued a similar theme, writing about the "end of history."[41] Fukuyama's claim was that the economic, technological, political, and moral achievements of liberal democracy and marketplace economics made ideological visions and struggles obsolete. History, understood as the battlefield of ideologies, had stopped.

To be sure, the global ideological battle between communism and capitalism has all but disappeared. Yet ideological visions persist, and ideological struggles—chiefly grounded in territorial, economic, ethnic, and religious claims—continue to flare up across the globe. Liberal democratic ideology, while increasingly pervasive, is not the only player left on the field of history. Indeed, nondemocratic regimes replaced democratic ones over fifty times in the last century—and that does not count democratic regimes toppled as the result of a foreign invasion.[42] Freedom House, the most widely acknowledged organization monitoring the health of democracy worldwide, observed in 2018 that we are entering "a period characterized by emboldened autocrats, beleaguered democracies, and the United States' withdrawal from its leadership role in the global struggle for human freedom. Democracy is in crisis." The remark was made as the world witnessed its 12th consecutive year of decline in "global freedom," with more than double the number of countries suffering net declines in political rights and civil liberties as those registering gains.[43] Clearly there is much history yet to be written.

Ideologies are sets of beliefs and values that conceptually and practically attempt to order or transform collective life. As long as individuals and groups have particular interests that can be better served by specific forms of social organization and political rule, their beliefs and values will be conceptually systematized in ways that justify these forms of organization and rule. The end of ideology is no more likely today or in the future than it was when Marx and Engels, echoing Saint-Simon, originally proposed to substitute a pragmatic "administration of things" for the strife-prone "government of men."

Nor would the end of ideology necessarily be a good thing. Ideologies are typically grounded in ideals, many of which are laudatory. Concluding his famous essay "Politics as a Vocation," Max Weber observed that politics was not for the weak of heart. "Politics," he wrote, "is a strong and slow boring of hard boards." Yet politics requires more than pragmatism and endurance: it demands the passionate pursuit of ideals. Weber writes: "Certainly all historical experience confirms the truth—that man would not have attained the possible unless time and again he had reached out for the impossible."[44] Notwithstanding their inherent dangers, ideologies can provide visions of a better future and encourage its pursuit. Ideologies are always dangerous—but so is a dearth of ideals.

Ideology may be used as a relatively neutral term or even a term of praise, as when Lenin speaks effusively of "socialist ideology." Nonetheless, it always denotes the beliefs or values of specific groups or classes of people. Ideologies are not impartial. To describe someone's views as ideological is to suggest that her beliefs and values legitimate her (group's) advantages within society. Consequently, the word *ideological* is often used as a synonym for biased or self-serving.

Are political theories merely ideologies dressed up in scholarly garb? The German social theorist Karl Mannheim (1893–1947) was one of the first thinkers to address this sticky issue. In his treatise *Ideology and Utopia*, Mannheim suggests that all economic classes and ruling groups necessarily propound systems of beliefs that justify their social status. To assess the ideological link between thought and power, he developed a "sociology of knowledge." Mannheim hoped to demonstrate that a group's claim to truth effectively derives from the need to protect and justify its social position and prerogatives.

Mannheim realized that a sociology of knowledge might be applied to the truth claims of the sociologist of knowledge, casting the validity of these claims into doubt. To avoid this problem, Mannheim argued that there was one group of people whose class position is not as "fixed" as that of wage-laborers or capitalists and therefore remains largely "unattached" or "unanchored" to particular economic interests. This *"relatively* classless stratum" of individuals are the intellectuals. Since intellectuals are less attached to economic interests than traditional classes, Mannheim believed they might rise above the ideological fray and supply a more objective and impartial view of the world. Mannheim writes that "a group whose class position is more or less definitely fixed already has its potential viewpoint decided for it. Where this is not so, as with the intellectuals, there is a wider area of choice. . . . Only he who really has the choice has an interest in seeing the whole of the social and political structure."[45] In escaping rigid class structures, intellectuals leave behind all the ideological baggage that others are forced to carry with them. Freed of this baggage, they may carry the torch for truth.

The problem with Mannheim's thesis is that it leaves itself open to the charge of being ideological in the most traditional sense of the term. As Marx and Lenin pointed out, each class attempts to portray its beliefs and values as objective, impartial, universal, free from hypocrisy, and beyond the taint of narrow self-interest. These claims constitute an ideology's public relations strategy. But ideologies are not simply lies people propagate to secure their interests and cover their tracks. They are complex systems of beliefs and values that people hold to be true and worthy, not only for themselves but for others as well. The power of ideology is that it allows (classes of) individuals to believe that their inherently biased beliefs *are* objective, universal truths. When Mannheim makes the claim of objectivity and impartiality for intellectuals like himself, he is doing exactly what Marx saw capitalists doing for their class and what Lenin encouraged proletarians to do for their class. Mannheim's notion of the "unattached" intellectual effectively protects and celebrates the interests of intellectuals, as merchants of ideas.

Are political theorists, as merchants of ideas, always propagating biased legitimations of their own particular interests and status? Can political theory ever escape ideology? Before attempting an answer, it will be helpful to examine an approach to political thinking that serves as a countervailing force to ideology.

## IRONY

It is tempting to ascribe ideological beliefs to others while holding oneself to have eminently defensible political convictions firmly grounded in reasoned arguments. Yet no theorist can completely divorce her interests and biases from the reasoning and concepts she employs. Still, to combat the most pernicious effects of ideology, theorists may employ irony.

While the ideological tendency to view the world through a single lens is ever-present in political theorizing, so is the opposing tendency of irony. Ideology systematizes the world to provide practical answers. Irony deconstructs the world to pose troublesome questions. Ironists acknowledge the essential contestability of both the concepts and principles that guide political life and the epistemological categories, such as reason and rationality, that ground concepts and principles.

Unlike the ideologist, the ironist is not very self-assured. She acknowledges that there is no single lens with which to best view the world, or at least admits that she has failed to discover it. This is not a shortcoming. Rather, by looking through many lenses, the ironist gains an increasingly expansive view of the world. The ironist reserves judgment and withholds support from ideological positions in order more deeply to explore and appreciate the inherent complexities and ambiguities of political life.

Socrates was one of the first ironists. Many still consider him to be the greatest. In the original Greek use of the term, an ironist was someone who leads others astray through rhetorical deception or sarcastic praise. The ironist (from the Greek *eiron*) was a dissembler. In many of Plato's dialogues, such as the *Symposium*, the *Apology*, and the *Republic*, the word irony is applied to Socrates as a term of abuse.

In the *Republic*, the description of Socrates as an ironist is used in exasperation by Thrasymachus, who finds Socrates' dialectic argument to constitute a tiresome beating around the bush. Socrates does indeed move in dialectical circles, often to no apparent purpose. Yet there is a method in his madness. To get the conversation started, Socrates admits that he has nothing to teach. He then flatters those who lay claim to knowledge, coaxing them to share their intellectual bounty. Socrates' flattery is often perceived as a mockery, for his persistent questioning inevitably undercuts his interlocutors' claims to knowledge. To be sure, Socrates is eager enough to poke holes in any inflated intellectual egos that come his way. Yet Socrates is ironic not so much because of what he reveals about others, but owing to what he reveals about himself. Irony, Aristotle states, is the opposite of boastfulness. Socrates denies his own possession of knowledge.

Socrates' irony validates the Delphic oracle's claim that he is the wisest of men. By admitting ignorance, Socrates demonstrates that he knows at least one thing—that he knows nothing. His interlocutors do not even know that. "Knowledge of ignorance is not ignorance," Leo Strauss remarks in his discussion of Socrates. "It is knowledge of the elusive character of the truth." Truth is not something one can grasp, only something one can approach. As Socrates demonstrates, the ironist tirelessly seeks truth by critically exploring the claims to knowledge made by others. He engages in this exploration because a firm sense of the limits of knowledge is only ever gained by the pursuit of knowledge itself.

In Plato's *Republic*, Socrates recites the famous allegory of the cave. He tells of a long-time captive who mistakes dim shadows on the cave wall for reality. The captive eventually breaks free of his chains and climbs up out of the cave into the bright sunshine. Here, after being initially blinded by the light, he comes to perceive things as they truly are. The allegory of the cave is typically interpreted as evidence of Plato's elitist belief that truth is available only for the few who break free of common opinions and perceptions and gain philosophic knowledge. This may indeed be Plato's intent.

Alternatively, there may be another message. Perhaps Plato is being ironic. The actual words that Plato employs in constructing the allegory of the cave, as all the words found in the *Republic*, are very much like the shadows dancing on the cave walls. These words are, at best, dim reflections of things. From this perspective, Plato's writing is ironic because it demonstrates a self-critical understanding of its own limitations. Perhaps Plato's works are not meant to persuade us of their truth with the rigor of a geometric proof. Perhaps the real message is that truth, be it philosophic or political in nature, may be glimpsed but never be grasped through the media of words.

An ancient Zen story tells of a teacher who directs students to look at the moon. To help focus their attention, he points skyward. The young students naively stare at their teacher's outstretched finger. Plato's words are like the teacher's finger. More enlightened readers, Plato may be suggesting, will understand that his writings do not speak for truth but are goads to the pursuit of deeper knowledge.[46]

Socrates states that "once a thing is put in writing, the composition, whatever it may be, drifts all over the place, getting into the hands not only of those who understand it, but equally of those who have no business with it; it doesn't know how to address the right people, and not address the wrong."[47] In a letter, Plato writes that "no intelligent man will ever be so bold as to put into language those things which his reason has contemplated, especially not into a form that is unalterable—which must be the case with what is expressed in written symbols."[48] Yet Plato chose to write, and so had to distinguish between suitable and unsuitable readers.

One means of meeting this challenge was to write dialogues rather than formal treatises. In a dialogue, where numerous voices are heard, the reader is never completely certain which voice, if any, represents the author. The reader never knows who speaks for truth. In turn, myth and metaphor are frequently deployed in Plato's dialogues when the limits of logic and reason are reached. Different readers receive different messages, in keeping with their dispositions and capacities. Dialogue is well suited to irony.

The genius of Plato is found in the multiple levels at which his dialogues operate. Infused with irony, they speak in multiple voices. Diverse interpretations of the texts will be unavoidable. Not all his readers will receive the same lessons. If we understand Plato to have adopted an ironic perspective, then our former interpretations of his politics—as guided by the pursuit of mathematical precision—must be reevaluated. We are left unsure whether Plato was serious about his political prescriptions for an authoritarian regime and rigid caste society. The reader of Plato's dialogues, like the philosopher, is subject to a "self-corrective" exercise that underlines both the imperative of reaching for truth and skeptical reserve concerning its grasp.[49] Plato's political theory is not straightforward. It is a lesson in irony. Appropriately, the import of the lesson remains undecided.

### BETWEEN IDEOLOGY AND IRONY

Wholly ideological thought is exceedingly rare. It could emerge only from a mind swept clean of all countervailing tendencies and confusions, incapable of original or independent thinking, and wholly ordered by a single, coherent system of beliefs and values. Perhaps wholly ideological thought is only temporarily evident in those who have been successfully brainwashed.

Wholly ironic thought is equally rare. To remain wholly ironic, one's mind would have to be swept every bit as clean of former beliefs and values as the ideologist's. But the sweeping would have to be continual and unending, leaving the cleansed mind without any firm beliefs or values to fill the void. To be a complete ironist would entail switching lenses with such rapidity that nothing would ever come into focus. The world would remain a blur. One could form no stable concepts, secure no attachments, and maintain no commitments.

Practically speaking, the complete ironist would be as a leaf in the wind, incapable of self-direction and settling nowhere. Since no one allows her life to be completely directionless, the pretension to be wholly ironic is hypocritical. One may be able to feign it in writing but could never practice it in life. Though the ironist attempts to hover above firm convictions, she still lives much like the rest of us, tied to her beliefs and biases and, despite any intellectual playfulness, usually quite serious in the pursuit of her interests.

In the *Republic*, Socrates resorted to telling myths and "noble lies" to achieve order in the city. In contemporary times, the theorist also tends to rely on mythic beliefs and values—ideological convictions—to bring conceptual and practical order to her world. Yet to the extent theorists engage in thinking, the ideological convictions they cannot wholly foreswear become challenged. Thinking, as Socrates demonstrated, is an inherently ironic exercise. It interrogates more than it settles. Thinking disturbs commitment. As poor Hamlet laments, "the native hue of resolution" is often "sicklied o'er with the pale cast of thought." Irony is not only a tactic deployed to challenge others' pretensions to knowledge. It is the inevitable product of deep thinking and undermines self-assured action.

It is said that one thinks through things to make up one's mind. But thinking more often leaves the mind less tidy than before, moving in circles and spirals rather than straight lines, as Socrates' dialogues well demonstrate. The political theorist Hannah Arendt (1906–75) observed that "thinking means that each time you are confronted with some difficulty in life you have to make up your mind anew."[50] Taking decisive action is difficult for those who think.

The thinker remains too unsettled to take a stand. The ideologue remains too committed to gain perspective. By making things seem simpler than they are, ideology promotes action. By demonstrating the complexity and ambiguity of the world, thinking induces reflection. To take decisive action, one has to stop thinking, at least for the moment. Acting interrupts thinking, just as thinking interrupts acting. As actors within political communities, complete irony is impossible for us. As thinkers, wholesale ideology is impossible for us.

Friedrich Nietzsche (1844–1900), the German philosopher and a deep ironist, acknowledged the appropriateness of the skeptic's statement, "I have no idea how I am *acting*! I have no idea how I *ought to act*!" But one cannot stop there. "You are right," Nietzsche responds to the skeptic, "but be sure of this: *you will be acted upon* at every moment!"[51] Those ironic thinkers who, for skeptical reasons, choose not to act are nonetheless always being acted upon. To live as a bystander is not to escape politics, just agency.

Exercising political agency does not necessitate intellectual dishonesty or self-deception. We might momentarily stop thinking in order to take action not because our beliefs and values suddenly seem incontestable to us but simply to cope with the demands of life. These demands include defending the just laws of the land, as Socrates consistently did—laws that safeguard the basic rights and responsibilities of citizens to think, speak and associate freely.

Politics demands action in the absence of firm foundations. To seek more than a "relative" validity for one's convictions, Isaiah Berlin (1909–97) writes, is perhaps a "deep and incurable metaphysical need." But to allow this necessarily unfulfilled need to thwart all practice, Berlin insists, is "a symptom of an equally deep, and more dangerous, moral and political immaturity."[52] Political theorists effectively navigate a position between ideology and irony, active commitment and skeptical thinking. They contribute to the search for political knowledge while asking questions that underline their ignorance. There is, as Richard Ashcraft acknowledges, a "very thin line, intellectually speaking, separating the political theorist from the ideologist."[53] That thin but crucial line is bound up with the theorist's commitment to questions that defy fully satisfying answers.

Ludwig Wittgenstein (1889–1951), an Austrian philosopher, once wrote that philosophy consists in the bumps on the head one gets from butting up against the limits of language. He meant to suggest that language takes us so far in assessing the quandaries of life and that philosophic wonder and speculation occur when these quandaries are experienced as unresolvable. Political theory consists in the bumps on the head that arise from attempts to understand and order political life in the face of its essentially contested concepts. These metaphoric contusions allow us to avoid the real bumps to the head that would be suffered were blows exchanged instead of words.

The pen is said to be mightier than the sword. One might applaud the thought behind this familiar maxim, which celebrates reasoned persuasion over violent coercion. Words are powerful things, as are ideas, concepts and theories. But words can also be formidable weapons.

A Spanish grammarian told Queen Isabella in 1492 that "language is the instrument of empire."[54] To control language is to control ideas and to control ideas is to control behavior. A few decades before the French Revolution, a scholar currying the favor of a ruler succinctly expressed this linkage:

> When you have thus formed the chain of ideas in the heads of your citizens, you will then be able to pride yourselves on guiding them and being their masters. A stupid despot may constrain his slaves with iron chains; but a true politician binds them even more strongly by the chain of their own ideas; it is at the stable point of reason that he secures the end of the chain; this link is all the stronger in that we do not know of what it is made and we believe it to be our own work; despair and time eat away the bonds of iron and steel, but they are powerless against the habitual union of ideas, they can only tighten it still more; and on the soft fibers of the brain is founded the unshakable base of the soundest of Empires.[55]

De Tracy had this sort of power in mind when he created his science of ideas. Ideology can be an impressive, and oppressive, force.

All ideologies imply, and more extreme ideologies insist, that there is only one correct lens with which to view social and political reality. This single-minded advocacy of a specific point of view has benefits. It may lead to insights that would not have arisen from a less dogged approach. The accompanying danger, however, is that ideology might blind one to more features of political reality than it reveals. Importantly, ideology gains its power not so much by telling people what to do but by telling them who they are. Ideologies define a person's place in nature, role in society, and mission in history. They generate identities, and tasks and duties to go with these identities. In doing so, ideologies typically foster hard-and-fast distinctions between friends and foes, "good guys" and "bad guys," the "in-group" and the "out-group."

The theorist does not deny that there are necessary and worthy struggles to be engaged in political life, and opponents to be challenged. But the distinction between allies and enemies is protean and ever subject to revision. In turn, key battles need to be waged within the self, as our limited capacities for certainty and truth are forced to confront a complex, contested world that will not stand still.

In *The Laws*, Plato warns of the problems faced in any attempt to establish a just city. "The real difficulty," the Athenian speaker in the dialogue states, "is to make political systems reflect in practice the trouble-free perfection of theory."[56] Practicing what you preach, having one's life conform to one's principles, is indeed a difficult task. Yet theory is hardly a trouble-free endeavor. Starting with Plato's own student, political theorists have engaged in the critical task of revealing troubling imperfections in the theories of their mentors and forebears.

The source of the trouble is twofold. First, any theoretical attempt to describe a complex world parsimoniously will do some violence to it. The Greek myth of Procrustes depicts a robber known for mutilating his victims. He would stretch or cut off their legs so that they would fit snugly into his bed. To call something Procrustean is to suggest that it produces uniform order by violent methods. Political theorists' efforts to make the world fit trimly into their conceptual schemes and reflect fully their normative standards may prompt them to lop off all those parts that prove unwieldy. Political theorists should be wary of Procrustean tendencies.

Second, political theorists can only understand social and political life if they participate in it. This participation leads theorists to adopt interests and identities that color perception and understanding. Without this color, much of the world would remain invisible. Yet the tinting often obscures as much as it reveals, as tensions, limitations, and contradictions in the theorists' lives work their way into their theories. William James observed that "a great many people think they are thinking, when they are merely rearranging their prejudices." Despite theorists' diligence as critical thinkers, there is no guarantee that their efforts do not amount to the rearrangement of biases born of personal interests and identities.

Karl Popper argues that reason in science is chiefly evidenced in the openness of a theory to its own contestation.[57] The physicist Richard Feynman observed that the "first principle [of science] is that you must not fool yourself—and you are the easiest person to fool. After you've not fooled yourself, it's easy not to fool other scientists." To avoid fooling colleagues, Feynman counsels, "try to give *all* of the information to help others to judge the value of your contribution; not just the information that leads to judgment in one particular direction or another."[58] In this way, Feynman observes, science is distinguished from advertising, which only ever provides information that contributes to increased sales. Unlike natural scientists, political theorists cannot avail themselves of the methodologically rigorous replication of experiments to reign in their biases. So they need to be especially welcoming of contestation, lest their theories degenerate into the political advertising of ideology.

Political theorists organize ideas and facts into reasoned propositions to gain both understanding of the domain of politics and moral footing within it. But political theorists do not occupy a privileged vantage point from which neutral descriptions and explanations of an objective reality might be obtained. Instead, they speak from specific points of view and evidence the effects that power has had upon them. Political theorists navigate the fertile and treacherous terrain between ideology and irony. While ideology is inescapable, theorists may avoid its deepest pitfalls by welcoming contestation of their concepts and reasoning, acknowledging the uncertainties of political life and their own biases, thinking deeply and critically, and well exercising practical judgment.

## REFERENCES

1   Michael Sandel, "The Procedural Republic and the Unencumbered Self," in *Communitarianism and Individualism*, eds Shlomo Avineri and Avner de-Shalit (Oxford: Oxford University Press, 1992), 12.

2   Quoted in John G. Gunnell, *The Descent of Political Theory: The Genealogy of an American Vocation* (Chicago: University of Chicago Press, 1993), 21.

3   Claude Henri de Saint-Simon, *Social Organization, the Science of Man, and Other Writings*, trans. Felix Markham (New York: Harper Torchbooks, 1964), 39–40. See also Robert Wokler, "Saint-Simon and the Passage from Political to Social Science," in *The Languages of Political Theory in Early-Modern Europe*, ed. Anthony Pagden (Cambridge: Cambridge University Press, 1987), 325–38.

4   John Stuart Mill, *Collected Works* (Toronto: University of Toronto Press, 1974), 8: 833.

5   James Shotwell, quoted in Bernard Crick, *In Defense of Politics*, 4th edn (Chicago: University of Chicago Press, 1992), 95–96.

6   Robert Michels, *Political Parties: A Sociological Study of the Oligarchical Tendencies of Modern Democracy*, trans. Eden and Cedar Paul (New York: Dover Publications, 1915), viii, 401.

7   Max Weber, *The Methodology of the Social Sciences* (New York: Free Press, 1949).

8   Max Weber, *The Protestant Ethic and the Spirit of Capitalism*, trans. Talcott Parsons (New York: Scribner's, 1958), 98.

9   Max Weber, *The Protestant Ethic*, 233.

10  See Charles Taylor, "Interpretation and the Sciences of Man," in *Philosophical Papers* (Cambridge: Cambridge University Press, 1985), 2: 15–57.

11  Sheldon Wolin, "Political Theory as a Vocation," *American Political Science Review* 63 (1969): 1076–77.

12  Philip Pettit, *Republicanism: A Theory of Freedom and Government* (Oxford: Clarendon Press, 1997), 102.

13  See Leslie Paul Thiele, *The Heart of Judgment: Practical Wisdom, Neuroscience, and Narrative* (Cambridge: Cambridge University Press, 2006).

14  Quoted in Charles R. Bambach, *Heidegger, Dilthey, and the Crisis of Historicism* (Ithaca: Cornell University Press, 1995), 161.

15  Hans-Georg Gadamer, *Truth and Method* (New York: Crossroad, 1975), 358.

16  Hans-Georg Gadamer, "The Universality of the Hermeneutical Problem," *Philosophical Hermeneutics* (Berkeley: University of California Press, 1976), 9.

17  Gadamer, *Truth and Method*, 238.

18  Tzvetan Todorov, *The Morals of History*, trans. Alyson Waters (Minneapolis: University of Minnesota Press, 1995), 15.

19  See Daniel Kahneman, Paul Slovic, Amos Tversky, eds *Judgment Under Uncertainty: Heuristics and Biases* (Cambridge: Cambridge University Press, 1982); Scott Plous, *The Psychology of Judgment and Decision Making* (Philadelphia: Temple University Press, 1993); Daniel Kahneman, *Thinking, Fast and Slow* (New York: Farrar, Straus and Giroux, 2011).

20  For the classic study, see Irving Janis, *Victims of Groupthink* (Boston: Houghton Mifflin, 1972).

21  See Dale Griffin and Amos Tversky, "The Weighing of Evidence and the Determinants of Confidence," in *Judgment Under Uncertainty: Heuristics and Biases*, 230; Philip E. Tetlock, *Expert Political Judgment* (Princeton: Princeton University Press, 2005).

22  Gadamer, *Truth and Method*, 273.

23  Hans-Georg Gadamer, *Reason in the Age of Science*, trans. Frederick Lawrence (Cambridge: MIT Press, 1981), 109–10.

24  Aristotle, *Nichomachean Ethics*, Book 2:2 (London: Penguin, 1953), 57.

25  Leo Strauss, *What Is Political Philosophy and Other Studies* (Westport, Conn.: Greenwood Press, 1959), 21.

26  Thomas Jefferson's letter to William Charles Jarvis, September 28, 1820, in Paul Leicester Ford, ed., *The Writings of Thomas Jefferson*, vol. 10 (New York: G.P. Putnam's Sons, 1899).

27  Sheldon Wolin, "Political Theory as a Vocation," *American Political Science Review* 63 (1969): 1064.

28  Judith Shklar, *The Faces of Injustice* (New Haven: Yale University Press, 1990), 16.

29  Quentin Skinner, "Meaning and Understanding in the History of Ideas," *History and Theory* 8, no. 1 (1969): 52–53.

30  Richard Ashcraft, "Political Theory and the Problem of Ideology," *The Journal of Politics* 42, no. 3 (August 1980): 702, 691.

31  George H. Sabine, *A History of Political Theory*, 3rd edn (London: George G. Harrap & Co., 1951), 7.

32  William E. Connolly, *The Terms of Political Discourse*, 3rd edn (Princeton: Princeton University Press, 1993), 1, 180.

33  Connolly, *The Terms of Political Discourse*, 227.

34  Aldous Huxley, *Brave New World* (London: Granada Publishing, 1932); and George Orwell, *Nineteen Eighty-four* (New York: Penguin Books, 1949).

35  George Orwell, "Politics and the English Language," in *A Collection of Essays* (Garden City, N.Y.: Doubleday, 1954).

36  Francis Bacon, *Selected Writings*, ed. H.G. Dick (New York: Random House, 1955), 435.

37  See E. Kennedy, *A "Philosophe" in the Age of Revolution: Destutt de Tracy and the origins of "ideology"* (Philadelphia: American Philosophical Society, 1978).

38  Francis Bacon, *The Advancement of Learning* (London, 1974), bk 2, sec. 23.49, quoted in Stephen Macedo, *Liberal Virtues: Citizenship, Virtue, and Community in Liberal Constitutionalism* (Oxford: Clarendon Press, 1990), 43.

39  Karl Marx, "The German Ideology," in *The Marx-Engels Reader*, 2nd edn, ed. Robert C. Tucker (New York: Norton, 1978), 154–55.

40  V.I. Lenin, "What Is to Be Done," in *The Lenin Anthology*, ed. Robert C. Tucker (New York: Norton, 1975), 28–29.

41  Francis Fukuyama, *The End of History and the Last Man* (New York: Free Press, 1992).

42  Frank Bealey, "Stability and Crisis: Fears about Threats to Democracy," *European Journal of Political Research* 15 (1987): 687–715. Cited in Robert Dahl, "Democratic Theory and Democratic Experience," in Seyla Benhabib, ed., *Democracy and Difference: Contesting the Boundaries of the Political* (Princeton: Princeton University Press, 1996), 337.

43  Michael J. Abramowitz, "Democracy in Crisis," Freedom House, 2018. Accessed May 2018 at https://freedomhouse.org/report/freedom-world/freedom-world-2018

44  Max Weber, *From Max Weber: Essays in Sociology*, ed. H.H. Gerth and C. Wright Mills (New York: Galaxy, 1958), 128.

45  Karl Mannheim, *Ideology and Utopia: An Introduction to the Sociology of Knowledge*, trans. Louis Wirth and Edward Shils (New York: Harcourt, Brace, 1936), 154–55, 161.

46  See Plato, *Phaedrus* (275c), in *The Collected Dialogues of Plato*, ed. Edith Hamilton and Huntington Cairns (Princeton: Princeton University Press, 1989), 521.

47  Plato, *Phaedrus* (275e), in *Collected Dialogues*, 521.

48  Plato, *Seventh Letter* (343), in *Collected Dialogues*, 1590.

49  Wayne C. Booth, *A Rhetoric of Irony* (Chicago: University of Chicago Press, 1974), 275.

50  Hannah Arendt, *The Life of the Mind* (New York: Harcourt Brace Jovanovich, 1978), 177.

51  Friedrich Nietzsche, *Daybreak: Thoughts on the Prejudices of Morality*, trans. R.J. Hollingdale (Cambridge: Cambridge University Press, 1982), 76–77. And see Leslie Paul Thiele, "Out from the Shadows of God: Nietzschean Skepticism and Political Practice," *International Studies in Philosophy* 27, no. 3 (August 1995): 55–72.

52  Isaiah Berlin, *Four Essays on Liberty* (Oxford: Oxford University Press, 1969), 172.

53  Ashcraft, "Political Theory and the Problem of Ideology," 695.

54  Quoted in Anthony Pagden, *European Encounters with the New World* (New Haven: Yale University Press, 1993), 118.

55  J.M. Servan, *Discours sur l'administration de la justice criminelle*, 1767, quoted in Michel Foucault, *Discipline and Punish: The Birth of the Prison* (New York: Vintage, 1977), 102–3.

56  Plato, *The Laws* (636a), trans. Trevor Saunders (New York: Penguin Books, 1970), 61; in *Collected Dialogues*, 1236.

57  See Karl Popper, *The Logic of Scientific Discovery* (New York: Basic Books, 1959), and *Conjectures and Refutations* (New York: Basic Books, 1962).

58  Richard P. Feynman, *Surely You're Joking, Mr. Feynman!* (New York: W.W. Norton, 1985), 387, 386.

## CHAPTER 2

# HUMAN NATURE, POWER AND POLITICS

Throughout the history of political thought, efforts to describe, explain, order and transform collective life have been grounded upon specific conceptions of the character and constitution of human being. This chapter addresses the relationship between human nature and politics. It explores the notion that memes and mores serve as the cultural counterparts to genes in the realm of human development and behavior. It subsequently investigates the core political concept of power and its relation to force and violence. In turn, the chapter examines the distinction between the public and private spheres as well as the relationship between rule and resistance, equality and elites.

## POLITICAL ANIMALS

Politics is often defined as the art of government. Government refers to the institutions and processes through which binding decisions are made for a society. Politics, then, pertains to the use of power to organize and order, regulate and transform collective human existence. Political theorists investigate the various forms and uses of power, and examine the rights and responsibilities of citizens and public officials. Most ground their understanding of power, rights, and responsibilities on implicit if not explicit theories of human nature.

It is often said that human beings are unique because they alone have language. But many other animals use sounds and gestures to communicate. Honeybees engage in an elaborate "waggle dance" to let their hive mates know precisely where sources of food are to be found. Dolphins employ a complex series of high-pitched tones to communicate, and whales "sing" to each other in conversations that can last for hours. Vervet monkeys warn each other whether snakes or eagles or leopards are approaching with distinct sounds that clearly identify each type of predator. Chimpanzees, gorillas and orangutans have been trained to communicate with rudimentary elements of human sign language. These apes not only respond to questions but also initiate communication, make basic requests, and have even taught each other to use sign language.[1]

Still, no other species employs original and extended combinations of words in a rule-governed fashion, employing syntax. Yet this skill comes naturally to human beings. Most of us speak grammatically in relatively complex sentences from the time we are three or four years old without any formal training. The complexity of human language allows for the development of reason. Reason is a process of separating, contrasting, and combining thoughts captured in words in a coherent and consistent manner, allowing for sustained chains of ideas as well as logical deductions and inferences. Language, in combination with reason, vastly extends our mental reach. Our linguistic and rational capacities make us unique among animals. Aristotle recognized this over two millennia ago. He defined human being as a *zoon logon echon*: a rational, speaking animal.

Aristotle is better known for a different definition of human being. He said human being was a *zoon politikon*, a political animal. Aristotle's definitions prove mutually supportive. The two key features of a human being—a linguistic, rational nature and a political nature—go hand in hand. One might say that we are political because we have language and reason, and we have language and reason because we are political.

In calling human being a political animal, Aristotle suggests that what makes us different from the rest of the animal kingdom is our capacity to live together in a manner that other animals do not and cannot achieve. He observes that we live politically, whereas other animals that sleep, travel, forage, or hunt together in groups only live collectively. Animal collectivities are often organizationally and behaviorally complex. Ant, bee and wasp colonies, for example, are extraordinarily well ordered with very efficient divisions of labor. Along with other social animals, they may engage in collective activities such as warfare and slavery. Mammals and primates evidence many of the tendencies basic to political life, such as struggles for leadership, reciprocity in relationships, punishment for rule-breaking, the mitigation of conflict, and mutual aid.[2]

What differentiates human communities from animal colonies, packs, and herds, therefore, is neither that humans organize themselves collectively nor that this organization results in complex social order. Ant, bee, wasp and termite colonies exhibit a much greater degree of order with much less disruption than human societies. Still, human communities are unique, Aristotle claims, and uniquely political.

The reason is that human communities are composed of beings that conceive themselves as unique parts within a complex whole. Some animals, such as ants, bees, wasps and termites, are fully collective beings. Other animals, such as spiders, snakes, and bears, are mostly solitary creatures. Some animals may engage in both a solitary and collective existence, like dogs and wolves, living sometimes as loners and other times as members of packs. Yet no other animal thinks, speaks, and acts self-consciously as a distinct individual within a community. Certain human cultures celebrate individuality, while others emphasize the importance of the community. Yet all political cultures evidence a fecund, and tensioned, relationship between individuality and community.

Conceiving oneself as an individual within a community is possible only for a self-conscious creature. Human beings not only desire and act but also evaluate their desires and actions self-reflectively. Only self-reflective thought allows us to gain distance from pressing desires, drives, and impulses. Consequently, we can indulge, deny, postpone, or reroute our desires, drives, and impulses, having judged them from more encompassing vantage points that allow present inclinations and behavior to be weighed against more distant or collective concerns. In this manner, we learn from the past and prepare for the future.

Abstract, self-reflective thought is never attained in isolation. Becoming self-conscious is a process that human beings only ever achieve when they develop among other human beings, in linguistic or language-speaking communities.[3] Consciousness, as the word itself indicates, is a "knowing with." We come to know things *with* others, by way of sharing the world in speech. Language allows us to understand others, and what others think of us. By this means, language prompts us to reflect upon ourselves. Self-consciousness arises when the human capacity to partake communicatively in the experiences of others is turned in on itself.

To summarize: The tensioned balance that exists between the self-conscious individual and the community constitutes the core of politics. Our experiencing and organizing ourselves in the light of this balance defines our lives as political animals. This requires a capacity for self-reflective thought. In turn, the capacity for self-reflective thought depends on the development of language and reason.

Political life is a historical achievement. It was unavailable to the evolutionary ancestors of human beings who had less sophisticated capacities of language and reason. Yet the development of language and reason depends on the existence of community. Which, then, came first, political life or language and reason? This quandary may never be solved. It is much like the puzzle of whether the chicken or the egg came first. There is no satisfying answer. Most likely, a rudimentary form of self-reflective language and reason developed simultaneously with a rudimentary form of political life in prehistoric human communities. The *zoon politikon* and the *zoon logon echon* always were, and remain today, one and the same animal.

### THE SIGNIFICANCE OF HUMAN NATURE

What is the relationship between biology and politics, nature and nurture? And to what extent does and should biology constrain and shape political life? These questions are as old as political thinking itself. "Few ideas," a historian writes, "have been recycled as often as the belief that the 'Is' of nature must become the 'Ought' of man."[4] From ancient through modern times, political theorists have attempted to erect political edifices upon the foundations of human nature.

Plato's politics follows directly from his understanding of human nature. He argues that the human soul is composed of three parts: an animal-like appetitive or desiring part, a humanlike emotional or spirited part, and a godlike intellectual or reasoning part. Plato structures the political realm to accommodate this tripartite division. In *The Republic*, three classes or castes of individuals represent the three facets of human nature. Merchants and tradespeople, who are mostly actuated by their appetites and base desires, form the lowest caste. Soldiers, who are mostly actuated by their spirited emotions and love of honor, form the middle caste. Philosophers and rulers known as guardians, who are mostly actuated by their reason or intellect, form the top caste. Through intensive education, children of lower castes may occasionally gain access to the upper castes. By and large, however, the political community is organized on the basis of enduring natural propensities. Indeed, Plato suggests that maintaining the best regime would entail a sophisticated program of eugenics or selective breeding. Human reproduction would have to be controlled to ensure the best stock for the ruling caste.

Integrating the Platonic (and neo-Platonic) distinction between the ideal and the real with Christian theology, Augustine of Hippo (354–430), a North African bishop and philosopher, distinguished between the "city of God" and the "city of man." Augustine writes that "everyone, since he takes his origin from a condemned stock, is inevitably evil and carnal to begin with, by derivation from Adam."[5] Based on this understanding of humankind's fallen nature, Augustine concludes that secular government, the "city of man," is inherently unstable and doomed to disruption. His prescriptions for politics are grounded in these beliefs about the inherited and indelible features of human nature.

Thomas Aquinas (1225–74) brought medieval theory to its height by integrating Aristotelian philosophy with Christian theology. Aquinas, an Italian Dominican friar and philosopher, argues that the government of a king is best because it follows the dictates of (human) nature. He writes:

> Whatever is in accord with nature is best, for in all things nature does what is best. In the multitude of bodily members there is one which is the principal mover, namely, the heart; and among the powers of the soul one power presides as chief, namely, the reason. . . . Wherefore, if artificial things are an imitation of natural things and a work of art is better according as it attains a closer likeness to what is in nature, it follows that it is best for a human multitude to be ruled by one person.[6]

Aquinas also argues that humankind's natural reason leaves it relatively well equipped to lead a peaceful, political life. His political prescriptions follow directly from his understanding of human nature.

In modern times, Thomas Paine (1737–1809), the American patriot, theorist and pamphleteer, argued for limited government based on his notion of the inherently social nature of humankind. Paine writes:

> To understand the nature and quantity of government proper for man, it is necessary to attend to his character. As Nature created him for social life . . . she made his natural wants greater than his individual powers. . . . She has not only forced man into society, by a diversity of wants, which the reciprocal aid of each other can supply, but she has implanted in him a system of social affections, which, though not necessary to his existence, are essential to his happiness. . . . If we examine, with attention, into the composition and constitution of man . . . we shall easily discover that a great part of what is called government is mere imposition.[7]

In an original twist to an Aristotelian theme, Paine invokes the social nature of human beings as an argument against overbearing government. Paine insists, in his endorsement of democratic politics, that "All the great laws of society are laws of nature."[8]

James Madison (1751–1836), an American patriot like Paine, contributed his famous essay on factions to *The Federalist Papers*. Here Madison explicitly attributes political strife to the fallibility of human reason and the effects of human passions and self-love. He writes that the "latent causes of faction are thus sown in the nature of man."[9] With this in mind, Madison aims to construct a government that will compensate for humanity's inherent shortcomings.

A contemporary of Paine and Madison, the German philosopher Immanuel Kant (1724–1804) likewise noted that political community is saddled with the task of achieving justice for individuals who are wont to act with biased self-interest. The rule of law goes some distance to ensuring justice. Still, who will enforce the law but an individual or group of individuals prone to self-serving bias? Of the prospects for just political communities in the face of this dilemma, Kant famously observed that "Nothing straight can be constructed from such warped wood as that which man is made of." Given the crooked timber theorists are working with, designing a "perfect solution" to the problem of justice is impossible. Fortunately, Kant observes, "Nature only requires that we should approximate to this idea," and this approximation can be achieved by constitutional government.[10]

Human nature provides the timber with which every politics is constructed. Many political theorists, like Kant and Madison, argue that such crooked timber requires sophisticated architectural engineering—the creation of a balanced government serving a hallowed constitution—to withstand the tests of time. Other theorists forgo tinkering with political institutions and set out instead to straighten the timber of humanity itself through revolution.

For Karl Marx, revolutionary activity cleanses participants of the selfishness that infects individuals who are enmeshed in inegalitarian social and economic relations. It restores them to their "species being." In 1835, Marx reflected on his own future, writing in a school essay that "man's nature makes it possible for him to reach his fulfillment only by working for the perfection and welfare of his society."[11] Marx sought his own fulfillment by theorizing how a perfect communist society might arise out of revolutionary

41

struggle. For Marx, no less than his predecessors, a theory of human nature serves as the prerequisite for a theory of politics.

Consider in greater detail how Thomas Hobbes (1588–1679) grounded politics on human nature. Hobbes, an English political theorist, was much impressed by Euclidean geometry, a science that deduced firm conclusions from self-evident axioms. Like Plato, Hobbes strove to make his political theory mathematical. Making and maintaining a commonwealth, Hobbes writes, entails discovering and applying the same sort of rules as are found in arithmetic and geometry.[12] Hobbes' theory of human nature is vastly different from Plato's, however, and consequently so is the politics he proposes. Hobbes departed from the ancient Greeks by embracing modern science. The sixteenth-century scientist Galileo observed, contrary to the longstanding tradition of Aristotelian thought, that objects stay in motion until acted upon by another force. Hobbes applied this tenet of modern science to the human animal. Our inner drives, Hobbes assumed, are constantly in motion and remain ever unsatisfied. Chief among our insatiable drives is the desire for power.

Hobbes was born in 1588 in an English coastal town then threatened by the Spanish Armada. He later wrote that fear and he were born twins. Indeed, Hobbes' political theory revolves around the notion that fear is the most fundamental human passion and the chief motivating force of politics. Human beings are subject to an endless pursuit of power, Hobbes insists, owing to their fear of death or deprivation at the hands of others. Even the strongest man can easily be struck dead in his sleep by the weakest man. Likewise, an individual's power can always be undermined or destroyed by another's greater power or by a lack of vigilance. To achieve security in this precarious world, the individual seeks ever-increasing power. Of course, everyone feels the same way and acts accordingly. The result is the endless and ubiquitous pursuit of power after power, which, in the absence of government, leads to violent anarchy. Without rules and rulers to enforce them, a war of all against all ensues. In this anarchic state of nature, Hobbes famously states, life is "solitary, poore, nasty, brutish, and short."[13]

Once we accept the premises of Hobbes' deductive theory, namely, that ever-fearful humans seek power after power "ending only in death," his conclusion inevitably follows. There is but one way to escape the constant fear of being killed or subdued. Everyone must agree to make one person (or a single governmental body) an all-powerful sovereign. This "Leviathan," as Hobbes calls the supreme governmental power, forcibly maintains peace and order among its subjects. The only alternative to anarchy, for Hobbes, is authoritarian government.

Why is the submission to despotism better than living in the state of nature? Submitting to arbitrary, authoritarian rule may seem like jumping from the frying pan into the fire. Hobbes' response is that once we have created a sovereign power at least we know where the heat is coming from. Moreover, the sovereign has no reason to fear his subjects because he is all-powerful. Accordingly, he has no reason to kill or otherwise harm them unless they get out of line. For individuals primarily motivated by fear of death and deprivation, a peaceful life under despotic rule is better than freedom in a state of endless war.

Hobbes had translated the writings of the ancient Greek thinker Thucydides (c. 460–400 B.C.), considered by many to be the first political theorist. Thucydides participated in and wrote about the Peloponnesian War, a conflict between the city-states of Athens and Sparta that lasted the better part of three decades. Hobbes appears to have well learned the lessons that Thucydides taught.

The islanders of Melos, in Thucydides account, requested that they be left out of the war and given liberty to pursue their own interests rather than pay tribute to Athens. The Athenians refused, responding that they could not, or would not, give up their imperial prerogatives. The Athenians justified their proposed destruction of the rebellious Melians by invoking a law of nature: "the strong do what they can and the weak suffer what they must."[14] Thucydides suggests that the pursuit of power is natural and endless, and only wavers in the face of greater force.

Hobbes accepted Thucydides' pronouncement as a universal law. Nevertheless, Hobbes wrote his masterwork, the *Leviathan*, at the time of the Peace of Westphalia in 1648, when the European territorial state declared its sovereignty after centuries of dominance by kingdoms and empires recently ripped apart by bloody religious wars. Hobbes believed that within the sovereign nation-state, the interminable human struggle for power might be curtailed. The law of nature that dictated the endless pursuit of power could not be thwarted, but it could be brought under control by a supreme national ruler.

Human nature, for Hobbes, inevitably creates a world wherein the fear of violent death binds men and women together into groups ruled by a sovereign power. With reason playing only a minor role among human motivations and with the appetite for power running rampant, Hobbes did not think it prudent to await the arrival of a wise and benevolent philosopher king. He deduces that the rational rule of philosophers is neither likely, necessary, nor recommendable. Peaceful despotism, in contrast, is acceptable and achievable. The despot need not be particularly intelligent, rational, or virtuous. By ending the anarchical war of all against all—the worst of all possible worlds—the sovereign, whatever his faults and shortcomings, deservedly gains the allegiance of all.

C.B. Macpherson was a strong critic of Hobbesian political thought and its impact. But Macpherson acknowledged that the overall merit of a theory largely rests on the depth of its insight into human nature.[15] This is an enduring truth. Today, many debates continue to rage about the relation between human nature and politics. Feminist political theorists question the biological basis of patriarchy or male domination and the cultural formation of gender identities. Environmental political theorists confront the "natural" human disposition for shortsighted behavior, examine its ecological costs, and speculate on its possible remedies. These and other examples of political theorists grounding their prescriptions for political processes and institutions on their understanding of human nature will be examined in each of the upcoming chapters. For now, we will dig deeper into the mechanisms by which nature and nurture prove interdependent.

## NATURE AND NURTURE

Genes are the building blocks of life. They are found on molecular coils, called DNA, that replicate themselves. Genes provide the biochemical codes, or blueprints, that regulate the development of an organism's features and characteristics. There are genes, for instance, that determine sex, eye and hair color, body type, and many other physical attributes. Human beings, like other animals, are largely products of their genes.

Over 90 percent of any person's genes are identical to those of every other human being. This sharing of genetic material is what makes us all members of the same species, *Homo sapiens.* Most of the codes within our genetic blueprint ensure that we develop as human beings. A small minority of our genes cause us to develop as different sorts of human beings. And most of this genetic variation makes us unique individuals. A much smaller amount of genetic coding makes us members of specific races or ethnic groups. There is over six times the amount of genetic variation, for example, between two individual Swedes chosen at random than there is between the average genetic composition of Swedes and that of, say, Aboriginal Australians or African Bushmen.[16] Our genes differentiate us as individuals, but most of our genetic makeup underscores what we have in common.

Unlike other animals, humans are genetically designed to grow large, complex brains and sophisticated organs of speech. Certain portions of our brains, specifically the neocortex and limbic systems, enable us to engage in reasoning, abstract conceptualization and speech, self-reflection, and extended emotional attachment. These attributes make humans eminently political creatures. We are biologically enabled, or rather, biologically induced, to live politically.

Our genetic blueprints make us political animals. But to what extent do they determine the specific nature of our politics? The shaping and constraining of political life by human nature is perhaps best illustrated by the metaphor of our biology holding our politics, and culture more generally, on a leash.[17] The leash is quite long and very elastic. Political life may develop freely in any number of directions, and its precise perimeters are unknown. But politics cannot totally free itself from its biological tether.

Genes determine the boundaries within which political life may develop, just as they provide the range within which our physiological and behavioral attributes allow us to manipulate and adapt to the environment. The genes that give us fingers and opposable thumbs, for instance, do not determine whether we will use them to plant potatoes or harvest grain, wield swords or ball-point pens, swing wooden clubs or peck out text messages on smart phones. They do make these and many other activities possible. Were we endowed with paws or hooves instead, our range of adaptation to the environment, the types of food we consume and things we do, would be very different and much more limited.

Importantly, politics—and culture more generally—stretches our biological leash. It expands the range of our activities. Were we genetically incapable of developing a sophisticated political and cultural life, our genes would determine much more of our experiences than they currently do. We would then find ourselves in the position of other animals, whose genetic leashes, being much shorter and stiffer, highly restrict their behavioral repertoires.

Among the erectly postured, apelike creatures that preceded the evolution of human beings some 12 million years ago, one may assume that culture and politics barely existed. Like the rest of the animal kingdom, the behavior of these early hominins was highly determined by their genes, which controlled their instinctive drives. Over millions of years of evolution, changes in genetic structure allowed rudimentary forms of culture and politics to emerge. As this culture and politics developed, the genetic leash in turn became increasingly stretched, allowing further and faster cultural and political development. Nature and nurture, for the human species, co-evolved.

Ethical discourse, for instance, was impossible before early humans gained the capacities for speech and reason. These capacities, in turn, could not develop until hominins underwent the physiological evolution that produced the uniquely structured human brain and larynx. Once the capacities for speech and reason allowed early humans to engage in moral thought and action, however, the boundaries of the activities that were circumscribed by their genetic blueprints were substantially enlarged. Morality restricted the types of behavior that instinct and appetite stimulated while inducing other practices. And these behavioral changes, in turn, impacted the genetic evolution of the species. The entire history of human development is largely a product of this pulling and tugging between nature and nurture, known as gene-culture co-evolution or interactionism.

For the direct ancestors of *Homo sapiens*, who lived over 300,000 years ago, the growth of the brain was not only the cause but also the effect of culture. Cultural development fostered and accelerated physiological evolution. The use of fire to cook food, for instance, allowed a greater range of things to be eaten and better absorption of nutrients. Big brains require lots of energy, and cooking food provided early hominins that surplus of available energy. In turn, the development of midwifery (aided childbearing) allowed baby hominins with larger heads, and hence larger brains, to pass more successfully through the relatively small pelvic cavities of their mothers. (Being upright walkers, hominins, like modern humans, had narrow hips.) These larger-brained children would eventually reproduce, passing on their genes for larger brains. "Whereas many accounts of the expansion of hominid evolution focus on male activities, such as hunting, group defense, or knowledge of the terrain," a political scientist observes, "an explanation based on social cooperation [of women during childbirth] emphasizes a factor that otherwise would have limited evolution toward larger brain size. . . . It is often argued that humans cooperate in society because they have big brains. Perhaps the truth is that we have big brains because we cooperate in society."[18] Biological and cultural development have always gone hand in hand for our species.

In William Shakespeare's *The Tempest*, the character Prospero describes Caliban as "a born devil on whose nature nurture will never stick." It was a harsh criticism. By and large, humans are very educable: nurture easily sticks to nature. Indeed, nature (genes) finds its expression by way of nurture, and nurture (cultural learning) builds upon nature's (genetic) foundation.

Biology, we observed, holds culture on a leash. But the obverse is also true. The development of myriad 'natural' capacities and traits depends on the environmental and cultural conditions that allow for the expression of specific genes, as the science of epigenetics demonstrates. At times, the appropriate image might be of a small child being pulled along by a Great Dane. At times, a powerful athlete is taking a tiny poodle for a walk. In both cases, nature and nurture are tethered. Neither can proceed without the other, notwithstanding all the pulling and tugging that takes place. Attempting to separate biology from culture as competing causes of human development is like trying to determine whether the area of a rectangle is caused more by its length or its width.[19]

To understand human beings, we must set aside the familiar but misleading trope of nature *versus* nurture and investigate instead the intertwined causes and effects of nature *via* nurture and nurture *via* nature. This truth was first recognized over over two millennia ago. "The moral virtues," according to Aristotle, "are produced in us neither *by* Nature nor *against* Nature. Nature, indeed, prepares in us the ground for their reception, but their complete formation is the product of habit."[20] Our culturally induced habits build upon and in turn redirect our natural dispositions. To explain human development, including political development, one must address both the biological and the cultural foundations of life.

## GENES AND MORES

Genes are the building blocks of organic life. As single units or in complex combinations, genes provide the information directives that produce and sustain organic development. In the realm of politics, the corresponding role is taken on by mores. Mores are the building blocks of political life. The term *mores* comes from the Latin translation of the Greek word for ethics. For the ancient Greeks, ethics was a broad concept. It pertained not only to matters of individual conscience and explicitly moral duties but to all standards grounded in custom. Likewise, mores pertain not only to the norms that regulate individual behavior but to all the concepts, conventions, principles, rules and ideals that maintain a social order and allow for its transformation.

Like all rules, mores restrict behavior. But they also serve as resources and stimulants. The rules of grammar, by way of comparison, restrict the ways in which we speak. We are forced to use nouns and verbs in a prescribed fashion. But these same rules allow us to speak intelligibly, to be understood and to solicit responses, and to be linguistically creative. Likewise, mores induce forms of behavior that are conducive to the formation and maintenance of a social order, impede other sorts of behavior that would prove destructive of this order, and allow for its creative transformation. There are revolutionary mores just as there are conservative mores, mores developed to help us survive the harsh realities of life and others that bespeak ideals for which we may strive.

What genes are to nature, mores are to culture and politics. Just as genes regulate the biological construction and maintenance of organisms, mores regulate the cultural construction and maintenance of societies. Yet mores are not immune to the effects of our genes. To retrieve the metaphor employed earlier, our genes hold our mores on a leash.

The genes that cause us to grow hair on various parts of our bodies do not determine how it will be cared for. Culture has an almost unrestricted latitude to prescribe variations in cutting, shaving, extracting, shaping, coloring, and adorning hair. Likewise, our genes determine us to be sexual reproducers (as opposed to asexual reproducers, like flatworms). These genes ensure that sex between men and women will occur in all cultures. Consequently, these genes effectively determine that all societies will develop mores to regulate and ritualize sexual relations and sexuality. Yet the expression of human sexuality is extremely varied. The kind of sexual mores that develop in a society is highly dependent on historical and cultural factors.

To take another example, our genes determine that children remain dependent during the first few years of their lives. Human babies and young children are incapable of fending for themselves and reproducing during this rather extended period. Mice, by way of contrast, not only nourish, shelter, and protect themselves, but start to reproduce by two months of age. Many different aspects of human culture have developed in response to this biological constraint. The institution of marriage, the celebration of family life, and the development of educational institutions are only a few of the more obvious cultural artifacts that compensate for and take advantage of the lengthy period of childhood immaturity and dependence. These cultural institutions, grounded in biological constraints, greatly impact political life. As Aristotle observed, the springs of politics and justice are to be found in the extended bonding of parent and child.[21]

The rules, principles, customs, conventions, and understandings surrounding marriage, family life, and education differ markedly from culture to culture, and even within the same culture. Yet the extent to which humans can wholly abandon these mores is circumscribed by the biological facts of human propagation and development. Until we can produce more viable infants by way of genetic engineering—a frightening thought for most people—culture will be forced to compensate for, and will be able productively to exploit, the extended helplessness of children.

Consider a more controversial issue. Only women bear children. That is genetically determined (at least for now). Historically, women have also filled the role of their children's primary caretaker. That is not genetically determined, but it is likely that genes heavily impacted the development of this cultural practice. A human being's genetic constitution largely determines the production of hormones and enzymes. Specific hormones and enzymes induce most boys from a very early age to be relatively more aggressive, while other hormones and enzymes induce most girls to be relatively more nurturing. Good evidence also suggests that in the aggregate women are genetically endowed with greater verbal ability, perceptual speed, and fine motor skills, while men have the edge in spatial perception and quantitative calculation. These differences are likely the product of hundreds of thousands of years of genetic adaptation among early hominins faced with the distinct demands of childrearing and hunting.[22] Yet even here, where genetic influences are ascertainable, the question of whether culture can and should attempt to augment, controvert, or ignore specific biological inheritances is left unanswered. The fact that genetics has produced a historical legacy of female childrearing does not mean that women should remain the sole or even primary caretakers of children today.

We are genetically constrained to grow legs and arms rather than fins, wheels, or wings. This explains why humans walk or run to get places. But that does not mean that we should never swim, ride bicycles, drive vehicles, or fly in airplanes. Humans are also genetically induced, owing to their bodies' production of certain hormones and enzymes, to respond aggressively in threatening situations. Nonetheless, culture and politics frequently curb, manipulate, and sublimate these aggressive tendencies, and rightly so. The extent to which we should stretch our genetic leash—and in which directions—remain open and very political questions.

Mores, and moral principles more specifically, are generally thought of as products of culture that allow human beings to overcome and channel natural tendencies. The development of morality itself, however, occurred in the context of the evolutionary struggle for survival. Competing tribes of hominins in a world of relatively scarce natural resources would gain an advantage, and hence be more likely to pass on and propagate their genes, if they developed and maintained solidarity in the face of external threats. Primatologist Frans de Waal observes that "In the course of human evolution, out-group hostility enhanced in-group solidarity to the point that morality emerged.... And so, the profound irony is that our noblest achievement—morality—has evolutionary ties to our basest behavior—warfare. The sense of community required by the former was provided by the latter."[23] While morality may have, at least in part, arisen out of the need to secure bonds within primitive tribes that faced the prospect of warfare with other tribes, those same mores of solidarity have been much expanded. In contemporary times, we are educated to experience solidarity with a global community. Historically, morality and politics made warfare possible and were employed to justify it. Today, morality and politics can serve as mechanisms for peaceful, planetary coexistence. Cultural mores born of natural impulses often come to channel, extend and challenge these impulses.

The development of political life is possible for humans and impossible for other animals for one simple reason: they do not have our genes. Yet political life rests upon a foundation of mores. That these mores at times appear to conflict with primitive, unmediated instincts speaks less to the antagonism between genes and culture than to the complex, age-old, and continuing interaction of nurture and nature. We are born genetically disposed to learn a great deal in this life and to alter our behavior based on this learning. Human culture does not stand in opposition to human biology. Nature and nurture are interdependent.

To the extent that our genes determine our nature they determine us to be cultural—and political—beings. It is no less natural for human beings to restrain or channel their behavior by way of mores than to act on unmediated instinct. Heeding ethical dictates is as natural as following appetites, at least for adult human beings who speak and reason together. Each human being has some 100,000–200,000 genes, composed of 6 billion nucleotides that form the letters of its genetic code. The brain, in turn, is made up of 100 billion cells, each containing thousands of synaptic connections. The amount of information stored in a human brain, assuming for the sake of argument that it corresponds to the number of its neural connections, is many thousands of times greater than the information stored in its owner's genes. One may interpret these biological facts to suggest that human beings are genetically destined to develop cultural mores that channel, extend and challenge their natural propensities and capacities.

Our genetic leash is sufficiently long to allow for self-consciousness and reasoned speech. Making use of these capacities is no rebellion against our genes. If anything, a creature biologically enabled for self-consciousness and reasoned speech that did *not* develop and adopt mores to regulate its individual and collective life would be the true rebel against nature. The fact that human genes constrain but do not determine the range and development of human activities and relationships presents us with enduring and complex dilemmas. These are the dilemmas of a political animal.

## BIOLOGICAL AND CULTURAL REPRODUCTION

Richard Dawkins, a zoologist, first suggested that genes had a cultural analog. He coined the word *meme*, from the Greek *mimeme*, which means "imitation," to define a unit of culture that replicates itself.[24] Memes serve as units of cultural transmission.

Genetic replication began billions of years ago in the primal soup of the earth's cooling seas. Here DNA molecules first appeared and started to replicate themselves. The diversity and sophistication of these primitive forms of life slowly increased, with each species bearing and reproducing its own unique "pool" of genes.

The transmission of memes, in contrast, only began millions of years ago, when tribes of primitive hominins began to produce and pass along expressions, information, skills, rules and rituals by way of gestures, speech and actions. The conglomerations of memes that get passed along through cultural reproduction may be understood as "symbol pools" that correspond to the "gene pools" passed along through biological reproduction. Gene pools are programs for transforming energy and matter into organic life. Symbol pools are programs for transforming energy and matter into cultural life.[25] Today we know a good deal about the chemistry that allows the genetic conversion of matter and energy into life. But what is the "chemistry" of culture? How do symbol pools maintain and transform themselves? In other words, how do memes reproduce?

Memes propagate through social interaction. As Dawkins writes, they leap

> from brain to brain via a process which, in the broad sense, can be called imitation. . . . When you plant a fertile meme in my mind you literally parasitize my brain, turning it into a vehicle for the meme's propagation in just the way that a virus may parasitize the genetic mechanism of a host cell.[26]

When we speak or act in a way that influences others to speak or act in a similar way, we are effectively propagating a meme. A good example might be the coining of a new word or phrase that goes "viral." Varied means of communication, such as books, journals, magazines, newspapers, radio, television, the internet, email, and social media dramatically increase the pace at which memes propagate. Indeed, a major advantage of memes over genes is the speed with which the former reproduce. This speed accounts for the growing comparative strength of culture over biology in its impact on human relationships and activities.

The propagation of memes may prove more successful than the propagation of genes for other reasons as well. Only half of each parent's genes gets passed on to its child. In turn, a grandchild carries only one-fourth of a grandparent's genes. This rate of diminishment continues indefinitely, such that distant descendants will be genetically little more related to forebears than complete strangers. Memes, in contrast, may survive relatively intact across countless generations. Dawkins explains that

> if you contribute to the world's culture, if you have a good idea, compose a tune, invent a sparking plug, write a poem, it may live on, intact, long after your genes have dissolved in the common pool. Socrates may or may not have a gene or two alive in the world today . . . but who cares? The meme-complexes of Socrates . . . are still going strong.[27]

Socratic thought is still taught in thousands of university classrooms; it continues to exert its effect on countless minds. One cannot claim the same sort of immortality for the genes that Socrates passed on to his children. Socratic genes today are as scattered as dust in the wind.

Like genes, memes that get passed along are likely to undergo mutation. Indeed, when it comes to political life, the most successful memes might not be those that faithfully replicate themselves across the generations but those that stimulate the development of altered and improved versions of themselves. Here, as with genetic transmission, mutation remains at least as important as faithful replication for the continuation and enrichment of life. If genes did not mutate over time, new species would not develop that were better suited to their environments. Soon biological diversity would dwindle as new forms of life failed to develop while old forms continued to perish in the face of environmental change. Likewise, memes that do not adapt to a changing world may have quite limited life spans. Those that mutate successfully, in contrast, may exercise an enduring influence.

Again, Socratic thought comes to mind. Socrates understood himself to be a midwife, aiding in the birth of thoughts and worthy ways of thinking. He produced a meme known as the "Socratic method." This is a way of teaching by means of posing probing questions that expose and challenge the unstated assumptions of interlocutors. The Socratic method is still widely employed today. But it fosters thoughtful exchanges that are quite different from those Plato recorded in his dialogues. Memes often achieve their greatest influence not through faithful reproduction but by stimulating adaptation and innovation. Indeed, a meme is perhaps most "alive" not when it is permanently etched in stone but when it serves as a midwife to the birth of new memes.

Memes are general cases of mores. Whereas memes refer to any cultural transmission (including technological inventions, artistic styles, and clothing fashions), mores refer more specifically to those concepts, conventions, principles, rules, and understandings that structure and transform social order and political life. Like genes, mores induce certain sorts of belief and behavior and dissuade others.

The mores systematized in political theories range from broad conceptual categories to particular rules or codes that prescribe or proscribe specific actions. Mores reflect the types of thought and behavior that individuals acknowledge or ignore and accept or reject as laudable, tolerable, or sanctionable within political life. The stakes for political theorists are quite high. In their efforts to understand, order, and transform political life, theorists may bear many intellectual offspring and practical reforms. Those who yearn for immortality might find the practice of political theory a more effective means of satisfying this ambition than the standard genetic route. Epistemological and ethical legacies may endure long after the theorist who bequeaths them has, to employ Hamlet's brooding phrase, "shuffled off this mortal coil."

As political animals, human beings face a unique challenge: we are the only species that consciously sets itself the task of reproducing and advancing its mores as well as its genes. That fact underlines the interminable task of political theory. Theorists have no way of assuring that their mores will be faithfully reproduced. Often they will be deployed in quite unanticipated ways. That is the fate of every technological artifact. Of course, genetic offspring—as every parent knows—are likewise full of surprises and not easily managed. The genes and mores we pass on eventually—and usually quite quickly—escape our control.

So there is no end in sight to the battles theorists wage for the hearts and minds of citizens and statespeople, and the determination of what constitutes the public good. The competition is stiff and the contestation interminable. That is a good thing. For any end to the epistemological and ethical struggles to understand, order, and transform political life would also be the end of human freedom and dignity.

## THE PUBLIC GOOD AND THE PRIVATE REALM

When Aristotle said man was a political animal, he was saying that it is human nature to engage in political life. Politics is to be found everywhere that humans are found. In turn, no facets of human life are completely beyond the reach of politics or wholly untouched by its effects. That does not mean everything is or should be political to the same degree. While politics pervades life, it is not the whole of life. As Jean-Bethke Elshtain observes, it would be a mistake to "collapse the personal into the political.... One does not demand of politics what it cannot give: wholeness, a complete self-identity, a uniform purpose."[28] In the same vein, Bernard Crick suggests that political thinking "inclines towards ideological thought" whenever it "abolish[es] the distinction between private and public."[29] Politics pertains to the organization and regulation of communities of distinct individuals whose private lives ought not be subject to overt political control. There are matters of individual conscience and personal choice that can and should be shielded from public scrutiny and interference.

To advocate for a private realm is not to suggest that private affairs have no public impact or importance. Most if not all business enterprises and exercises in household management have an impact on the public. The energy and resources consumed, the pollution created, and the trash generated by the very acts of running a business or sustaining a private life are legitimate issues of public concern. Only the inhabiting of a cave by a hermit in an unpopulated hinterland might be thought to have no public impact, assuming the hermit left no dependents to become wards of the state, did not disturb any endangered wildlife or consume scarce resources, and did not contribute to climate change by lighting fires that emitted carbon dioxide. In an increasingly populated and ecologically precarious world, few activities do not in some way affect public welfare. To the extent that private activities—where and how we live and travel, what we buy and sell, produce, consume and discard, and how we interact with others—impact the public, they are proper subjects for political oversight and regulation.

In countries where government is grounded on liberal principles and constitutional order, private matters are often protected by Bills of Rights. Individuals, and groups of individuals who voluntarily associate, are protected from intrusions by the government. That is because a political society, as the liberal theorist John Rawls insists, is not a homogenous community. It is not a group of people who have uniform values and beliefs and affirm a comprehensive doctrine to direct their lives. For Rawls, political life is defined by its pluralism: the existence of distinct individuals and voluntary associations of individuals over which political power is rightly limited. Notwithstanding its inherent pluralism, a political society must organize itself. At its best, for Rawls, it organizes itself according to a "fair system of cooperation."[30] That system of cooperation, constitutionally enshrined, dictates how a people defined by its pluralism can secure the public good while protecting the privacy of individuals.

But how can we say that politics is pervasive if there exists, and should exist, a constitutionally protected private realm? The answer is straightforward: politics determines which parts of our lives can and should remain private. It is politics, moreover, that safeguards these realms, effectively guarding them from governmental intrusions. The constitutional rights that protect the privacy of individuals and families and voluntary associations from state interference are themselves created through political processes and are maintained through political institutions.

Like the constitution in which they are embedded, rights to privacy are politically decided, politically instituted, and politically preserved. Civil liberties, the freedom from governmental interference enjoyed by individuals, have government as their guarantor. Politics is pervasive because it is involved in creating and maintaining the separate yet interrelated public and private spheres. Politics is pervasive not only because it brings many concerns into the public realm but because it determines what things are to remain, as much as possible, within the private realm.

Take the issue of religious freedom. Freedom of religion, at least in modern, liberal states, is an important civil liberty. Where religious freedom is maintained, the question of if, how, when, where, whom or what one chooses to worship remains a matter of individual conscience and personal choice. The government neither promotes religious dogma nor prescribes religious ritual. There remains, as is commonly said, a separation of church and state. Individuals can practice any religion, or none, so long as their practices do not interfere unduly with the lives of others. A religion that called for forced conversion of infidels or the burning of heretics, for instance, would be politically intolerable. Here the church would be encroaching on a prerogative uniquely held by the state in modern times, namely, the use of physical force to protect its citizens and defend its interests.

Many political communities of the past were theocratic, that is, they were governed by rulers who claimed to be the vicars or representatives of a deity or deities. Typically, this meant that the head of state was also the high priest of an officially sanctioned and promoted religion. Even today, fundamentalist religious leaders and parties continue to secure political power and maintain theocratic rule. In the United States, as in many other countries, the separation of church and state is explicitly enshrined in a constitution that sets out the structure and boundaries of political life. When the American Constitution was written in 1787, however, only two states—New York and Virginia—did not have religious qualifications for public office. Most of the other states required that one be a Protestant to hold office. The separation of church and state is itself a historical, political achievement. *Without* politics, the safeguarding of many private realms of life *from* politics would be impossible.

Economic freedom is also an important right in modern societies. It allows citizens to hold private property and to engage in financial enterprises of their own choosing. Like religious freedom, economic freedom is a crucial aspect of individual freedom and autonomy. Like religious affairs, economic affairs in modern, liberal states remain largely privatized. And, like religious freedom, economic freedom has its limits. These limits are politically established and maintained through laws, regulations and customs.

Economic freedom allows us to earn and spend money in various ways. Nonetheless, our economic transactions should not interfere unduly with the rights and freedoms of others. One may not spend money any which way one wants. It is illegal, for instance, to buy a slave. Nor can one legally buy votes. In many countries, there are also strict limits on the media coverage and advertising that one can buy to run a campaign for election to public office. Similarly, the ways one may earn money are restricted. Wealth must be gained in some legitimate fashion rather than by means of fraud of extortion. In turn, one may manufacture goods to be sold for profit, but one cannot sell anything one wants or manufacture things in any way one wants. One cannot legally sell contaminated food, or dangerously pollute the land, air, or water during the processes of manufacturing. Goods manufactured and sold should truly be goods, that is, they ought not harm the consumer or damage the public domain.

These restrictions are necessary to ensure that economic rights and freedoms do not overstep their boundaries, interfering unduly with the enjoyment of other rights and freedoms. Establishing boundaries between potentially conflicting rights and freedoms entails crafting and implementing constitutions and legislation. It is a matter of politics.

Recall that the study of politics, for Aristotle, does not allow for the certainty, exactitude, or generalization that may be gained through mathematics or natural sciences such as physics. Despite this apparent shortcoming, Aristotle maintains that the study of politics is the master science. His reasoning is straightforward. Politics orders the whole of the social realm, allotting diverse activities and relationships their proper place and prerogatives. Though politics does not determine how every human endeavor, such as religious worship, economic enterprise, artistic creation, or philosophical reflection, ought to be pursued, politics does demarcate the appropriate boundaries of these activities. Political theory is an intellectual and moral effort to identify and justify these boundaries.

Politics is about how the power employed to order collective life is accumulated, exercised and distributed. Most generally put, we may say that politics is about power that is primarily public rather than private in its exercise and in its ends. Indeed, the word *politics* derives from the Greek *politica*, which means that pertaining to the *polis*, or city-state. To be political is to be of concern to the public citizen, or *polites*. When the Romans translated the works of Greek political theorists, they settled on the words *res publica*, or republic, to denote the political realm. The *res publica* literally means the "public thing" or "public affair." Likewise, the word *commonwealth*, often considered synonymous with republic, refers to that which pertains to the public good or, in Old English, the *common weal*. The public sphere, in the modern sense of the term, and the notion of "public opinion" to which elected representatives give ear, arose in Europe during the late 1700s and developed markedly the following century.[31] It extended the ancient Greek and Roman notion of the republic and the commonwealth for an increasingly democratic age. Politics is activity that sustains the public sphere and, optimally, pursues the public good.

There is a great irony in today's pejorative use of the word politics. Candidates for office often speak of the need to end "politics as usual." Likewise, public officials and elected representatives are criticized for pursuing "political interests," which suggests they are focused on narrow partisan or other self-serving ends. These deprecatory uses of "politics" and "political" represent a reversal of the etymological meaning of the terms. Rather than suggest a concern for the public good, "politics" and "political" now connote a complete lack of such concern.

This denigration of politics has a long history. Abraham Lincoln already observed in 1837 that politicians were thought of as "a set of men who have interests aside from the interests of the people, and who, to say the most of them, are, taken as a mass, at least one long step removed from honest men."[32] At the turn of the last century, politics was wittily defined as "a strife of interests masquerading as a contest of principles. The conduct of public affairs for private advantage."[33] This pejorative connotation has gained the upper hand in common parlance today. It will likely persist, given the extent to which the pursuit of individual power, narrow partisan interests, and wealth dominate the political process.

## POWER, FORCE AND VIOLENCE

The history of politics is the history of the efforts of individuals or groups of individuals to accumulate, exercise and distribute power. Questions of power figure into discussions of most, if not all, other political concepts. Who should wield power? That is the question of leadership or rule. How should power be (institutionally) distributed? That is the question of the best form of government. How can power be exercised fairly? That is the problem of justice. What should the limits of power be? That is the question of individual liberties and rights.

Politics, first and foremost, is about power. Political theory is the study of the nature of power—its uses, abuses, effects and limits. Reflecting on the importance of power to the study of politics and society, the British philosopher Bertrand Russell (1872–1970) wrote that

> the fundamental concept of social science is Power, in the same sense in which Energy is the fundamental concept in physics. Like energy, power has many forms, such as wealth, armaments, civil authority, influence or opinion. No one of these can be regarded as subordinate to any other, and there is no one form from which the others are derivative.... To revert to the analogy of physics: power, like energy, must be regarded as continually passing from any one of its forms into any other, and it should be the business of social science to seek the laws of such transformations.[34]

Power, for Russell, is the capacity to produce intended effects. It is the ability to get what one wants. Figuring out how people get what they want, individually and collectively, is the job he assigns to political scientists.

Using power to get what you want is generally thought of as "power over." One exercises power by influencing people to do, say, believe, or value specific things. One may pay them (the power of wealth); win them over in speech (the power of eloquence); appeal to their sense of duty or rightful obedience (the power of authority); rely on one's reputation (the power of prestige); exercise the prerogative to carry on a legacy (the power of tradition); or intimidate them (the power of coercion). Each of these forms of power—wealth, eloquence, authority, prestige, tradition, and coercion—has its own mechanisms and limitations.

The power of rational debate and persuasion typically displays its limits once battle lines have been drawn and active hostilities begin. Wealth may get you much of what you want in this world. As the saying goes, however, you can't buy love. Most often, the limits of one form of power are established in confrontation with other forms of power. A popular musician may influence tens of thousands of people to drink a particular brand of soda. Yet his fame or prestige may be quite ineffective when marshaled to promote a specific moral position. In ethical matters, rational persuasion, the power of tradition, or the influence of authority may prove more effective.

Some political theorists believe that force is a form of power, and violent force, as evidenced in military or police action, is the ultimate form of power. The "power of might" is a familiar phrase reflecting this understanding. It enjoys a wide currency.

Thomas Hobbes, adopting the tough-minded orientation of political realism, insists that violence is the natural and ultimate expression of political power. Promulgating the rules, regulations and laws needed to order collective life does little to secure the peace, Hobbes argues, unless these rules, regulations and laws are backed by force. Some form of punishment for lawbreakers and transgressors is necessary. Covenants without swords, Hobbes tersely remarks, are mere words.

The Florentine political theorist Niccolò Machiavelli (1469–1527) maintained that good politics ensue from good laws. Yet Machiavelli, who along with Hobbes established modern realism, also insisted that "there cannot be good laws where there are not good arms." Force, for Machiavelli, always lurks in the shadows of politics. Indeed, he believed that it was often necessary for leaders to create a show of force. Machiavelli advises rulers or princes to become feared by their subjects.[35]

For better or worse, political rulers often employ force. They also deny that option to others. Max Weber proposed that the modern state is best defined as that political entity having a monopoly on the legitimate use of violence. All modern states, and most other forms of national or imperial government throughout history, have claimed the exclusive prerogative to exercise force within their borders. This prerogative is justified as the only viable means to secure internal peace. In the seventeenth century, for example, King Louis XIII of France forbade dueling to consolidate his power, that is, to gain a state monopoly on the use of force. States also claim the prerogative to exercise force beyond their borders to defend against aggressors or secure national interests. As one theorist of state power observed, "what each state forbids its citizens to do to one another, all states must stand in readiness to do to each other."[36]

Today, as in times past, most political power is backed up by the force of arms. With the exception of pacifists, people generally consider the use of force by political rulers legitimate in principle if it secures internal peace and defends against foreign threats. In practice, however, the use of force is usually subject to criticism or condemnation from some quarter, and often for good reason. Governmental abuse of the prerogative to employ force is an all too common affair. Regimes often wage needless wars or other unjustified acts of aggression against foreign nations. In turn, violence and deadly force are often exercised by states within their own borders, against their own citizens. From ancient times, monarchs, tyrants and oligarchs have employed brutal violence to keep their subjects obedient and passive. Unfortunately, it remains an all-too-common practice. Governments in the twentieth century killed many times the number of their own citizens (for political reasons, that is, excluding nonpolitical, criminal executions) than they killed foreign combatants.[37] Authoritarian governments in particular rely extensively on force to maintain their rule. Violence and political power are certainly no strangers.

Is there an alternative to force for those who wield state power? Hobbes and Machiavelli maintained that force was always necessary to back up the rule of law. And most political theorists concur that the power to legislate rests on the power to coerce. While one might deplore its abuses, the threat of force is required for political rule, just as political rule is necessary to order collective life.

Anarchists disagree. The word *anarchism* first appeared during the French Revolution. It was employed to characterize those who opposed the heavy-handed rule of the Jacobins and argued for the formation of communes. The French social theorist Pierre-Joseph Proudhon (1809–65) revived the term in 1840, though most of his followers preferred to describe themselves as "mutualists." By the early 1870s, while struggling with the disciples of Karl Marx for the heart and soul of the First International Workingman's Association, the Russian thinker and activist Mikhail Bakunin (1814–76) proudly embraced the term anarchism and developed its principles.

Much in keeping with the ideas of Proudhon and Bakunin, the well-known American anarchist Emma Goldman (1869–1940) defined anarchism as "the philosophy of a new social order based on liberty unrestricted by man-made law; the theory that all forms of government rest on violence and are therefore wrong and harmful, as well as unnecessary."[38] Anarchy literally means the absence of rule. It is based on the utopian hope that in the absence of rulers, people will lead peaceable, cooperative, and non-violent lives. These lives would be blessed with greater freedom and happiness than could be achieved through the institution of a coercive government.

According to Robert Dahl, the denial of the legitimacy of law and force makes "anarchism . . . not so much a *political* philosophy as a *moral* doctrine."[39] In their effort to safeguard the independence and autonomy of individuals, anarchists argue that all coercion within the political realm is illegitimate. They consequently advocate the abolition of government. The abolition of government, Dahl maintains, means an end to politics, and an end to political theory.

Dahl effectively embraces Weber's famous distinction between the "ethic of responsibility" that is appropriate for political affairs and the "ethic of ultimate ends" that pertains to matters of conscience. The ethic of ultimate ends holds that good intentions are of paramount concern in judging the rightness of actions; the unintended consequences of good actions may be ignored. The ethic of responsibility, in contrast, takes heed of the "foreseeable results of one's action." It regretfully accepts that to achieve good ends, "one must be willing to pay the price of using morally dubious means or at least dangerous ones."[40] The use of force for Dahl and Weber constitutes the dangerous but necessary means to protect civil liberties and social order. The option of employing force is inherent to an ethic of responsibility, and an inescapable feature of political life.

To insist that a theory of politics cannot ignore the need for force is not to say that politics amounts to the rule of the strong and the law of the jungle. Political power bears an intimate relationship to force. Most forms of political life—certainly all that occur within nation states—would never arise and could not persist without the threat of force. Politics, whose essence is power, concerns the control of force as well as its legitimation.

But force and violence should not be equated with political power. Indeed, politics ends where force and violence begin.

"What we should consider as unique to political power, as conceptually intrinsic to it," Gianfranco Poggi observes, "is control over the means of violence, rather than the direct and frequent recourse to their employment."[41] While control of the means of violence is a defining characteristic of a political regime, the frequent reliance on force demonstrates the absence of political rule. Well-functioning states utilize shared values, institutions, and economic incentives to secure order, strengthen community, and achieve prosperity. They engage multiple forms of power short of physical force to achieve these goals. When force is deployed, it signals the limits, and failure, of political power. Violence is substituted for influence.

The matter is complex because nonviolent forms of influence may be so compelling that they seem to constitute a kind of force. The power of wealth, for instance, when used to influence the actions of the desperately poor, may prove virtually irresistible. The power of authority, when unquestioned, may be overwhelming. Of course, intimidation, in the form of a coercive threat, explicitly flirts with force. If these forms of power can be so unyielding, one might ask, then why should the compulsion of actual force not be considered a form of power?

Power rather than force is wielded if the object of influence can resist or refuse without facing a direct threat to life or limb. Power does not destroy or deny the freedom of the individual over whom it is exercised, though power may and often does make the exercise of freedom more difficult or dangerous. If I shackle someone to a wall to keep him from voting in an election, then I am not exerting a form of power. I am exerting force. The individual's potential for effective resistance has been negated and his freedom has been denied. In contrast, if I persuade this person not to cast a ballot, arguing that his voting will not make any difference to the outcome of the election, then I have exercised power.

But what if a rich landowner to whom a peasant family is heavily indebted announces that it will greatly displease him were anyone to vote or otherwise participate in an upcoming election. To be consistent with our definition, we would say that the land-owner is exercising power, specifically the power of coercion. In this case, the peasants, unlike the person shackled to the wall, retain the option of ignoring the intimidating threat, casting their ballots, and awaiting the hinted-at reprisals.

Admittedly, the line drawn between force and the power of coercion in this case is very thin and probably of little consolation to the intimidated peasants. But the distinction remains important. If a robber persuades you to hand over your wallet by pointing a loaded gun at your head, you remain at liberty to retain your wallet (for the moment) and pay the consequences. However, the threat of violence is clear and imminent. You are justified in interpreting such a threat not as a form of coercive power but as an exercise of force. Once power gains enough coercive strength to deny all effective forms of (non-violent) refusal, it effectively ceases to be power. For rule to be grounded in power, the opportunity for resistance must persist.

## RULE AND RESISTANCE

Hobbes considered the use of violence by rulers legitimate because everyone has an interest in internal peace and external security. This peace and security could not be assured without a Leviathan threatening the use of force and occasionally employing it. For Hobbes, the sovereign can be said to rule in the public interest simply by meeting the minimum requirement of preventing a war of all against all. Consequently, Hobbes argues that the sovereign can never be justly punished in any way for any acts he commits. In becoming sovereign, the ruler gains the prerogative to do as he pleases.

When the Leviathan is recognized, Hobbes maintains, each subject states: "*I Authorise and give up my Right of Governing my selfe to this Man.*" This act of submission, carried out simultaneously by all, unites the multitude of actors milling about the state of nature into a single commonwealth. The Leviathan is considered a *"Mortall God"* to whom its subjects owe their lives and loyalty.[42] King James I of England (1566–1625) took this sort of claim quite seriously, though he had a religious, as opposed to purely pragmatic, justification for his despotic reign. If confronted by unjust and tyrannical rule, James states, "the people may do no other than flee unresistingly from the anger of its king; its tears and sighs are the only answer to him allowed it, and it may summon none but God to its aid."[43] A king has a divine right to rule, James was saying. This rule is absolute and must meet with no resistance whatsoever.

Few people today accept James' defense of absolute monarchy on religious grounds. Most would also argue that Hobbes' legitimation of sovereign power and violence is excessive and that his understanding of the public good is far too narrow. Ruling for the public good requires more than the mere prevention of anarchy or war. Establishing basic order is a necessary condition for good government, but it is not a sufficient condition.

Tyrannies may be orderly states, but they are not political ones. That is because tyranny is a form of rule grounded in violence rather than power. Tyrants rule by force. They deny their subjects any sort of meaningful resistance short of armed revolt. They deny subjects the opportunity to influence the organization and regulation of their collective life. Tyrants do not acknowledge their subjects as citizens capable of exercising political power.

The sharing of political power begins through the rule of law. The English political theorist James Harrington (1611–77) references Aristotle in asserting that "ancient prudence" dictates that government consists in "an empire of laws, and not of men." [44] Indeed, the *sine qua non* for political life within the state is law. In the absence of law, one is left with arbitrary rule or despotism, and the frequent force required to back it up.

Within the republican tradition—exemplified by the Roman orator and politician Cicero (106–43 B.C.), Machiavelli, Harrington, the French political philosopher Baron de Montesquieu (1689–1755), and the American Founding Fathers—the peace, security and freedom of citizens were secured by law rather than the arbitrary and uncontestable rule of a single man or oligarchic group. While citizens may not play an active part in writing, promulgating, or enforcing the law, their political status as citizens is manifested when they abide by the law, and, from time to time, when they contest it.

When citizens obey the laws or the constitution of a state they are, in some minimal sense, participating in politics. In effect, they are influencing rulers to carry on business as usual. Compliance to law, then, remains a mitigated form of the public exercise of power. When laws or constitutions are too frequently ignored, disobeyed, or subverted, rulers must respond to keep order, either by changing the laws or constitution, persuading citizens to remain compliant, or enforcing the laws or constitution more strictly or repressively. The latter response, if met with yet more resistance by citizens, transforms political rule into brute force and pushes citizens into open rebellion.

The English philosopher and political theorist John Locke suggested that citizens effectively "consent" to their rulers and become obligated to their governments simply by inhabiting the territory, using its roads, and observing its laws. This public compliance or tacit consent is not to be equated with submission to force. Tacit consent may always be withdrawn. When the injustice or inequity of law becomes intolerable, citizens may contest its legitimacy and resist its enforcement.

Political rule's vulnerability to resistance helps ensure, in Philip Pettit's words, that "public decision-making tracks the interests and ideas of those citizens whom it affects."[45] Political power is evident wherever there is rule of law not only because the law constrains the actions of rulers, but because it makes their rule available to public scrutiny and contestation. At the point where citizens' compliance with law gives way to their subjection to force with little or no potential for non-violent resistance, we are justified in saying that power and hence politics have ebbed to the point of nonexistence.

While Machiavelli advocated the occasional necessity of rule by a strong prince, he acknowledged that force alone cannot sustain the polity. He accordingly counsels the prince not only to cultivate respect by instilling fear but also to seek the love and avoid the hatred of his subjects. This latter task is best achieved when the prince abides by his own laws. Machiavelli also observed that while most citizens do not want to rule, they do want to live in freedom from arbitrary rule.[46] For both the rulers and the ruled, lawfulness is crucial to politics.

Endorsing this republican sentiment, Pettit observes that democracy does not entail the involvement of all citizens in lawmaking or other forms of rule. Rather, it is based "on the contestability by the people of everything that government does: the important thing to ensure is that governmental doings are fit to survive popular contestation, not that they are the product of a popular will."[47] In a despotism, there is no room for contestation, and no sharing of power. Political rule shares power. As we will see, however, seldom if ever is power shared equally.

While order might be established and maintained through force alone, other aspects of the public good, such as freedom, can be established and maintained only through the exercise of power. Different forms of political rule offer more order or more freedom, depending on their nature. Montesquieu held that monarchical states place more value on order, while republican states place more value on freedom. Similarly, Plato argued that democracy raises the pursuit of freedom to the highest level and enshrines it as its first principle. By Plato's reckoning, democracy's infatuation with freedom leads to intolerable breakdowns in social order. He opts for the monarchical rule of philosopher kings.

Tyranny, the violent and arbitrary rule of a single individual, is not a political form of rule. It stands in contrast to monarchy (the rule of a king or queen), aristocracy (the rule of the best or most qualified), oligarchy (the rule of the rich or select few), and democracy (the rule of the people). As Aristotle observed, what distinguishes the king from the tyrant is that the tyrant rules only in his own interest, while the king has the public good in mind. The king's concern for the public good makes monarchical rule at least minimally political in its ends. In turn, as ancient Greek thinkers also maintained, the king, unlike the tyrant, is expected to consult with his subjects, or at least their representative leaders and elite members. He is not supposed to rule arbitrarily. The king's solicitation and heeding of public opinion makes monarchy at least minimally political in its means.

What differentiates the monarch from the tyrant, then, is that the latter's rule is based solely on his subjects' surrender to force, while the former's rule, though also absolute, is based on his subjects' compliance with power. Of course, a king or autocrat, like any other political ruler, may deceive the public into believing that he rules in their interest, all the while abusing his prerogatives and filling his own coffers. Yet even such deceit constitutes a form of power. By succeeding in his deception, the political ruler avoids the need to rule by force. By no means is political power always benign or good. Nonetheless, political power is always distinguishable from brute force. It remains susceptible to public influence and solicitous of public compliance.

Political rule is not democratic rule or even just rule. Indeed, democracy and justice are seldom if ever to be found at the origins of political rule. However, once political rule is established the growth of public influence is usually accompanied by demands for greater justice and the greater sharing of power. The concentration of power comes first, typically deployed in the narrow interests of those who wield it. Demands for rule oriented to the public good and attentive to the public voice follow.

Sovereignty typically precedes legitimacy, Thomas Nagel observes:

> First there is the concentration of power; then, gradually, there grows a demand for consideration of the interests of the governed, and for giving them a greater voice in the exercise of power. The demand may be reformist, or it may be revolutionary, or it may be a demand for

reform made credible by the threat of revolution, but it is the existence of concentrated sovereign power that prompts the demand, and makes legitimacy an issue.[48]

When political rule—the concentration of power—does not accede to the demands for greater consideration of the interests of the governed and their greater role in the exercise of power, rebellions and revolutions are not uncommon. Nor are they unjustified. With an eye both to the American Revolutionary War and the broad swath of history, Thomas Jefferson observed that "the tree of liberty must be refreshed from time to time with the blood of patriots and tyrants. It is its natural manure."[49] To say that violent revolt is natural, however, is not to say it is particularly effective. Insurgencies and revolts often fail to achieve their aim of toppling autocratic governments. And even when successful in this aim, violent rebellions often do not achieve the enduring justice their participants crave.

Revolutions often eat their children. Victims of the violence typically extend well beyond the autocrats and their acolytes. Revolutionaries who seize control of the state may lay waste to former colleagues who resist their consolidation of power. The Reign of Terror that followed the French Revolution is a case in point, no less than the Stalinist purges that followed the Bolshevik Revolution in Russia. Many former comrades in arms, and innocent bystanders, have died at the hands of their revolutionary brethren.

In describing the struggle against violent and oppressive colonial power, Frantz Fanon observed that a colonized people is

> ready at a moment's notice to exchange the role of the quarry for that of the hunter. The native is an oppressed person whose permanent dream is to become the persecutor.... The colonized man finds his freedom in and through violence... The violence of the colonial regime and the counter-violence of the native balance each other and respond to each other in an extraordinary reciprocal homogeneity.... The development of violence among the colonized people will be proportionate to the violence exercised by the threatened colonial regime.[50]

Violence begets violence. Of course, not all rebellion need employ force. Mahatma Gandhi, fighting British colonial rule in India, and Martin Luther King, Jr., fighting racism and segregation in the United States, initiated non-violent campaigns that were ultimately successful. These are not isolated cases. Empirical research demonstrates that nonviolent campaigns against oppressive regimes in the twentieth century were twice as likely as violent insurgencies to achieve their strategic objectives, with the latter having only a 25 percent rate of success. In turn, violent insurgencies often have negative impacts on their societies, and are less likely to lead to civil peace or the creation of democratic institutions.[51] While it may well be natural for force to be met with force, there are (often more effective) alternatives.

The more political the rule, the more it avoids the use of force. It cannot avoid the exercise of power. Historically, a greater sharing of power provided greater legitimacy to rule, allowed the dictates of law and other means of securing justice to gain sway over force, and staved off rebellion. To say that rule becomes more political when power is shared, however, is not to say that power is ever shared equally.

## EQUALITY AND ELITES

In liberal democracies, it is a constitutional right to be treated as an equal. Discrimination against specific individuals or groups—whether it is legal, political, economic, or social—constitutes the systematic denial of equal treatment. It is a form of injustice.

Formal equality means that all individuals, regardless of sex, race, religion, or class, stand before the law with the same rights and privileges. Formal equality is established through procedural (or formal) justice. Procedural justice exists when everyone is subject to the same rules, and the same punishments when these rules are broken.

Procedural justice or *equality under the law*, whether pertaining to legal, economic, or political affairs, does not necessarily translate into *equality of opportunity*. The French novelist Anatole France (1844–1924) sarcastically marveled at "the majestic equality of the laws, which forbid rich and poor alike to sleep upon the bridges, to beg in the streets, and to steal their bread."[52] Equality of the law, in this case, benefits the rich more than the poor. The wealthy have their well-prepared food and posh accommodations, whereas the poor who abide by the law are left cold and hungry. The equal opportunity to sufficient nourishment and shelter is not guaranteed—indeed it may be undermined—by equality under the law that, for both rich and poor, forbids stealing bread, begging in the streets, or sleeping upon bridges.

Likewise, equality under the law may give each citizen the equal right to dine in fancy restaurants, live in fashionable neighborhoods, and attend prestigious universities. For poorer citizens, however, such formal equality seldom translates into fine dining, luxurious suburban dwelling, or an Ivy League education. All other things being equal—which seldom if ever is the case—not eating in fancy restaurants and not living in fashionable neighborhoods will not unduly restrict opportunities in the economic or political world, assuming one is well nourished and one's neighborhood is safe and secure. Not receiving a good education, however, might substantially diminish opportunities to achieve financial success and political office.[53] In turn, where one eats, sleeps, and works will largely determine whom one associates with, and social associations impact economic and political opportunities. Sorting out when equality of opportunity is crucial to the maintenance of political rights, and when such equality is not adequately secured through formal, procedural means, is intrinsic to the pursuit of justice.

Equality of opportunity, most broadly understood, means that all individuals receive the same chance to develop fully as human beings. That entails, at a minimum, a basic level of nourishment, housing, health care, emotional support, and education. Equality of opportunity, for this reason, is often understood as a form of substantive justice. Unlike procedural justice, substantive justice requires that each person receive more than the due process of law. It requires that each person also receive the material, emotional, and educational support required for self-development. In most cases, substantive justice entails a redistribution of resources such that the basic needs (economic, medical and educational) of all are met by government programs financed through taxation.

Achieving equality of opportunity would not be so difficult if disadvantages in one area of human endeavor were naturally offset by advantages in another. More frequently, however, disadvantages beget further disadvantages. Economic privation typically translates into political impotence. Wealth allows for the greater leisure, education and influence that facilitate the pursuit of political power. It is not simply a matter of having a large bank account. Most political leaders first hone their skills and gain their reputations in their careers. Those who are disadvantaged in the professional or business world will likely be disadvantaged in the political world.

Liberal political institutions and culture maintain that each person has an equal right to life, liberty, and the pursuit of happiness. Some argue that formal or procedural justice adequately secures this equality of rights. Others insist that the right to life, liberty, and the pursuit of happiness remains a hollow slogan unless people enjoy the equal opportunity to make full use of these rights. Equal opportunity in the realm of employment, for example, entails not merely the equal right to apply for a job but the equal opportunity to acquire the education and training that would make one's application for this job truly competitive. Substantive justice, understood as equality of opportunity, is a more demanding and more elusive achievement than procedural justice.

Equality under the law does not ensure equality of opportunity. Some argue that equality of opportunity can only be achieved by *in*equality under the law. At least, that is how the argument for affirmative action might be characterized. Originally, affirmative action was aimed at the removal of "artificial barriers" to the employment of women and members of minority groups. Eventually it came to mean special efforts to recruit, hire, and promote members of disadvantaged groups, effectively compensating for the enduring effects of past discrimination. Affirmative action aims to offset a tradition of discrimination against specific groups by offering compensatory opportunities.

Those opposed to affirmative action argue that it legislates favoritism and constitutes an unjustifiable "reverse discrimination." They maintain that affirmative action is unnecessary because equality of opportunity merges with equality under the law when laws forbidding discrimination are both extensive and well enforced. Economic opportunities would theoretically be equal if laws forbidding discrimination in education, recruitment, hiring, promotion, wages, and benefits were strictly upheld. Many proponents of affirmative action deny that current laws forbidding discrimination will end the economic privation of minority groups. Under conditions of enduring injustice, they view reverse discrimination as not only permissible but morally required.[54] The legitimacy and effectiveness of affirmative action will likely remain a contested issue.

The pursuit of economic, racial and gender equality will be addressed extensively in Chapter 4. For now, we will limit our attention to the pursuit of political equality. In liberal democracies, each citizen has one vote and access to public office. Political equality is fundamental. In ancient times, political power was mostly held by monarchs or aristocrats, who passed on the right of rule to their sons. With the development of democracy, the opportunity to compete for political office became available to more people. In turn, the right to vote gave citizens a voice, albeit an indirect one, in the way laws and policies were crafted. Such formal political equality, however, seldom translates into substantive political equality.

"Water, water every where, Nor any drop to drink," wrote Coleridge of the salty sea. One might say something similar about democracy in many nations, including the United States of America. It ostensibly surrounds us. Yet for many there is very little of it to be tasted. While the US is often celebrated as a model of democratic politics, Americans' participation in politics remains severely limited.

Only about 160,000 people out of the nearly 4 million inhabitants of the American colonies voted for the delegates who ratified the 1790 constitution. That amounts to about 4 percent of the population. At the time, a large proportion of people were explicitly excluded from political participation, while others (white men without property) were restricted in their manner of participation. Most restrictions on white male suffrage were lifted in the early 1800s. African Americans were not constitutionally enfranchised until 1870, women in 1920, and aboriginal peoples in 1924. (Likewise, Britain has been considered a democracy since the end of the eighteenth century, though at that time only one adult in twenty had the right to vote.) Though the franchise in the US legally extends to all adults today, whether at municipal, state, or national levels, less than two out of three citizens regularly take advantage of it. Voter turnout is lower in the US than in most other developed countries.[55]

Notably, some groups vote more than others. A much greater proportion of people with high incomes vote than do people with low incomes. Economic power and political power go hand in hand. This relationship should be assessed in tandem with the fact that economic inequality in the United States has increased dramatically in recent decades. The top 1 percent of US income earners have more than doubled their share since the middle of the twentieth century, and now average over 40 times as much income as the bottom 90 percent of income earners.[56] In light of these trends, the prospects for political equality are not promising.

Economic hardship is not the only factor diminishing participation in politics. Many citizens, rich and poor, simply choose to avoid politics and focus on other pursuits. Some may be apathetic. Others find politics not to their tastes. In any case, with the partial exception of referendums that institute specific policies or laws, citizens in democratic nations do not directly engage in self-government. Instead, citizens periodically decide who shall govern for them. Such representative systems of government, effectively, is government by elites. The fact that most forms of government constitute rule by elites is undeniable. Whether elite politics is good or bad, invariable or amenable to transformation, remains a topic of debate.

Some would argue that rule by elites is simply a reflection of human nature, as most primate and other mammalian groups are dominated by *alpha* members. Hierarchies are natural. Thucydides recorded his native Athenians' invocation of a law of nature—namely that "the strong do what they can and the weak suffer what they must"—to legitimate their imperial domination of the Mediterranean world. Likewise, in Plato's *Republic*, Socrates' philosophic appeals to justice are harshly derided by Thrasymachus, who observes that justice is merely "the advantage of the stronger."[57] Justice, Thrasymachus argues, is a concept developed by elites to serve their own interests. Those who practice injustice on a "sufficiently large scale," he suggests, become the rulers of a country and gain the power to redefine words like justice to serve their interests. Might makes right.

Throughout history, elites—whether politicians, bureaucrats, business leaders, the clergy, the media, or officers of the armed forces—have played a preponderant role in wielding power. Recall Robert Michels "iron law of oligarchy," which stipulates that all human organizations will develop a hierarchical structure wherein a minority rules over a majority. Elites, Michel argued, were inevitable. Some political theorists, such as C. Wright Mills, sharply oppose all forms of elitism despite its acknowledged tenacity.[58] Other social and political theorists, often informed by the work of Gaetano Mosca (1858–1941) and Vilfredo Pareto (1848–1923), accept elite power as an unavoidable fact of life. But they defend it selectively, arguing that there are better and worse forms of elite rule.

Mosca and Pareto were concerned with the propensity of the ruling class to become hereditary. They advocated the "circulation of elites" as a means of ensuring that social and political leadership remained vibrant. In the absence of elite rule continually recharged with the most skilled and talented individuals, social order might collapse and with it the liberties it allowed.

In this vein, and in the wake of totalitarian forms of rule in the twentieth century, Giovanni Sartori argued that the major threat to democracy was not an aristocracy or elite. Democratic rights and liberties are threatened, Sartori maintained, because the masses are susceptible to demagogues, and demagogues are increasingly likely to gain power when the authority of traditional elites is undermined. Sartori's argument can be employed to explain the rise of populist demagogues who bill themselves as champions of the people and promise to drain the elite-filled swamp of politics. Once in power, however, populists frequently subvert constitutional order and pursue ever-increasing personal power. Along with Mosca and Pareto, Sartori defends rule by elites as a necessary, if imperfect, means to secure constitutional order and the rule of law, notwithstanding the political inequality of elite rule and its corruption.

Many theorists supportive of elite politics assume the exercise of power to be a "zero-sum game." They believe that any increase in the power held by one person or group means a decrease in power held by another, with the net sum always being zero. Other political theorists, such as Hannah Arendt, insist that cooperative activity—acting in concert—constitutes an exercise of power wherein common interests are served. As social order is established, mutual influence grows, and so does power. Cooperation begets a positive-sum game of power. Power in the political realm is not only a "power over." It can be understood as "power with." Power is seldom if ever shared in a wholly egalitarian manner, but it need not be zero-sum. All may benefit from its exercise.

In a world of scarce resources, the ubiquitous concern for self-interest stimulates competition and, frequently, conflict. In such a world, the exercise of power is unlikely to be fully reciprocal and actors' interests will seldom be equally served by it. Competition and conflict is inherent to politics. But so is cooperation. Indeed, the attempt to manage conflict through politics brings people together to form political parties, groups of cooperating individuals who are engaged in a competitive quest for power. Politics is a means of managing conflict so that it does not deteriorate into the brute force of authorities, private feuding, or mob violence.

Politics has been called the art of compromise. The political actor accepts limitations to conflict to avert violence. Likewise, the political actor makes concessions and adjustments to achieve cooperation among diverse individuals and groups. Through the exercise of power and the art of compromise, political actors muster cooperation and manage conflict.

It is said that nature abhors a vacuum. Power also abhors a vacuum. If a form of power is diminished or dies out, some other form of power quickly fills the void. What makes for political rule, then, is not the diminishment of power but the multiplicity of its forms, its vulnerability to contestation, and its shared exercise.

## REFERENCES

1   See Donald Griffin, *Animal Minds* (Chicago: University of Chicago Press, 1992), 219.

2   See Frans de Waal, *Good Natured: The Origins of Right and Wrong in Humans and Other Animals* (Cambridge: Harvard University Press, 1996).

3   See Daniel C. Dennett, *Darwin's Dangerous Idea: Evolution and the Meanings of Life* (New York: Simon and Schuster, 1995), 379.

4   Donald Worster, *Nature's Economy* (Cambridge: Cambridge University Press, 1994), 335.

5   St Augustine, *The City of God* (New York: Penguin, 1972), 596.

6   St Thomas Aquinas, *The Political Theories of St Thomas Aquinas*, ed. Dino Bigongiari (New York: Hafner Press, 1953), 180.

7   Thomas Paine, *The Rights of Man* (Garden City, N.Y.: Doubleday, 1961), 398–99.

8   Thomas Paine, *Common Sense, Rights of Man and Other Essential Writings of Thomas Paine* (New York: Signet, 2003), 273.

9   Alexander Hamilton, James Madison and John Jay, *The Federalist Papers* (New York: Mentor, 1961), 79.

10  Immanuel Kant, *Political Writings*, 2nd edn, ed. Hans Reiss (Cambridge: Cambridge University Press, 1991), 46, 47.

11  Karl Marx, *Writings of the Young Marx on Philosophy and Society*, trans. L. Easton and K. Guddat (Garden City, N.Y.: Doubleday, 1967), 39.

12  Thomas Hobbes, *Leviathan*, ed. C.B. Macpherson (New York: Penguin, 1968), 261.

13  Hobbes, *Leviathan*, 186.

14  Thucydides, *The Peloponnesian War* (New York: Modern Library, 1951), 334, 331.

15  C.B. Macpherson, *Democratic Theory: Essays in Retrieval* (Oxford: Clarendon Press, 1973), 202.

16  Steven Pinker, *The Language Instinct* (New York: Morrow, 1994), 430.

17  See Edward O. Wilson in *On Human Nature* (Cambridge: Harvard University Press, 1978), 78–79.

18  Roger D. Masters, *The Nature of Politics* (New Haven: Yale University Press, 1989), 26.

19  Cited in Masters, *The Nature of Politics*, 35.

20  Aristotle, *Nichomachean Ethics* (Book 2:1) (London: Penguin Books, 1953), 55.

21  Aristotle, *Nichomachean Ethics* (Book 8:12), 249–52. See also Larry Arnhart, "The New Darwinian Naturalism in Political Theory," *American Political Science Review* 89 (June 1995): 390.

22  Melvin Konner, *The Tangled Wing: Biological Constraints on the Human Spirit* (New York: Holt, Rinehart and Winston, 1982), 111.

23  Frans de Waal, *Primates and Philosophers: How Morality Evolved* (Princeton: Princeton University Press, 2006), 54–55.

24  See Richard Dawkins, *The Selfish Gene* (Oxford: Oxford University Press, 1989). Charles Lumsden and Edward O. Wilson, *Genes, Mind, and Culture: The Coevolutionary Process* (Cambridge: Harvard University Press, 1981).

25  See Masters, *The Nature of Politics*, 109.

26  Dawkins, *The Selfish Gene*, 192.

27  Dawkins, *The Selfish Gene*, 199.

28  Jean Bethke Elshtain, *Public Man, Private Woman: Women in Social and Political Thought*, 2d edn (Princeton: Princeton University Press, 1993), 357–58.

29  Bernard Crick, *In Defense of Politics*, 4th edn (Chicago: University of Chicago Press, 1992), 84.

30  John Rawls, *Justice as Fairness: A Restatement* (Harvard: Harvard University Press, 2001), 3–4.

31  Jürgen Habermas, *The Structural Transformation of the Public Sphere* (Cambridge: MIT Press, 1989).

32  Quoted in Jay M. Shafritz, *The HarperCollins Dictionary of American Government and Politics* (New York: HarperCollins, 1993), 368.

33  Ambrose Bierce, *The Devil's Dictionary (1906)*, quoted in Shafritz, *HarperCollins Dictionary of American Government and Politics*, 369.

34  Bertrand Russell, *Power: A New Social Analysis* (New York: Barnes and Noble, 1962), 9–10.

35  Niccolò Machiavelli, *The Prince and the Discourses* (New York; Random House, 1950), 44, 61–62.

36  Gianfranco Poggi, *The State: Its Nature, Development and Prospects* (Stanford: Stanford University Press, 1990), 25.

37  R.J. Rummel, "War Isn't This Century's Biggest Killer," *Wall Street Journal*, 7 July 1986, 12.

38  Emma Goldman, "Anarchism: What It Really Stands For," in *Anarchism and Other Essays* (New York: Dover, 1969), 50.

39  Robert Dahl, *Democracy and Its Critics* (New Haven: Yale University Press, 1989), 50.

40  Max Weber, *From Max Weber: Essays in Sociology*, trans. H.H. Gerth and C. Wright Mills (New York: Oxford University Press, 1958), 120–21.

41  Poggi, *The State*, 5. See also Jane Mansbridge, "Using Power/Fighting Power: The Polity," in Seyla Benhabib, ed., *Democracy and Difference: Contesting the Boundaries of the Political* (Princeton: Princeton University Press, 1996), 46–66.

42  Thomas Hobbes, *Leviathan*, ed. C.B. Macpherson (New York: Penguin, 1968), 227, 232.

43  Quoted in Bertrand de Jouvenal, *On Power: The Natural History of Its Growth* (Indianapolis: Liberty Fund, 1993), 36.

44  James Harrington, *The Oceana and other Works of James Harrington with an Account of his Life by John Toland* (London: Becket, Cadell and Evans, 1771), 35.

45  Philip Pettit, *Republicanism: A Theory of Freedom and Government* (Oxford: Clarendon Press, 1997), 184.

46  Niccolò Machiavelli, *The Prince and the Discourses* (New York; Random House, 1950), 163.

47  Pettit, *Republicanism*, 277.

48  Thomas Nagel, "The Problem of Global Justice", *Philosophy and Public Affairs* 33 (2005): 145, 146.

49  Thomas Jefferson, *Thomas Jefferson on Democracy* (New York: Mentor, 1939), 168.

50  Frantz Fanon, *The Wretched of the Earth* (New York: Grove Press, 1963), 42, 67, 69.

51  Erica Chenoweth and Maria J. Stephan, *Why Civil Resistance Works: The Strategic Logic of Nonviolent Conflict* (New York: Columbia University Press, 2011), 201.

52  Anatole France, *The Red Lily* (London: John Lane, 1908), 95.

53  See Jonathan Kozol, *Savage Inequalities: Children in America's Schools* (New York: Crown, 1991).

54  Iris Marion Young, *Justice and the Politics of Difference* (Princeton: Princeton University Press, 1990), 197.

55  See "US Trails Most Developed Countries in Voter Turnout," Pew Research Center, May 15, 2017. Accessed April 2018 at www.pewresearch.org/fact-tank/2017/05/15/u-s-voter-turnout-trails-most-developed-countries/

56  See https://inequality.org/facts/income-inequality/

57  Plato, *Republic* (344c), in *The Collected Dialogues of Plato*, eds Edith Hamilton and Huntington Cairns (Princeton: Princeton University Press, 1989), 594.

58  See James Burnham, *The Machiavellians* (New York: John Day, 1943); Giovanni Sartori, *Democratic Theory* (New York: Praeger, 1965); Peter Bachrach, *The Theory of Democratic Elitism: A Critique* (Boston: Little, Brown and Company, 1967); and C. Wright Mills, *The Power Elite* (New York: Oxford University Press, 1959).

## CHAPTER 3

# ANCIENT, MODERN AND POSTMODERN POLITICAL THOUGHT

The tradition of political theory is multifaceted and ever evolving. Perhaps its most pronounced boundaries are those distinguishing ancient, modern and postmodern political thought. This chapter explores continuities and innovations within the tradition of political theory. It addresses and integrates the ancient concern for the cultivation of virtue and the formation of character, the modern effort to set politics upon the foundations of science to more effectively build institutions and regulate interactions, and the postmodern focus on the social construction of identity. The chapter demonstrates that border crossings can make for good theory.

## STATECRAFT AND SOULCRAFT IN ANCIENT GREECE

In describing the character of a citizen, the ancient Greeks employed the word *psyche* or soul. Plato maintained that politics is "that concerned with the soul."[1] Differently constructed political regimes, he held, produce specific sorts of souls. For the ancient Greeks, statecraft was a form of soulcraft.

Greek legislators involved in managing the city-state, Plato held, were engaged in ordering of the souls of citizens. The name given to this endeavor in the classical world was *padeia*, the shaping of character. *Padeia* was a form of education, namely, an education in virtue. Both Plato and Aristotle agreed that this sort of education constituted the greatest part of politics and was the primary task of the legislator. Indeed, Plato suggests that the responsibility for a people's wickedness lay not with the people themselves but with the politicians responsible for their education and government. "In such cases," he states, "the planters are to blame rather than the plants."[2] He complains that even Pericles, the greatest of Athens' political leaders, frequently pandered to the citizenry's base desires rather than properly educating and improving them.

In the absence of an education in virtue, an extensive legal system becomes necessary to control vice. The attempt to rule citizens with heavy-handed legislation, Plato writes, is like trying to kill the Hydra by cutting off its head. In Greek mythology, every time a head of the Hydra was severed, two more grew in its place. Likewise, every time a law is enacted to restrain a vice, another vice emerges to take its place, requiring yet more laws. If souls are not properly ordered, laws and punishment only alleviate the symptoms of decay and postpone catastrophe. Laws cannot produce justice. An education in virtue is required. And this ordering of souls must begin at an early age. Plato went so far as to suggest that a truly just city could only be created if everyone over ten years of age was cast out. The remaining youth, bearing uncorrupted souls, could then be properly mentored in the life of virtue.

The first task for a philosopher is to put his own soul into order, with reason ruling over passion and appetite. The philosopher also may take on the task—or may be compelled to take on the task—of ordering the souls of his students and fellow citizens. Were the job of shaping souls well done, the harmony *within* individuals would produce a harmony *between* individuals. Well-ordered souls would produce a well-ordered city. The name Plato gives to this order, both within the soul and within the city, is justice.

For a just political order to be achieved, statecraft and soulcraft must be practiced in tandem. That is because the customs of the political realm mold the characters of its citizens, while the character of citizens determines what sort of political regime will be formed and maintained. As uneducated and vicious citizens cannot adequately organize their collective life, statecraft depends upon soulcraft. As an ill-organized polity will corrupt the characters of its citizens, particularly the youths whose souls are most susceptible to influence, soulcraft depends upon statecraft.

Plato's *Republic* depicts Socrates and a few young men constructing a hypothetical political regime, a "city in speech." But the dialogue begins with a conversation oriented to discovering justice in an individual, the order of the soul. Socrates remarks that the individual's soul is too small and obscure to see well into its nature. Magnifying lenses are required for the young theorists. The construction of a city in speech is proposed as a means to view justice at a sufficiently large scale to make it comprehensible.

From the middle of Book II onwards, the largest portion of the dialogue focuses on justice in the city, the soul writ large. Only at the end of Book IX are we explicitly reminded of our starting point, that founding the city in speech was only meant to make possible the investigation of justice within the soul. The entire theoretical enterprise of organizing the city-state was simply a "pattern . . . laid up for the man who wants to see and found a city within himself."[3] Despite the time and effort spent discussing the nature of the just regime, the person who knows what is best for himself, Plato concludes, "won't mind the political things." He will concern himself solely with "his own city," that is, with his soul.

Is the *Republic* primarily a political program for establishing the just state or a philosophic investigation of the just, well-ordered soul? If the latter, was it necessary for Socrates to spend so much time talking about the polity when his concern all along was the psyche? It has been suggested that Socrates' proposal to found a city in speech was simply a devious way of securing the abiding interest of his politically ambitious interlocutors. Perhaps Socrates' purpose was to shape their souls. The only way he could get them to stick around long enough to undergo this philosophic therapy was to entice them with the prospect of becoming the glorious theoretical founders of a new city-state. If this is true, then the *Republic*, like many of Plato's other dialogues, is an ironic piece of writing harboring multiple messages and multilayered meanings.

### ORDERING THE SOUL AND STATE

The word *philosophy* literally translates as the love of wisdom. The lover of wisdom seeks wisdom because he does not already possess it. As Socrates observes, no one who is truly wise desires wisdom, for no one seeks to become what he already is.[4] Though the philosopher is not wise, neither is he wholly ignorant. For the philosopher knows that it is best to seek wisdom above all else. The ignorant man does not even know that.

Platonic philosophy was the practice of performing reconstructive surgery on the soul. The chief surgical instrument was reason.[5] Reason provides the route to wisdom and insight. It is the spark of the divine in man, separating him from the beasts. But reason is not the only force within us. There are also the passions and appetites, which seek to go their own ways. Passions and appetites, Plato insists, must be kept in line and put to good use. Otherwise there will be inner anarchy and nothing much can be accomplished. An ordered soul is one in which reason rules unchallenged. It subjugates the passions and appetites, like a charioteer whose firm grip on the reins keeps his horses running straight and true.

The means to develop and strengthen reason is by way of a type of conversation called dialectic. Dialectic, also known as the Socratic method, begins when someone asks a simple question about some fundamental issue. One might ask, for instance, What is the nature of justice? All answers given in response are subject to interrogation. This interrogation uncovers unstated assumptions and logical inconsistencies and subsequently submits these assumptions and inconsistencies to further inquiry. In this way, dialectical argument exposes and rejects ungrounded opinions.

At the end of the dialectic process, one usually finds oneself back where one started. The original question remains unanswered. But one is no longer able to avail oneself of all those opinions and beliefs that formerly produced a sense of stability. At this point, an admission of ignorance is in order. Such an admission is the prerequisite for knowledge. Now the path is cleared. The mind is no longer cluttered with a hodgepodge of groundless assumptions. Instead, one may rely on reason to catapult one into the realm of knowledge.

Plato suggests that moral and political truths are of the same eternal and unchanging nature as mathematical truths. Such truths can only be apprehended through the intellect by way of reason. Dialectic clears the intellect of the debris of prejudice and false opinions so that true knowledge may be gained. Yet we are confronted with a paradox. Only by achieving mastery over one's appetites and passions can one follow the rule of reason. Yet only by following reason can one secure "immunity" from the appetites and passions.[6] In other words, only those with well-ordered souls are capable of ascending through dialectic to knowledge. Yet only those who already have knowledge can well order their souls. As Plato remarked in one of his letters, knowledge of the "Good" can be engendered with the careful use of reason, but only in a soul that is itself "naturally" good.[7] A soul must already be reasonably well-ordered for philosophy to carry out its dialectic therapy.

As the function of philosophic speech is to influence the soul, the philosopher must first ascertain the sort of person he is addressing in order to tailor his speech to achieve the best results.[8] Very disorderly souls are not worth the bother. In the *Republic* Socrates appears to choose his partners for conversation based on his sense of which souls are naturally good and hence have the potential for further philosophic sculpting. His decision to carry out the project of constructing the city in speech was based on his pleasant surprise at the natural orderliness of the souls of those young men available to take part in the conversation, namely Adeimantus and Glaucon, the brothers of Plato.[9]

In the *Republic* and other dialogues, Plato affirms that human beings are reincarnated after they die. Before being reborn, they are allowed a glimpse of the divine. This experience is mostly forgotten at birth, though remnants of it linger in memory. If Plato is taken at his word, then every human soul shares some basic degree of order because it has been privileged to behold cosmic order at the end of a former life.[10] Its glimpse of the cosmic order, however, does not guarantee a philosophic disposition. Very few individuals remember their brush with divinity. Once reborn, most people smother the spark of cosmic order under opinion and belief and custom. For the select few whose souls are naturally well-ordered, the philosopher kindles the spark into the raging fire of knowledge.[11] Dialectic reasoning is the philosophic art that leads "the best part of the soul up to the contemplation of what is best among realities."[12]

Since education is the better part of politics, Platonic soulcraft is also a form of statecraft. Socrates considered it a relatively safe form. Athenians took their religious and political mores seriously, and they were wary of philosophers with radical ideas. Eventually, Socrates' efforts to educate fellow citizens landed him in a court of law facing charges of impiety and corrupting the youth. At 70 years of age, Socrates was condemned to death and forced to drink hemlock. But had he engaged in standard political practices such as seeking public office, Socrates observed, he likely would not have lived as long.

Plato maintains that political regimes mirror the order or disorder found in the souls of their citizens. He proposes that there are as many types of political regimes as there are types of souls. Aristocracy corresponds to the soul that loves goodness and justice, timocracy to the soul that loves honor and glory, oligarchy to the soul that loves wealth, democracy to the soul that loves freedom and pleasure, and tyranny, the worst of all regimes, to the soul that loves domination.

The best regime is not democratic, according to Plato. He believes that the democratic love of freedom leads to anarchy, and anarchy eventually leads to tyranny. But democracy, Plato admits, is the "fairest" or most beautiful regime owing to its inherent complexity and diversity. Still, its sensual appeal should not be overvalued. The problem is that democracy's celebration of freedom leads to disorder in souls. The democratic defense of liberty deteriorates into the toleration of license. Democratic freedom amounts to a freedom to let the passions and appetites rule unchecked. Rather than promote a freedom that invites licentiousness, Plato advocates a monarchical or aristocratic rule that maintains authoritarian control. He argues that citizens must not get into the habit of acting independently. They must remain under the command of a leader who instructs their actions "to the least detail." Freedom from such strict control, Plato insists, must be expelled "root and branch from the lives of all mankind."[13]

In the *Republic*, the role of reason in the city is modeled on its role in a well-ordered psyche. Just as reason rules over the passions and appetites, so the most rational member of society, the philosopher-king, rules over its spirited and appetitive parts, its warriors and merchants. As embodied in the rule of the philosopher king, reason ensures the welfare of the whole city in the same manner that the rule of reason in the well-ordered soul ensures the happiness of the individual. Justice in the soul and state is achieved through the authoritative rule of reason.[14] Notwithstanding Socrates' deployment of a city in speech to serve as a model for justice in the soul, in the end the individual soul provides the model for justice in the city.

Dialectics, Plato states, is the art of discerning "unity and plurality" as they exist in the nature of things.[15] Yet Plato fails to discern the inherent plurality of political community. Accordingly, many political theorists, starting with Aristotle, have criticized Plato's attempt to model the political realm on the soul. The problem, Aristotle observes, is that the polity is defined by its plurality, while the individual is defined by its organic unity. Reducing plurality to unity is a dangerous ambition. For one, it requires deception. Plato's philosopher kings resort to propagating myths and "noble lies." The citizens must be tricked into believing that the rigid caste system that structures their society is the creation of infallible gods. Duped by what amounts to an ancient form of ideology, the citizens of the *Republic* allow the philosopher kings to rule with unquestioned authority.

Even in Plato's much more practical work, *The Laws*, we find a uniform and docile citizenry. "All should agree, without a dissonant voice," Plato writes, that the laws "are all god-given and admirable, flatly refusing a hearing to anyone who disputes the point."[16] Inquiry into the merits of the laws is strictly forbidden, except for private conversations that elders may hold with magistrates.

Theorists throughout the ages have worried about the concentration of power that the rule of philosopher kings would entail. With the onset of modernity, this worry was translated into sustained efforts to design political institutions that could thwart the abuse of power. Attentive to the history of the rise and fall of the Roman republic, Montesquieu understood the importance of political institutions in both generating power and disabling its misuse. "Constant experience shows us that every man invested with power is apt to abuse it, and to carry his authority as far as it will go," Montesquieu writes. "To prevent this abuse, it is necessary from the very nature of things that power should be a check to power."[17] Montesquieu's insight became the basis for the American system of "checks and balances" between executive, legislative and judiciary branches of government. John Adams, concerned with potential abuse of power, included in the 1780 Constitution of Massachusetts a provision that forbade the legislature, executive and judiciary from overstepping their respective prerogatives. This ensured that the state would remain, in Adam's now famous rewording of Harrington, "a government of laws and not of men."

With a similar concern, Benjamin Constant (1767–1837), a French-Swiss political thinker, maintained that whenever unlimited power was exercised, regardless of who wielded it, the results were unfortunate. The problem, he states, rests not with the holder of power but with the amount of power held. "There are weapons," Constant writes, "which are too heavy for the hand of man."[18] Perhaps the most famous statement of this sort was made by the English historian and moralist Lord Acton (1834–1902), who observed that "all power tends to corrupt, and absolute power corrupts absolutely." Like Montesquieu and Constant, Acton cautions against the consequences of the concentration of power.

One does not have to be a cynic about human nature, or politics, to appreciate the prudence of these thinkers. It is not the case that everyone yearns or strives for despotic power, nor even that all politicians are crooked or tyrants in waiting. As Pettit observes, "people in power are not inevitably corrupt but are inherently corruptible: while they may actually make their decisions on a proper impartial basis, they cannot be relied upon to continue to do so if there are no blocks or checks on the abuse of their power."[19] Creating political institutions that provide checks and balances to the exercise of power is an acknowledgment of the frailty of the human condition: not everyone is corrupt, but all are corruptible. It is also a celebration of the human capacity to create artifacts, such as constitutions, that compensate for these frailties. Kant may have voiced the strongest variant of this claim, observing:

> As hard as it may sound, the problem of setting up a state can be solved even by a nation of devils (so long as they possess understanding). It may be stated as follows: "In order to organize a group of rational beings who together require universal laws for their survival, but of

whom each separate individual is secretly inclined to exempt himself from them, the constitution must be so designed that, although the citizens are opposed to one another in their private attitudes, these opposing views may inhibit one another in such a way that the public conduct of the citizens will be the same as if they did not have such evil attitudes. A problem of this kind must be soluble. For such a task does not involve the moral improvement of man; it only means finding out how the mechanism of nature can be applied to men in such a manner that the antagonism of their hostile attitudes will make them compel one another to submit to coercive laws."[20]

For Kant, we should not hope that well-ordered souls will produce well-ordered states. Rather, we should endeavor to create constitutional regimes that encourage fallible and often selfish citizens and statespeople to act justly. While the ancients were primarily concerned with the cultivation of character and virtue, modern political theorists, like Kant, became preoccupied with the design of political institutions that could effectively regulate the interactions of citizens and statespeople. Understanding and exploiting the "mechanism of nature" so that it might better order human affairs was central to the project of modernity.

Whether a nation of devils might be adequately restrained by well-crafted institutions is debatable. There are good reasons to believe that political community cannot be sustained without the cultivation of good character among citizens and their regular exercise of virtue. While well-crafted political institutions are not omnipotent, they nonetheless remain crucial. They are the necessary but not sufficient conditions of just polities. In this vein, the American religious and social thinker Reinhold Niebuhr (1892–1971) argued that democracy was the only viable solution to the problem of concentrated power. "Man's capacity for justice makes democracy possible," Niebuhr said, "but man's inclination to injustice makes democracy necessary."[21] Democratic checks and balances, constitutionally enshrined, limit the power a political leader can exercise and hence the corrupting effects of this power.

Plato was not unaware of the problem. After all, he declared tyranny to be the worst of all regimes. But Plato believed philosophers were immune to the corruption of power. Philosophers like nothing better than to philosophize. They are mostly concerned with the order of their souls, not the ordering of the city. Political power would be a dangerous burden and an unwanted distraction. Indeed, philosophers would have to be forced to take office by citizens who recognized their wisdom and wished to benefit from it. If philosophers agreed to steer the ship of state, Plato held, they would do so not for the love of power but to fulfill their obligations to the city.

Common sense suggests that we should not put too much faith in the purity of the souls of our leaders, even those with philosophic dispositions. While the character of those who rule is important, a more reliable safeguard against the abuse of power are well-crafted institutions. In any case, corruption may occur not only among the rulers, but among the ruled.

We might revise Acton's well-known adage by saying that just as power corrupts so does its dearth, and an absolute lack of power corrupts absolutely. To be constantly subjected to power while remaining wholly powerless oneself is to be transformed from a responsible citizen into a resentful slave. A political realm built on servitude and resentment is ripe for revolution. To rule over powerless citizens is to sow the seeds of corruption throughout a regime.

An exploration of modern political thought will help us chart the development of efforts to design political institutions that account for the exercise and effects of power. In large part, the modernist conviction that such institutions could be crafted was grounded in the supplanting of traditional authorities by scientific inquiry, and the belief in the power of such inquiry to advance the progress of humanity.

## MODERN POLITICAL THOUGHT

Modernity arose out of the Renaissance, the Protestant Reformation, and the Scientific Revolution, events of the fourteenth to seventeenth centuries that marked a radical transformation of the artistic and literary world, the religious world, and the world of inquiry and knowledge. These three events produced a widespread challenge to tradition and authority. They marked a vibrant assertion of the growing power of the human mind.

The word *modern* refers to that which is recently in existence. A modernist is someone who prefers the new to the old-fashioned. The term modernist was first used with this connotation in the sixteenth century. It referred, often pejoratively, to someone who spurned tradition and advocated either new techniques of scientific inquiry or the study and use of vernacular or contemporary languages rather than classical Greek or Latin. Modernism stood in contrast to traditionalism.

The term modernist may never actually have been used in his own day to describe the Italian astronomer, mathematician, and physicist Galileo Galilei (1564–1642). Nonetheless, this key figure of the Scientific Revolution embodied the central features of modernism. Galileo abandoned traditional authorities and standards of inquiry. He took exception to Aristotle, who until that time had stood as the chief authority in matters of science no less than in matters of philosophy. Galileo argued that bodies do not fall with velocities proportional to their weights, as Aristotle held. Were it not for the effects of (air) friction, Galileo insisted, heavy objects would fall at the same speed as light ones. He also rejected the Ptolemaic understanding of the earth as the center of the solar system. Instead, he embraced the theory of the Polish astronomer Nicolaus Copernicus (1473–1543) that the earth revolved around the sun. Copernicus developed his heliocentric theory based on extensive examination of ancient astronomical charts. Though eventually banned, Copernicus' thesis was initially unopposed by the Catholic church, perhaps because it was a highly academic treatise and did not seem likely to gain widespread support. Galileo, however, made the "Copernican revolution" come to life. In 1632, he published a defense of the heliocentric theory based on empirical evidence, namely, the observations he had made through a device of his own construction, the astronomical telescope.

In 1633, Galileo was brought to Rome and forced to renounce heliocentrism, which was held to contradict the teachings of Catholicism. The church's effort to force Galileo to recant was the first, and most infamous, attempt by the forces of tradition to stifle the nascent forces of modernism. While the traditionalists won the battle—Galileo regretfully recanted— they would lose the war. The tide of modernism proved unstoppable.

Modernism largely developed in the Western world owing to the growing power of science. This was a new, empirical science, no longer grounded in the metaphysical musings of ancient authorities or in religious creed. "I think in the discussion of natural problems," Galileo wrote, "we ought to begin not with the Scriptures, but with experiments, and demonstrations." From this point on, nothing was to be taken for granted or accepted on faith. Everything was to be validated through reason and grounded in repeated observations and experimental investigation. As Albert Einstein wrote, the leitmotif of Galileo's work was "the passionate fight against any kind of dogma based on authority."[22] In the wake of this battle, modern science was born.

Francis Bacon, Galileo's contemporary, stated that "ancient times were the youth of the world." Bacon believed that there was much growing up to be done. He wrote the *Novum Organum*, or New Logic, to replace the old logic developed by Aristotle (who had composed a work called the *Organum*). Bacon's new logic was also meant to supersede the metaphysical speculation that developed within the medieval theological philosophy of scholasticism. Scholasticism aimed to complement and strengthen faith in the Christian God with a good dose of Aristotelian logic. In proposing a new form of logic to guide inquiry, Bacon challenged both the authority of Aristotle and the relevance of religious faith. Bacon's new logic was based on induction, the process of reasoning from the particular to the general. It stood in contrast to the ancient logical methods based on deduction. Deduction is argument that proceeds from the general to the particular, from cosmological principles, for example, to specific moral imperatives.

Voltaire (1694–1778), a French philosopher and man of letters, called Francis Bacon the "father of experimental philosophy."[23] Bacon's work on induction was particularly well suited to the emerging empirical sciences. Instead of beginning with a general principle, which was often theologically grounded or based on the metaphysical speculations of ancient authorities, Bacon started with numerous concrete observations of the real world. These observations would allow the scientist to discern patterns or regularities in the workings of nature. Employing observed regularities, the scientist would then form hypotheses and theories that described the general laws of nature. Scientific theories were held to function in strict accord with logic, and they could be tested and refined by repeated observation and experimentation. To understand the natural world, one no longer required religious revelation. Science was enough.

The heliocentric movement of the planets was discovered by Copernicus, empirically validated by Galileo, theoretically refined by Johannes Kepler (1571–1630), who calculated the mathematics of planetary motion, and effectively explained by Isaac Newton (1642–1727), who addressed the role of gravity. The Scientific Revolution inaugurated by these men yielded the laws of physics, which applied equally to the heavens and the earth. In contrast to ancient authorities, scientists viewed the world solely in terms of mechanical forces that acted causally on material objects. These forces could be rationally inferred, empirically measured, and mathematically expressed. Gods, theologians, and metaphysical philosophers had little to add. The book of nature was written in the language of mathematics, Galileo said, and scientists had taken over the task of reading it.

Modernism was grounded in the assumption that the order of the universe is natural, accessible to reason and observation, and describable in impersonal, mathematical terms. Bacon famously maintained that "knowledge itself is power." Modernism flourished in the wake of the power accumulated through scientific knowledge and technical engineering. Nature can be commanded, Bacon wrote, only by obeying her laws. Learning nature's laws was the first step to mastering her. Mastering nature became a central goal for the modernists.

The modern celebration of science had roots in scholasticism. The scholastics relied on Aristotle, who, unlike Plato, attempted to combine rational inquiry with empirical investigations of the natural world. Modernists were receptive to the empirical orientation of Aristotle. Scholastics took Aristotle as an authority, however, and were preoccupied with deductive argument and its relationship to religious faith. Modernists rejected ancient authority. Moreover, modernists advocated a humanistic orientation that was opposed to the theocentric or God-centered orientation of the scholastics.

This "secular" humanism was a legacy of the Renaissance, a period that broadly marks the transition from the Middle Ages to modernity. The Renaissance, which literally means "rebirth," began in the fourteenth century as a rediscovery of the humanistic orientation of the Greeks and Romans. These ancient people were admired for their celebration of human beauty, intelligence, and individual greatness. Such values stood in marked contrast to the traditionalism advocated by the medieval church, which roundly condemned the sinfulness of human pride and was suspicious of human ingenuity.

The Renaissance reached its peak in Galileo's and Bacon's time. By then the privileged throne of humankind at the center of God's creation, like the privileged position of the earth at the center of the solar system, was crumbling. Yet humanism could maintain the celebration of human values and the human spirit because it unlocked the secrets of the universe through human reason and ingenuity. Humankind was gaining the power to control more and more of its world through science and the development of technology. America had recently been "discovered" by Europeans, the globe was being circumnavigated, and the human mind, it appeared, was beginning to exercise its full potential. This age was unique, the famous French historian Jules Michelet (1798–1874) reflected, in achieving both the "discovery of the world" and the "discovery of man."

In addition to its scientific and humanistic orientation, modernity was characterized by progressivism. To be progressivist is to believe that the world is constantly changing for the better through the power of the human mind. As the French philosopher René Descartes (1596–1650) observed in his effort to ground the Scientific Revolution philosophically, if humankind puts its "long chains of reasoning" to work in a methodical, empirical fashion then "there can be nothing so remote that we cannot reach to it, nor so recondite that we cannot discover it." In exercising the full power of the human mind, Descartes concludes, we can "render ourselves the masters and possessors of nature."[24] Modernists believe that there will be steady growth in the accumulation of knowledge and in the capacity to better humanity's condition.

With the Enlightenment, at its height in Europe during the eighteenth century, the progressivist celebration of reason took a new turn. Rational capacities were increasingly applied not only to the conquest of the natural world but also to the management of the social and political world. The attempt was made to duplicate in culture the mastery increasingly achieved over nature. Modernists suggested that humanity's moral stature and political organization, not simply its material condition, might undergo constant improvement.

Such progressivism was given dramatic voice in the work of the Marquis de Condorcet (1743–94), a French philosopher who wrote a work entitled *Outlines of a Historical View of the Progress of the Human Mind*.[25] Condorcet traced the development of humanity through nine epochs and predicted a tenth in which the "indefinite" perfectibility of the human race would become irreversible. Most modernists do not share Condorcet's utopian belief in humanity's imminent moral and intellectual perfection, but they do believe that humanity can steadily achieve progress. Like Condorcet, they attribute this progress to the benefits of scientific inquiry and the ever-increasing power of technology to steadily improve the lot of humankind.

The great strides in scientific and technological progress that have been made since the onset of modernity might be contrasted to the rather meager results achieved in moral development. Indeed, the argument might be made that humanity's ever-increasing power in science and technology accentuated the moral immaturity of our race, while exacerbating its destructive effects. The modern epoch was marred by the ruthless exploitation of peasants and wage-laborers, the growth of slavery, and numerous genocides and wars, including two world wars in the twentieth century. Moral progress is, at best, not a linear phenomenon for our species. In turn, modernity undermined many traditional sources of order and meaning without developing ready replacements.

The modernist celebration of rationality to the detriment of traditional authority and religious faith, Roxanne Euben claims, has led to widespread alienation, the collapse of community, and, in some cases, outright nihilism. Euben observes a "transcultural pre-occupation with the limits of modern rationalism" in contemporary Western political thought no less than in Islamic fundamentalism.[26] Without the anchors of stable identity offered by scripture and tradition, life may become increasingly directionless and meaningless. Whenever that happens, reactionary forces fill the vacuum, with fundamentalist religious leaders and demagogues promising their followers a return to better times.

Critiques of modernity often exhibit nostalgia for the good old days. But when rose-tinted glasses are exchanged for the instruments of inquiry, we discover that the good old days were not all that good. The historical record prior to modernity evidences a great deal of brutality, bigotry, domination, cruelty, ignorance, disease and early death. Many things have gotten better. There is no doubt that modernity has produced a world of increasingly rapid change and placed a heightened burden on the individual to find his or her own way in life. But science, public reason, equality and liberty are better than the alternatives, at least to the extent that we can agree, as Steven Pinker concludes his well-grounded endorsement of Enlightenment values, that "life is better than death, health is better than sickness, abundance is better than want, freedom is better than coercion, happiness is better than suffering, and knowledge is better than superstition and ignorance."[27] Still, the modernist celebration of the rational individual pursuing its self-interest en route to endless progress bears further scrutiny.

## Individualist Theories of Politics

Western political thought is primarily individualist in its orientation. As either the wielder or object of power, the individual is held to be an independent actor and autonomous moral agent engaged in voluntary and rational acts that serve its self-interest. The way individuals interact, and how political institutions are formed and transformed as a product of these interactions, become the foci of study.

The individualist understanding of power is generally directed to three central concerns:

(1) the nature and degree of power held by particular individuals (e.g., studies of presidents, prime ministers, legislators, or other political elites);
(2) the nature of the political processes and institutions that distribute and manage the power held by individuals (e.g., studies of elections and the various branches of government); and

(3)  the moral and rational standards that the individual ought to apply to the exercise of power or its resistance (e.g., studies of civil rights and duties, the nature of justice and liberty, and other concerns of normative political theory).

Each of these otherwise distinct fields of investigation focuses on individual actors as the autonomous wielders or resisters of power. Collective political existence, in turn, is viewed as the aggregated sum of the actions taken by individuals.

Such an orientation is evident in Hobbes. Individuals in the state of nature unanimously decide to give up their weapons and rights to a Leviathan, who then rules absolutely. Whether in an anarchical state of nature or in a society ruled by a sovereign, Hobbesian individuals intentionally wield power and make choices as autonomous agents.

Of course, the result of individualist theorizing need not be a Hobbesian form of politics. Most liberals accept the tenets of individualism. Yet the liberal tradition—from the English philosopher John Locke through contemporary champions of individual rights and freedoms—has taken a strong stand against the political absolutism promoted by Hobbes. The perspective of the autonomous individual is deployed to promote liberal democratic politics grounded in constitutionalism, limited government, and inalienable civil rights and liberties.

One of the more widely accepted individualist definitions of politics forms the title of Harold Lasswell's classic book, *Politics: Who Gets What, When, and How*.[28] Politics is about the power to decide who gets his interests served, according to what processes, and on whose timetable. It is about the struggle of individuals to secure their needs or wants. Lasswell is primarily concerned with the allocation of scarce resources because conflict over their pursuit is understood to be inevitable. Governmental regulation of social interaction is also inevitable, lest violence (and injustice) rule the day. For Lasswell, politics is about the use of governmental institutions to regulate the interactions of individuals and allocate scarce resources.

This modern definition of politics has proven very useful for political theorists and scientists, allowing them to chart the exercise of power and argue for its appropriate limits. It often fosters elegant theorizing. Yet, like all theories, it demonstrates a limited perspective.

Politics is not only about how individual needs become satisfied in a world of scarce resources. Politics also plays a role in determining how these needs are created, how they are understood and articulated, and how they are transformed. Politics influences how we come to perceive our needs as needs and how we come to perceive our rights (to see these needs fulfilled) as rights. Politics precedes and exceeds the distribution of scarce resources and the pursuit of individual interests because it concerns the ways we define and understand our resources, our interests, our relationships, and ultimately ourselves.

A common assumption of individualists is that the autonomous agent is, as it were, prepolitical. For liberals who accept this premise, individuals make politics, politics does not make individuals. Communitarian theorists disagree. As Michael Sandel writes: "By putting the self beyond the reach of politics, [liberalism] makes human agency an article of faith rather than an object of continuing attention and concern, a premise of politics rather than its precarious achievement."[29] Communitarian theorists argue that liberals ignore the way political communities shape the attitudes, values and behavior of their members. The proper cultivation of these attitudes, values and behavior, communitarians insist, is required to sustain social and political life.

Communitarians believe that social order is currently being undermined owing to an uncritical celebration of individual autonomy. At least this is the case in certain societies. Liberals who champion individual autonomy, sociologist Amitai Etzioni argues, tend to present their principles as ahistorical and transcultural truths. Yet the need for either increased social order or increased individual autonomy in any given society depends on historical and cultural circumstances. While contemporary China may be better served by an increase in individual autonomy, Etzioni states, contemporary America is in desperate need of greater social order. This does not necessitate increased levels of (state) coercion. Indeed, to the extent that social order is achieved through moral education and an appeal to common values, Etzioni argues, coercive means become less not more necessary.[30]

Politics, for communitarians, is not simply the Lasswellian process of divvying up the collective pie. Politics also entails an ongoing debate and struggle over the way we become identified as pie makers, pie cutters, and pie eaters. Communitarian political philosopher Alasdair MacIntyre argues that to answer the question "What ought I to do?" one must first answer the question "Who am I?"[31] What one wants and what one does is largely a product of who one understands oneself to be. Politics, it follows, is not only about doing what you do to get what you want; it is also a question of how you become who you are.

Communitarians tend to focus on reinvigorating traditional means of cultivating moral selves. They advocate the strengthening of the family, the intervention of the state in fostering cultural and ethical life, and the need for a robust social order. Like the ancients, they are concerned with the characters and virtues of citizens, and the power of the cultural environment to shape character and instill virtue. Still, communitarians constitute a relatively small minority amongst contemporary political theorists. Liberal individualism remains the dominant approach.

### STRUCTURALIST THEORIES OF POLITICS

Communitarians focus on the impact of the cultural environment, which is constituted by custom and tradition as well as a panoply of other practices and institutions. Collectively, these practices and institutions are known as social structures. Social structures influence the way we understand ourselves and our world, but they often do not have identifiable origins or specific authors. Those who concern themselves with the power of social structures—in distinction to individualist theorists who emphasize the power of human agency—are known as structuralists. Structuralism paved the way for postmodernism.

Those who reject structuralism and adopt the modern, individualist orientation are often known as methodological individualists. For methodological individualists, the whole is defined by its parts. One starts with the actions and relationships of individuals, and subsequently aggregates these actions and relationships to explain political processes, patterns, and institutions. A key characteristic of structuralism, in contrast, is the belief that the whole is greater than the sum of its parts. Society is more than an aggregate of individuals. Social structures have features that cannot be understood simply by adding up the features of its component parts. But how can a whole gain a quality that is absent in its parts? How can society have a life of its own, so to speak, apart from the various comings and goings of the individuals that compose it?

Émile Durkheim (1858–1917), a French sociologist, believed that society did indeed have a life of its own. His work inaugurated structuralism. Durkheim explained the nature of society by way of a biological metaphor. He writes:

> The living cell contains nothing but mineral particles, as society contains nothing but individuals; and yet it is patently impossible for the phenomena characteristic of life to reside in the atoms of hydrogen, oxygen, carbon and nitrogen. . . . Let us apply this principle to sociology. If, as we may say, this synthesis *sui generis* which every society constitutes, yields new phenomena, differing from those which take place in individual minds, we must, indeed, admit that these facts reside in the very society itself which produces them, and not in its parts, i.e., its members.[32]

In one bowl, we have a fish swimming in water. In another bowl, we have a small pile of minerals and other elements lying on the bottom of a bowl filled with water and gas bubbles, the same types and amounts of minerals, elements and gases as are found in the fish. It is obvious that the whole (the live fish) is indeed greater—not only more complex but qualitatively different—than the sum of its parts (a few grams of minerals, other elements and gases). Piling together an assortment of molecules will not produce a living creature. The organism has behaviors and capacities, such as self-directed movement and reproduction, that exceed what its constituent molecules are capable of on their own or in aggregate form. Yet, from the methodological individualist perspective, a living organism is simply a collection of molecules.

Applying this understanding to the study of society, Durkheim argues that social structures far exceed in power and scope the aggregated activities of the individual members that compose them. Social structures largely determine how individual members of a society behave and interact. They do so just as the physical constitution of a fish or any other living organism largely determines how the tissues and organs that compose it will interact.

"Society does not find the bases on which it rests fully laid out in consciences; it puts them there itself," Durkheim insists. He goes on to state that "although society may be nothing without individuals, each of them is much more a product of society than he is its maker."[33] Social structures produce the observable regularities of the social world. These regularities are rigid in the sense that most individuals cannot alter them. As individuals, we cannot appreciably change kinship systems, matrimonial patterns, the rate of unemployment, and enduring hierarchies organized around class, race, gender, or age. Yet as individuals we may be greatly affected by these structures. They influence our behavior and contribute to our identities.

Durkheim suggested that the way people think in primitive societies mimics the social order of their society. Individual cognitive systems and mental schemata are patterned upon the existing social structure of the group. This understanding has been extended to contemporary times by Pierre Bourdieu, a French sociologist. Bourdieu argues that individuals internalize the organization of social reality as "mental dispositions" and "schemes of perception and thought." The word Bourdieu uses for these dispositions and schemes is *habitus*. Habitus is a matrix of internalized cultural orientations, skills and practices. Bourdieu uses the word *field* to describe a network of social arrangements that embody and distribute positions and relations of power. The mental structures composing one's habitus, then, are reflections of the social structures composing the fields in which one participates.

Habitus is an internalization of social fields much like the soccer player's repertoire of behavior reflects the constraints (rules and boundary markers) of the soccer field. Unlike the rules for the game of soccer, however, the rules of social fields are seldom explicit or codified. They are learned, mostly without effort or intent, simply by living in a complex network of social relations. Following Durkheim, Bourdieu insists that these structural configurations are *sui generis*, which is to say, they are unique entities unto themselves. They are not merely the aggregate sum of individual actions and "cannot be reduced to the interactions and practices through which they express themselves."[34] Social structures often remain undetected by those they affect. Individuals in society do not generally notice the structures that channel their behavior. They fail to perceive these structures because they are focused on the behavior of other individuals like themselves. Effectively, they cannot see the forest for the trees.

Claude Lévi-Strauss, a French structural anthropologist, observes that we think and communicate according to set mental patterns, such as binary oppositions or dichotomies. Totemic and kinship systems also evidence these structured patterns, which reproduce themselves and their effects in all cultures.[35] For Lévi-Strauss, cultural institutions are the external projections and manifestations of universal structures, just as sentences are external manifestations of general grammatical rules. While individuals may create innumerable "original" sentences, they can do so intelligibly only by following rather strict grammatical rules that determine how words and phrases can be combined. Likewise, while individuals may create various cultural arrangements, they can do so, Lévi-Strauss suggests, only by following strict yet unwritten rules that dictate how the phenomena of cultural life are structured.

This line of thinking might be traced back to Immanuel Kant, who argued that the human mind has innate faculties that organize its perceptions of the world according to certain "rational" constraints and categories. Without these faculties, which determine the "mode of our knowledge of objects" and maintain the stable categories of space and time, experience would be reduced to a haphazard mishmash of largely incommunicable sensations.[36]

Structural Marxists likewise hold that individuals are epistemologically and behaviorally molded by deep patterns that transcend culture and time. For structural Marxists, such as Louis Althusser, these patterns are set neither in the collective mind, as Lévi-Strauss proposed, nor in innate mental categories, as Kant proposed. Instead, they are found in concrete economic relations that undergo logical and predictable transformations.[37] These economic patterns and their transformations depend on the level of a society's technological development. For structural Marxists, individual agents bear a resemblance to puppets on strings. The strings are being pulled by historically patterned economic forces that are beyond any individual's control. For the most part, these strings remain invisible to the individual agents themselves. It takes the demystifying work of theorists to illuminate the deeper structural forces.

Structural Marxists tend to deny the importance of human individuality, volition and freedom. Durkheim, Bourdieu, Lévi-Strauss, and the sociologist Anthony Giddens, do not take such a hard line. They propose a more balanced tension between the social structures that constrain us and the freedom we demonstrate as individuals.

Greater individuality and freedom, Durkheim insists, arises with the division of labor and the development of larger, more complex societies that allow individuals to escape the constraints of both instinct and convention. Lévi-Strauss similarly insists that the true value of liberty only arises once we understand that liberty itself is a cultural creation.[38] In turn, Bourdieu argues that habitus, though a reflection of social structures, is also creative and subject to change. Though "durable," it is "not eternal."[39] Individuals may transgress, redefine, invent and improvise within the boundaries of their field. Indeed, this is all part of the game. As a structuralist, however, Bourdieu maintains that these redefinitions, transgressions, inventions, and improvisations are neither limitless nor completely free-floating. They are conditioned by the rewards and sanctions typically meted out in social fields. Likewise, Giddens insists that structures are involved in the generation of our daily practices but that these practices, taken together, also generate and maintain social structures. His theory of "structuration" holds that social structures are both the "medium and result" of human practices.[40] Human agency continues to play an important, albeit constrained, role.

Structuralism has contributed important insights to political thought. Individuality and freedom arise only through human interaction, and human interaction only ever occurs within social structures that constrain, channel, and enable behavior. The greatest freedom arises when we become aware of the structures that both constrain us and make our actions viable and intelligible. Only by understanding the power of our social environment do we become well equipped to navigate and transform it.

From the 1940s until well into the 1970s, the social sciences were animated by debates between social structuralists and methodological individualists. For the most part, and particularly in America, methodological individualism gained the upper hand and contemporary liberal political theory remains closely aligned with it. Debates about the relative importance of social structure and human agency persist, however. The debate will probably never be resolved wholly in favor of one side or the other. The question as to how social and political life is best understood and explained—by way of the social structures that mold individual behavior or by way of the aggregated individual behavior that generates social structures —will continue to perturb theorists.

## POSTMODERN THOUGHT

Beginning in the late 1960s, structuralism itself underwent a challenge from an upstart movement that came to be known as *poststructuralism*. Poststructuralists reject the idea that social structures are invariant or evolve according to fixed cultural or historical patterns. Unlike methodological individualists and like structuralists, they maintain that power is not always or even primarily a tool willfully employed by the individual actor in pursuit of freely chosen interests. The social environment is assumed to play a larger role. Unlike structuralists, however, poststructuralists do not view power as emanating solely from stable kinship systems, mental faculties, or economic classes. They reject the notion that powerful institutions or traditions transform social life across time and space according to an identifiable, ahistorical and transcultural logic. Rather, they see power as widely dispersed and always in flux, and they explore how particular forms of power achieve specific effects.

Postmodernism is the direct heir to poststructuralism. Effectively, postmodernism is the more encompassing cultural expression of the theoretical sensibilities and scholarship of poststructuralists. Postmodernists are far from a unified bunch. They have been usefully described as a "constellation" of thinkers, that is to say, a cluster that resists reduction to a common core.[41] The thinkers and writers commonly considered to be postmodernists—such as Jean Baudrillard, William Connolly, Gilles Deleuze, Jacques Derrida, Michel Foucault, Frederic Jameson, Jean-François Lyotard and Richard Rorty— have all criticized certain tendencies of postmodernism and have denied that the term neatly applies to their own efforts.[42] They approach the practical and theoretical world from varied perspectives and seldom see eye to eye among themselves. Nonetheless, like structuralists and unlike methodological individualists, postmodern theorists are primarily concerned with the social construction and contestation of identities. In turn, like structuralists and unlike methodological individualists, postmodern theorists do not so much celebrate the power of human agency as worry about its vulnerability.

Modernist individualists generally assume, to employ the language of social science, that identities are independent variables. Identities are the stable cause rather than the changing effect of political actions and relationships. Postmodernists maintain, in contrast, that identities are complex in their constitutions and remain susceptible to transformation. Identities are not independent, static variables: they are the dynamic and protean effects of social forces. Identities are continually being constructed and contested within social environments owing to the exercise of power.

Postmodernists are critical of modern theorists who assume the polity to be an aggregate of stable, preformed, unchanging selves. And they worry about the suppression of difference that occurs whenever theorists assume that identities are stable and homogeneous. They insist that identities are fluid, multifaceted, overlapping, and cross-cutting. Every individual's identity might be multiply hyphenated, even though one or another of its many facets typically becomes prominent. In turn, identities are always relational. They develop in relationship to difference, in the sense that we gain an identity by differentiating ourselves from something or someone which is "other." If our identities are extremely unified and closed, it is likely that this rigid rendering of ourselves is achieved by maintaining an equally one-dimensional understanding of others. In turn, we are all constantly involved in negotiating which parts of our identities will be privileged and accentuated, which parts will be suppressed or ignored, how our identities will be transformed, and what sort of relationship our identities will form with difference.

Postmodern theorists, like communitarians, insist that liberal modernists mistakenly assume individuals to be autonomous agents. However, postmodern theorists criticize the normative commitment of communitarians. The communitarian celebration of a well-ordered social whole within which everyone plays their prescribed part, postmodernists worry, valorizes a rigid and homogenizing collective identity that suppresses difference and undermines diversity.[43]

Postmodernists study discourses (systematized collections of mores) that permeate society and generate social identities. Unlike structuralists, however, postmodernists reject the development of a comprehensive theory that describes enduring patterns. The French philosopher Jean-François Lyotard (1924–98) observed that postmodernity is chiefly characterized by an "incredulity toward metanarratives."[44] A metanarrative is a story that subsumes all other perspectives to produce a singular, all-encompassing account of the world—an account that implicitly or explicitly legitimates certain social norms, political structures and positions of power. Postmodernists are skeptical of all grand theories that seek to explain everything. Rather, they investigate how identities, cultural practices and institutions develop as the products of diverse mechanisms of power.

Like many modern individualists, structuralists had hoped to develop a social science that would yield objective truth along the lines of the natural sciences. Postmodernists suggest that we can never achieve an objective, scientific overview of the social forces that shape us. Consequently, many postmodernists spurn social science in favor of the deconstruction of texts. The roots of deconstruction may be traced back to the Swiss structuralist linguist Ferdinand de Saussure (1857–1913). Saussure's theory of language held that meaning is not determined by the stable relation of words (signifiers) to concrete things or even to conceptual representations of these things (the signified). Rather, meaning is determined by the intricate relation of words to other words. It is a structured play of signs. Deconstruction focuses on this unstable relativity of language. For the French deconstructionist philosopher Jacques Derrida, a text does not have an intrinsic meaning grounded in its accurate representation of reality. Rather, the meaning of a text is found in its differential relation to other texts.

Deconstruction utilizes the rhetorical features of a text to undermine or cast suspicion on its manifest content or argument, particularly if the text asserts or legitimates stable categories of experience or structures of social existence. Deconstructionists demonstrate that any effort to neatly conceptualize these categories or structures harbors self-contradictory tendencies. In turn, deconstructionists emphasize that certain rhetorical forms, such as binary oppositions—between subject and object, appearance and reality, mind and body, male and female, self and other, speech and writing—insidiously establish hierarchies of values.[45] Deconstructionists disrupt the strategies of exclusion and inclusion that are generated by such binary oppositions.

Like much of modern philosophy, deconstruction exhibits what philosopher Richard Rorty refers to as "the linguistic turn." It focuses on language. Deconstructionists assert that the world is a text, or rather a constellation of interwoven texts in the ongoing process of being written and rewritten. Deconstruction is concerned not only or even primarily with the capacity of language to represent reality. It focuses on the capacity of language to construct reality—from particular perspectives.

This leads postmodernists to endorse perspectivism. Perspectivism was originally proposed by Friedrich Nietzsche, the German philosopher commonly credited with blazing the trail for postmodernism. Nietzsche maintained that "objectivity" as traditionally conceived was a "nonsensical absurdity." He denied that there was "knowledge in itself" that did not bear the marks of the situated individuals who created it. Nietzsche insists that "there is *only* a perspective seeing, *only* a perspective 'knowing.'"[46] Likewise, postmodernists deny that there are universal, timeless structures or patterns that operate according to a stable logic or scientific laws. They insist that institutions and identities are the products of protean forms of social power. Their own investigations, postmodernists acknowledge, necessarily reflect the impact of particular relations of power theorized from particular vantage points. This perspectivism contributes to an ironic demeanor.

For the postmodernist, a "God's eye view" of the world is simply not attainable. One can only ever see things from a specific viewpoint; and one's perspective always already reflects the effects of power. Perspectivism generates a kind of skeptical reserve, and skeptical reserve begets irony. Rather than search for a "final vocabulary" with which to construct an objective description of reality, the postmodern ironist accepts, as Richard Rorty maintains, that many different "language games" are being played simultaneously in the competitive attempt to shape reality. There is no neutral or final vocabulary that might allow the ironist to decide once and for all how best to view, understand or describe the world.[47] So the ironist playfully challenges all authoritative statements.

The postmodern ironist lacks all certainty, including the certainty that there is no truth. Michel Foucault speaks of leaving "as little space as possible" in his own research for assumptions about underlying truths that might ground knowledge once and for all. At the same time, he cannot exclude the possibility that "one day" such a truth will be discovered.[48] Foucault acknowledges that "there is no way that you can say that there is no truth."[49] That conviction should leave the postmodern ironist, like the first ironist, Socrates, engaged in the avid pursuit of knowledge.

Postmodernists challenge the notion of a single, uniform human nature. What makes humans what they are, postmodernists insist, is not some metaphysical or even biological human essence, but a specific form of historical development, one that has been and remains grounded in social processes. As Richard Rorty states, the postmodern assumption is that "socialization, and thus historical circumstance, goes all the way down—that there is nothing 'beneath' socialization or prior to history which is definatory of the human."[50] The loci of socialization are legion: family and friends; places of study, work and worship; clubs and teams; professional, philanthropic, political, religious and ethnic affiliations; business associations and interest groups; radio, film, television, print, the internet and social media; municipal, state, national and international movements, organizations and institutions. Our embeddedness in this complex and diverse social environment largely defines who we are by both constricting and enabling our experiences, influencing what we feel, believe, know and do.

In rejecting the notion that there is a stable essence that defines humanity, postmodernists are not saying (though sometimes their rhetoric belies them) that people can simply choose who or what they want to be. Identities are not just roles people whimsically play, roles that can be given up or exchanged at will from one day to the next. Identities are complex patterns of norms and desires, and modes of thinking and behaving, formed over time owing to the integration of individuals within dense social networks. Individual and collective identities are intricately constructed and not easily transformed.

Many political theorists and scientists who do not consider themselves postmodernists are also concerned with how attitudes, beliefs, values and identities are formed by social environments. Arguing against the individualist view that people are independent agents that always act in accordance with their preexisting beliefs and values, Murray Edelman writes:

> The common assumption that what democratic government does is somehow always a response to the moral codes, desires and knowledge embedded inside people is as inverted as it is reassuring. This model, avidly taught and ritualistically repeated, cannot explain what happens; but it may persist in our folklore because it so effectively sanctifies prevailing policies and permits us to avoid worrying about them.[51]

Edelman investigates how economic and political elites shape political agendas and public opinion, effectively embedding moral codes, desires and knowledge in citizens rather than responding to them. In like fashion, many political scientists address the "continued, insistent, and ubiquitous process" of communication and intimidation through which elites "win minds" and establish in the public a predilection for "order, obedience, the status quo, deference, political docility, and inequalities of income and wealth."[52] Modernist students of political behavior study how elites manipulate political agendas and exploit the media to form and shape the opinions, attitudes, and values of the public, making it more receptive to their control.

These investigations of elite power follow the lead of the Italian neo-Marxist Antonio Gramsci, who was concerned with the "hegemony" enjoyed by the political class controlling the state apparatus.[53] Gramsci formulated his theory to account for specific historical developments, namely, the longevity and increasing strength of capitalism in the twentieth century. Its unabated growth contradicted orthodox Marxist theory (particularly as elaborated by the Second International), which predicted a proletarian revolution and the quick demise of capitalism. Gramsci attempted to explain the anomaly. He focused on how the dominant class used political and cultural tools to manipulate the other strata of society into accepting, and even endorsing, unjust and exploitative social relations. While orthodox Marxism often spoke with the voice of economic determinism, Gramsci pointed to the power of elites and elite institutions to postpone social revolution indefinitely.

Postmodernists have many of the same concerns as Gramsci and contemporary theorists of political behavior. They would concur with a specialist on the media who wrote: "The best way to control and manipulate an individual is not to tell them what to do; that always generates resistance, hostility and defiance. Instead, tell a person *who* and *what* they are. They will end up eating out of your hand."[54] Postmodernists investigate how people become who and what they are. While acknowledging the power of elites to manipulate the public, however, they tend to focus on more ambiguous forces—modes of discourse and other systems of mores—that shape identities.

Postmodernists believe that the process of socialization goes deeper than most modernist theorists of political culture and behavior would be willing to admit.[55] While modernist theorists of political behavior and culture observe that people tend to ignore information until it is conveniently and perhaps misleadingly packaged for them by elites,[56] postmodernists suggest that there are no independent "facts" or "data" about the world at all. Knowledge always develops with a social context, as a product of diverse mechanisms of power. Postmodernists, in this regard, adopt a "constructivist" perspective. Reality itself, they suggest, is a social construct.

## IDENTITY AND THE EXERCISE OF POWER

Postmodernists' preoccupation with diffuse forms of social power, critics suggest, leave them blind to the concrete forms of power exercised—ruthlessly at times—by elites. In turn, critics charge that the perspectivism of postmodern theorists undermines moral and political engagement. Postmodernists display great skill and insight exposing the contingencies of our current social and political practices. But perspectivism delegitimizes any suggested improvements, since the criteria for better and worse forms of collective life depend solely on one's point of view. Irony, in turn, may keep postmodernists from taking seriously the need for social change, not withstanding their belief that reality is a social construct. Moreover, the postmodernist claim that there are no objective facts or data suggests that all news is, at some level, "fake news." In this respect, postmodernism opens the gates to demagoguery. Its dismissal of Enlightenment values such as truth, reason and democracy grounded on widely shared public values is not simply an intellectual exercise in skeptical reserve. It prepares the ground for reactionary ideologies naively or duplicitously extolling the better days of yesteryear when identities were satisfying and stable, and everyone knew their place.[57]

Environmentally oriented theorists also worry that the notion of socially constructed reality may undermine needed efforts to protect the natural world. "If nature is only a social and discursive construction," one critic of postmodernism rhetorically queries, "why fight hard to preserve it?"[58] Voicing similar concerns, another critic suggests that postmodernism has become "an excuse not to believe in anything, to avoid both personal and political involvement and take refuge in apathy, despair, or mere ambition."[59]

Postmodern deconstructions of social reality may be the privileged pastime of relatively affluent intellectuals exercising their academic freedom. Whether they much improve the world is unclear. And while postmodern theorists are severely critical and at times disdainfully dismissive of modernity, most take full advantage of the economic opportunities, scientific advancements, political freedoms, and basic rights that are modernity's crowning achievements. Is postmodernism, then, parasitic upon modernist values and victories that it rejects?

Postmodernists have not been able to provide wholly reassuring responses to these charges. At the same time, their work offers keen insights. Michel Foucault has frequently been subject to the sorts of criticisms mentioned above. A brief look at his efforts to theorize power allows us to investigate these charges, examine his insights, and further illustrate the difference between postmodern theory and modern political science.

In describing the nature of contemporary power, Foucault offers the image of a spider's web without a spider. Because everyone is embedded in the social whole, everyone is caught in the web of power. Foucault writes that power is not so much "possessed" by elites as it is exercised in "capillary" form throughout society.[60] Power is always in play, creating interests and identities wherever it circulates.

It is difficult to imagine a spider's web in the absence of an actual spider that constructed it and sits in control over it. We generally think of power as being exercised by a specific agent. Foucault suggests that the difficulty arises because our understanding of power remains under the "spell of monarchy." In our political thinking and theorizing, Foucault graphically states, "we still have not cut off the head of the king."[61] Ancient and modern notions that power is either held by a sovereign ruler (monarchical power) or embodied in the rule of law (juridical power) are persistent. These monarchical and juridical views of power are outdated. Power now extends well beyond the influence of law and government. The strands of power entangle us from all sides. We are all caught in its web. Power is woven into the very fabric of social life. Indeed, it binds the social fabric together.

Foucault's understanding of this network of social control bears a striking resemblance to the sort of power that Alexis de Tocqueville (1805–59), a French political theorist, observed in America in the early nineteenth century. Tocqueville was concerned with the "tyranny of the majority" that arose in the United States owing to its citizens' conformity to custom and public opinion. The pressure to conform, in Tocqueville's judgment, was more powerful than the rule of kings or the rule of law in shaping the lives of the citizenry. In his famous analysis of American democracy, Tocqueville wrote:

> The authority of a king is physical and controls the actions of men without subduing their will. But the majority possesses a power that is physical and moral at the same time, which acts upon the will as much as upon the actions and represses not only all contest, but all controversy.... Under the absolute sway of one man the body was attacked in order to subdue the soul; but the soul escaped the blows which were directed against it and rose proudly superior. Such is not the course adopted by tyranny in democratic republics; there the body is left free, and the soul is enslaved.

Tocqueville goes on to contradict popular belief about the form of liberty enjoyed in the absence of monarchical power by stating: "I know of no country in which there is so little independence of mind and real freedom of discussion as in America."[62] Likewise, Foucault suggests that power today impinges on us not only through the rule of elites or legal sanctions but by way of our enmeshment in a ubiquitous network of relations. Like Tocqueville, Foucault maintains that power often exercises its greatest influence when it remains largely hidden from view. In these invisible mechanisms, power enchains not the body but the soul.

When postmodernists insist that power permeates the social environment, they are not suggesting that there are no elites exercising influence. Foucault agrees that from an individualist perspective, power remains the product of a "calculation" made by individuals or groups of individuals. It is always exercised as an "intentional" act with definite "aims and objectives" in mind.[63] Nevertheless, Foucault argues that relations of power between individuals and groups of individuals eventually amalgamate into larger, more complex relationships that remain "anonymous and almost unspoken." By the time these complex networks further coalesce into the major "apparatuses" of power that structure society at large (or the "discourses" on which apparatuses ground themselves), they are no longer directed by individuals. While invested with power, and while serving the interests of certain individuals more than others, these networks—such as scientific, medical, penal, military, academic or political institutions, class or caste structures, and their respective discursive disciplines—defy individual control. They take on a life of their own.

Seldom if ever is political power equally exercised by all; and seldom if ever is political power exercised in the equal interests of all. So even if we accept the postmodern argument that the web of power is relatively anonymous, we still need to investigate how relations of power serve specific interests. Whenever power is in play, one should always ask the eminently political question, first articulated by the ancient Romans, "Cui bono?"—"Who benefits?" This is true not only regarding the development of policy, laws and institutions. It is also true of beliefs and values. Specific beliefs and values benefit some individuals more than others even if the key beneficiaries are not solely responsible for their formation and propagation.

Consider respect for the law, which is cultivated throughout society—by parents, schoolteachers, employers, policemen, judges, jailers, and politicians. Such reverence for legal rules often benefits the rich a good deal more than the poor. Respect for the law forbidding sleeping upon bridges, begging in the streets, and stealing bread, to recall Anatole France's concerns, saves the rich the annoyance of petty theft and the discomforting sight of tattered beggars. The poor, for their part, have few obvious gains. The beliefs and values that buttress such laws do not equally serve the interests of all. Yet they are held in place by a vast and relatively anonymous web of social relations.

As with respect for the law, many other opinions and beliefs, norms and desires, modes of thinking and behaving, interests and identities are created and shaped by a wide variety of diffuse social forces. Perhaps in very small, isolated communities, one might still observe the overt construction of identity by a small number of elites. Within isolated religious sects or cults, for instance, leaders might successfully control the hearts and minds of followers. Yet in complex societies, the formation of identity is anything but a straightforward affair. Today, our sense of self is molded by the subtle interplay of innumerable social, political, cultural, economic and technological relations and forces.

Foucault's postmodern analysis is illuminated by contrasting it to Hobbes' modern project. Hobbes hoped to escape the anarchical war of all against all that erupts among fearful, isolated individuals in a state of nature. A despotic Leviathan is chosen to establish and enforce the rules and norms by which all must abide. Foucault attempts to demonstrate that our identities are already largely formed, our thought and behavior largely circumscribed, by a diffuse social Leviathan. The rules and norms structuring social life—including its political apparatuses, its technological developments, its cultural traditions, its intellectual discourses, and its economic relations—contribute to making us who we are, determining the interests we have and how we pursue them.

Hobbes assumed that individuals were independent, autonomous agents on whom power needed to be exercised by a despot to avoid anarchy. For Foucault, the chief problem is neither anarchy, nor even a sovereign power. In the contemporary world, he argues, we need to encourage and equip all individuals to struggle for their autonomy in the context of a potentially despotic yet diffuse social network of power. Hobbes endorsed the designation of a governmental Leviathan to safeguard society. Foucault urges us to contest the social Leviathan to safeguard the individual. Yet unlike Hobbes, and going well beyond Tocqueville, Foucault rejects the notion that power is limited to something wielded *against* individuals. In contemporary society, he insists, power creates and shapes individuals. He writes:

> The individual is not to be conceived as a sort of elementary nucleus, a primitive atom, a multiple and inert material on which power comes to fasten or against which it happens to strike, and in so doing subdues or crushes individuals. . . . The individual, that is, is not the *vis-à-vis* of power; it is, I believe, one of its prime effects. The individual is an effect of power, and at the same time, or precisely to the extent to which it is that effect, it is the element of its articulation. The individual which power has constituted is at the same time its vehicle.[64]

For postmodernists, power is not only or even primarily a repressive force that constrains us. It is a creative force that makes us who we are. Power produces us as much as we produce power.

Following Foucault, postmodernists argue that social power does not limit itself to constraint and prohibition. Social power stimulates desire. Power is not solely a repressive force, symbolized by a king or the law, restricting the movements of its subjects. Increasingly, power manifests itself as a creative force, evidenced in the social, political and technological networks that shape identities. The postmodern concern is that we have become the vehicles and chief effects of power, not simply the objects of its repression.

## SOCIAL CONTROL AND INDIVIDUAL FREEDOM

Postmodernists are concerned with the mores that structure thought and behavior. While mores are needed to order and regulate social life, they also restrict the freedom and autonomy we desire and cherish as individuals. Foucault, like many other postmodern theorists, encourages us to struggle against the ubiquitous forces of "normalization" that impinge on our lives. We are encouraged to resist the webs of power that envelope us.

But why should we resist? The German philosopher Jürgen Habermas sums up his objection to postmodern theory by asking why we should keep struggling against power if one can never extract oneself from its web. If power is truly inescapable, why fight?[65]

Foucault understands resistance to normalization as the essence of freedom itself. Power is not force. It is a form of influence that induces and constrains. Those who are enmeshed in relations of power, while often passive and compliant, retain options. Power is grounded on the freedom of the individual to respond in any number of ways, even though its exercise makes certain responses more or less likely—more or less profitable, pleasurable, or prudent—than others. For Foucault, it remains indispensable to every power relationship "that 'the other' (the one over whom power is exercised) be thoroughly recognized and maintained to the very end as a person who acts; and that, faced with a relationship of power, a whole field of responses, reactions, results, and possible inventions may open up."[66] Attitudes, values, behavior, and the formation of identity are never exhaustively determined by the exercise of power. In the absence of outright violence, the opportunity for resistance persists.

While postmodern theorists advocate resistance to normalization, they also remind us that unmitigated autonomy is an illusion. To exercise individual autonomy one must first become an individual. Yet one only ever becomes an individual through immersion in a (normalizing) culture. One's identity as a free, independent, and autonomous agent, in other words, is already the product of power exercised within a social environment. To be human means, first and foremost, to develop within a web of social relations permeated by power. From the day of our birth we never wholly escape relations of power; we simply shift our position within them.

Certain postmodernists, such as Jean Baudrillard, meld postmodernism with a form of structuralist determinism, maintaining that individuality and agency have been destroyed in the contemporary world. Today, Baudrillard suggests, we are wholly enslaved to commodities and images. There is no meaningful freedom left.[67] Other postmodernists, like Foucault, argue that power and the freedom to resist go hand in hand. Freedom is a precondition of power. That is why power degenerates into sheer force in the absence of freedom. The political problem, therefore, is not the impossible task of wholly doing away with relations of power so that we might finally be free. Neither is it the Hobbesian project of wholly sacrificing freedom to a sovereign so that we might escape anarchy. The political challenge is determining which specific forms of power to resist, and how to exercise power cooperatively and constructively.

Our problem today, Foucault stated, "is not that everything is bad, but that everything is dangerous, which is not exactly the same as bad. If everything is dangerous, then we always have something to do.... I think that the ethico-political choice we have to make every day is to determine which is the main danger."[68] Power is always dangerous. But that does not mean we should forego its exercise or attempt to escape its reach, which is impossible in any case. We could not live without power. At the same time, we should be wary of the ways we live with power. Power allows us to create mores, to act in concert, and to develop as individuals. Yet these mores may be overly constraining or obnoxious, cooperative action may be unjust or inequitable, and the identities we develop as individuals may be limiting or vicious. That is why vigilance is required. To acknowledge that we are products of power is not to become mindless pawns of the system. Though we may serve as vehicles for power, we cannot abdicate the responsibility of being, at times and to a degree, in the driver's seat.

Comparing postmodern thought to the modernist science of behaviorism is illuminating in this regard. Like postmodernists, behaviorists investigate the power of the social environment to shape individual values and behavior. The roots of modern behaviorism go back to John Locke's empiricist theory that human beings are born as "blank slates" whose worldly experiences imprint them with knowledge and dispositions. Modern behaviorists aim to create a science of human behavior that can predict the way individuals will react given certain environmental stimuli.

Any such attempt to understand human behavior scientifically, postmodernists worry, may lead to efforts to control human behavior technologically. To achieve such control, much that is spontaneous, unpredictable, and variable in human beings might become suppressed. To the extent that postmodern theorists adopt a moral perspective, then, it is frequently oriented to a "responsibility to otherness."[69] Behaviorism, they suspect, might intensify efforts to repress diversity and difference in pursuit of a normalized homogeneity.

The modern science of behaviorism found one of its foremost advocates in B.F. Skinner, an experimental psychologist. Skinner illustrated the hoped-for benefits of applying behavioral science to the organization of society in his utopian novel *Walden Two*.[70] The novel portrays an isolated community that secures an idyllic life through the extensive application of behavioral techniques. Its inhabitants achieve their utopia by manipulating and reconstructing both the natural and social worlds. They engage in the "conquest of nature" as well as the "conquest of man."

The "tyranny" of bad weather, for example, is overcome at Walden Two through mechanical engineering that makes most everything accessible indoors. In turn, the tyranny of antisocial drives and habits and dysfunctional social conventions is overcome through behavioral conditioning that reinforces useful behavior and discourages noxious conduct. In this way, benign drives, habits and beliefs are scientifically inculcated through a technique of psychological reinforcement called "operant conditioning." Walden Two, as its chief engineer quips, is really a "Walden for Two." It is an idyllic existence that, unlike Henry David Thoreau's original retreat by Walden Pond, does not merely escape the vexing problems of modern life but solves them.

We learn from Skinner's protagonist that "religious faith becomes irrelevant when the fears which nourish it are allayed and the hopes fulfilled—here on earth." To this end, priests have been replaced by psychologists to guide the flourishing community. In turn, Walden Two is considered a "world without heroes," and for much the same reasons that it is a world without gods. We find that "a society which functions for the good of all cannot tolerate the emergence of individual figures" that might disrupt its equilibrium. More important, the inhabitants of this utopia have forsaken belief in the freedom that heroic individuals incarnate. At Walden Two everyone knows that there is no such thing as free, uncontrolled, or undetermined, and therefore heroic human behavior. Everything one does is a direct product of behavior modification, of networks of power.

The denizens of Walden Two do not pine for freedom because they maintain that those who live outside their technological utopia are no freer than they are. It is simply a question of *who* is doing the controlling or conditioning. At Walden Two, conditioning is carried out by well-informed scientists, psychologists and social engineers. In the outside world, it is carried out by priests, parents, hucksters and demagogues. Walden Two is considered the "freest place on earth." It deserves this distinction not because its behavioral technicians have made human beings free. They simply offer a more functional and benign form of control. As behavior is successfully modified through techniques of positive reinforcement, physical coercion is no longer needed to achieve harmony. Power does all the necessary work by creating and maintaining socially useful mores. Force and violence are completely absent. At Walden Two, people do things that benefit society not because they are punished if they refuse but because they have been trained to *want* to secure social welfare. In this way one may simultaneously "*increase* the feeling of freedom" while providing all the benefits of a well-ordered, social life.

The central challenge of the behavioral revolution, and its tentative resolution, is most straightforwardly described by Skinner in his subsequent work, *Beyond Freedom and Dignity*. The book begins with a litany of environmental woes: the population explosion, the nuclear threat, world famine, pollution. These are the global problems that confront contemporary humanity. After explaining the theory and benefits of operant conditioning, Skinner concludes with a plea that we abandon the unnecessary and ultimately fatal prejudices about freedom and autonomy that prevent the timely resolution of our worsening crises. Skinner proposes that we abolish

autonomous man . . . the man defended by the literatures of freedom and dignity. His abolition has been long overdue.... He has been constructed from our ignorance, and as our understanding increases, the very stuff of which he is composed vanishes. Science does not dehumanize man, it de-homunculizes him, and it must do so if it is to prevent the abolition of the human species. . . . Man himself may be controlled by his environment, but it is an environment which is almost wholly of his own making. The physical environment of most people is largely man-made . . . the social environment is obviously man-made. . . . An experimental analysis shifts the determination of behavior from autonomous man to the environment—an environment responsible both for the evolution of the species and for the repertoire acquired by each member. . . . We have not yet seen what man can make of man.[71]

Behaviorism does not assume human life to be wholly predictable any more than meteorology assumes weather to be wholly predictable. There are simply too many variables that defy measurement and management. Still, much can be known, and, at least in the case of human behavior, much can be controlled. The object of the behavioral revolution, here placed in its extreme form in the work of B.F. Skinner, is the betterment of society and the conquest of nature through technological manipulation. The age-old conflict between the (autonomous) individual and its environment becomes a working relation between the scientist and the natural and social environments that are the crucibles of humankind.

The contrast between postmodern theorists and behaviorists is illuminating because of their many, seldom-noted similarities. Postmodernists, like behaviorists, assume that the individual is wholly malleable, a function of its social environment. For both postmodernists and behaviorists, the webs of social power are inescapable. We are all necessarily caught in the game of mutual manipulation and control. Power is the medium in which humans exist, a medium that both shapes and sustains us. We may resist power to be sure, but not because there are realms of absolute freedom we might discover or create. Resistance is the substitution, or offsetting, of one form of power by another. Freedom is simply the word we employ to denote the experience of exchanging forms of control.

The end of human freedom and dignity at the hands of a scientific elite is applauded by Skinner. Foucault, in contrast, opposes the centralization of power required for such a project, likening his writings to tool kits from which his readers may select conceptual artifacts for short-circuiting the system. Foucault advocates a "hyper- and pessimistic activism" on the part of all who are enmeshed in power networks.[72] Skinner advocates a hyper- but *optimistic* activism on the part of social engineers involved in constructing ever stronger and stickier webs of power. Foucault, like Skinner, argues that we create and perpetuate the social environment that inevitably creates, constrains, and enables us. But the goal for Foucault is to proliferate and diversify struggle. The object for Skinner is to strengthen technologies of power to control human behavior ever more efficiently and benevolently. The ever-increasing power of technological systems to shape our lives, and the task of political theory in the face of this growing power, will be further addressed in Chapter 6.

### THEORIZING AT THE EDGE OF MODERNITY

Postmodernists spurn the modern faith in progress. Foucault insists that "humanity does not gradually progress from combat to combat until it arrives at universal reciprocity, where the rule of law finally replaces warfare; humanity installs each of its violences in a system of rules and thus proceeds from domination to domination."[73] Modernists reject such statements, arguing that postmodernists ignore the fact that not all forms of domination are equally oppressive. Progress may occur, for instance, not because we have escaped all forms of social control but because we have developed less cruel or less harsh forms of social control. Most of us, for instance, would consider it a sign of progress that we no longer draw and quarter criminals or burn those accused of witchcraft at the stake. Yet we cannot deny that power is still exercised, often quite insidiously and for unjust purposes, through the media, the economy, and the rule of law.

Our theorizing can benefit by partaking of both the modern and postmodern perspectives. Indeed, the two orientations complement each other much more than is generally recognized. Just as modernism grew out of and remained nourished by scholasticism, so postmodernism grew out of and remains nourished by modernism. While the difference between modernism and postmodernism is real enough, overlapping concerns persist. Many of the early polemics exchanged between modernists—those who carry on and critically reconstruct the unfinished Enlightenment project of transforming the world in the name of rational progress—and postmodernists—those who suggest that the Enlightenment project is historically exhausted, epistemologically bankrupt, and ethically censorable—are now giving way to more synthetic efforts of accommodation and dialogue.

Michael Walzer, a political philosopher, writes in a modernist vein that "the central issue for political theory is not the constitution of the self but the connection of constituted selves, the pattern of social relations."[74] It is certainly important to inquire into the pattern of social relations. Ultimately, however, political theory is about both the constitution and connection of selves. It is about the formation of identity and the regulation of interaction. That is because identities are formed through interaction, and the nature of these interactions, in turn, largely depends upon the identities of the actors.

Postmodernists acknowledge that identity is formed through interaction. So they should share the modernist concern for the regulation of interaction by way of institutions grounded in rational processes, attentive to standards of justice, and mindful of the prerogatives of freedom. In turn, modernists build their theories of social interaction on shaky ground unless they inquire how the identities of the actors in question are constructed, sustained and transformed. And this inquiry into identity ought not ignore the political importance of character and the cultivation of virtue, as ancient political theorists insisted.

Aristotle said that democracy entailed ruling and being ruled in turn. The democratic exercise of power, in other words, implies not only acting and effecting change, but also being acted upon and undergoing change. Democratic life engages citizens in co-crafting the political institutions and culture that will structure and transform their own behavior. Democracy—notwithstanding its acute concern for individual agency and liberty, indeed owing to it—is an experimental exercise in soulcraft and statecraft.

## REFERENCES

1 Plato, *Gorgias* (464b), in *The Collected Dialogues of Plato*, eds Edith Hamilton and Huntington Cairns (Princeton: Princeton University Press, 1989), 246.

2 Plato, *Timaeus* (87b), in *Collected Dialogues*, 1207.

3 Plato, *Republic* (592b), trans. Allan Bloom (New York: Basic Books, 1968), 275. In *Collected Dialogues*, 819.

4 Plato, *Symposium* (204a), in *Collected Dialogues*, 556.

5 See Martha C. Nussbaum, *The Therapy of Desire: Theory and Practice in Hellenistic Ethics* (Princeton: Princeton University Press, 1994).

6 Plato, *Phaedo* (84a), in *Collected Dialogues*, 67.

7 Plato, "Letter VII" (343e), in *Collected Dialogues*, 1591.

8 Plato, *Phaedrus* (271b), in *Collected Dialogues*, 516.

9 Plato, *Republic* (368a), in *Collected Dialogues*, 614.

10 Plato, *Phaedrus* (249e–250a), in *Collected Dialogues*, 496.

11 Plato, *Phaedrus* (249e–250a), in *Collected Dialogues*, 522–23.

12 Plato, *Republic* (532c), in *Collected Dialogues*, 764.

13 Plato, *The Laws* (942), in *Collected Dialogues*, 1488–89.

14 Plato, *Republic*, in *Collected Dialogues*, 701.

15 Plato, *Phaedo* (89d-e), in *Collected Dialogues*, 71–72.

16 Plato, *The Laws*, in *Collected Dialogues*, 1235.

17 Baron de Montesquieu, *The Spirit of the Laws*, trans. Thomas Nugent (New York: Hafner Press, 1949), 326.

18 Quoted in Bertrand de Jouvenal, *On Power: The Natural History of Its Growth* (Indianapolis: Liberty Fund, 1993), 326.

19 Philip Pettit, *Republicanism: A Theory of Freedom and Government* (Oxford: Clarendon Press, 1997), 210-11

20 Immanuel Kant, *Political Writings*, 2nd edn, ed. Hans Reiss (Cambridge: Cambridge University Press, 1991), 112–13.

21 Reinhold Niebuhr, *The Children of Light and the Children of Darkness: A Vindication of Democracy and a Critique of its Traditional Defense* (New York: Charles Scribner's Sons, 1944), xiii.

22 Quoted in Peter Coveney and Roger Highfield, *The Arrow of Time* (New York: Fawcett Columbine, 1990), 49.

23 Voltaire, *Lettres Philosophiques*, XII, *Oeuvres Complètes* (Paris: Garnier, 1879), 22: 118.

24 René Descartes, *A Discourse on Method*, trans. E. Haldane and G. Ross (New York: Washington Square Press, 1965), 89, 117.

25 *Outlines of a Historical View of the Progress of the Human Mind.* Accessed May 2018 at http://oll.liberty fund.org/titles/condorcet-outlines-of-an-historical-view-of-the-progress-of-the-human-mind

26 Roxanne L. Euben, *Enemy in the Mirror: Islamic Fundamentalism and the Limits of Modern Rationalism* (Princeton: Princeton University Press, 1999), 167, 123-53.

27 Steven Pinker, *Enlightenment Now: The Case for Reason, Science, Humanism, and Progress* (New York: Viking, 2018), 453.

28   Harold Lasswell, *Politics: Who Gets What, When, and How* (New York: Meridian Books, 1958).

29   Michael J. Sandel, *Liberalism and the Limits of Justice* (Cambridge: Cambridge University Press, 1982), 183.

30   Amitai Etzioni, *The New Golden Rule: Community and Morality in a Democratic Society* (New York: Basic Books, 1996).

31   Alasdair MacIntyre, *A Short History of Ethics* (New York: Macmillan, 1966), 187.

32   Quoted in Anthony Giddens, *Capitalism and Modern Social Theory: An Analysis of the Writings of Marx, Durkheim, and Weber* (Cambridge: Cambridge University Press, 1971), 88.

33   Émile Durkheim, *The Division of Labor in Society*, trans. George Simpson (New York: Free Press, 1933), 350.

34   Pierre Bourdieu and Loic J.D. Wacquant, *An Invitation to Reflexive Sociology* (Chicago: University of Chicago Press, 1992), 113.

35   See, for example, Claude Lévi-Strauss, *The Savage Mind* (London: Weidenfeld and Nicolson, 1966) and *Structural Anthropology* (New York: Basic Books, 1963).

36   Immanuel Kant, *Critique of Pure Reason*, trans. Norman Kemp Smith (New York: St. Martin's Press, 1929), 59.

37   See, for example, Louis Althusser, *For Marx* (New York: Vintage Books, 1969).

38   See Claude Lévi-Strauss, "Reflections on Liberty," in *The View from Afar*, trans. Joachim Neugroschel and Phoebe Hoss (New York: Basic Books, 1985), 279–88.

39   Bourdieu and Wacquant, *An Invitation to Reflexive Sociology*, 133.

40   Anthony Giddens, *Central Problems in Social Theory* (Berkeley: University of California Press, 1979).

41   Richard J. Bernstein, *The New Constellation: The Ethical-Political Horizons of Modernity/Postmodernity* (Cambridge: MIT Press, 1991), 8.

42   See Steven Best and Douglas Kellner, *Postmodern Theory: Critical Investigations* (New York: Guilford Press, 1991).

43   See Iris Marion Young, *Justice and the Politics of Difference* (Princeton: Princeton University Press, 1990), 226–56.

44   Jean-François Lyotard, *The Postmodern Condition: A Report on Knowledge*, trans. G. Bennington and B. Massumi (Minneapolis: University of Minnesota Press, 1984), xxiv.

45   See, for instance, Jacques Derrida, *Writing and Difference*, trans. Alan Bass (Chicago: University of Chicago Press, 1978).

46   Friedrich Nietzsche, *On the Genealogy of Morals*, trans. Walter Kaufmann (New York: Vintage, 67), 119. And see Leslie Paul Thiele, *Friedrich Nietzsche and the Politics of the Soul: A Study of Heroic Individualism* (Princeton: Princeton University Press, 1990).

47   Richard Rorty, *Contingency, Irony, and Solidarity* (Cambridge: Cambridge University Press, 1989).

48   Michel Foucault, *Foucault Live: Interviews, 1966–84*, trans. John Johnston (New York: Semiotext(e), 1989), 79.

49   Quoted in William Connolly, "The Irony of Interpretation," in *The Politics of Irony*, eds Daniel W. Conway and John E. Seery (New York: St. Martin's Press, 1992), 144.

50   Rorty, *Contingency, Irony, and Solidarity*, xiii.

51   Murray Edelman, *The Symbolic Uses of Power* (Urbana: University of Illinois Press, 1964), 172–73.

52   Charles E. Lindblom, *Inquiry and Change: The Troubled Attempt to Understand and Shape Society* (New Haven: Yale University Press, 1990), 89.

53   Antonio Gramsci, *Selections from the Prison Notebooks of Antonio Gramsci*, eds and trans. Q. Hoare and G.N. Smith (New York: International Publishers, 1971).

54   Wilson Bryan Key, *Subliminal Seduction: Ad Media's Manipulation of a Not So Innocent America* (Englewood Cliffs, N.J.: Prentice Hall, 1973), 70.

55   See Gabriel Almond and Sidney Verba, *The Civic Culture* (Boston: Little, Brown, 1963).

56   Edelman, *The Symbolic Uses of Politics*, 172–73.

57   See Pinker, *Enlightenment Now*.

58   K. Katherine Hayles, "Searching for Common Ground," in *Reinventing Nature: Responses to Postmodern Deconstruction*, eds Michael E. Soulé and Gary Lease (Washington, D.C.: Island Press, 1995), 47.

59   Robert Solomon, "Nietzsche, Postmodernism, and Resentment: A Genealogical Hypothesis," in *Nietzsche as Postmodernist: Essays Pro and Contra*, ed. C. Koelb (Albany: SUNY, 1990), 292.

60   Michel Foucault, *Discipline and Punish: The Birth of the Prison*, trans. Alan Sheridan (New York: Vintage Books, 1977), 26.

61   Michel Foucault, *The History of Sexuality*, vol. 1, *An Introduction*, trans. Robert Hurley (New York: Vintage Books, 1978), 88–89.

62   Alexis de Tocqueville, *Democracy in America* (New York: Vintage Books, 1959), 1: 273–74.

63   Foucault, *The History of Sexuality*, 94–95.

64   Michel Foucault, *Power/Knowledge: Selected Interviews and Other Writings, 1972–1977*, ed. Colin Gordon (New York: Pantheon Books, 1977), 98.

65   Jürgen Habermas, "The Genealogical Writing of History: On Some *Aporias* in Foucault's Theory of Power," *Canadian Journal of Political and Social Theory* 10 (1986): 7. See also Nancy Fraser, "Foucault on Modern Power: Empirical Insights and Normative Confusions," *Praxis International* 1 (1981): 2762–87.

66   Michel Foucault, "The Subject and Power," in Hubert L. Dreyfus and Paul Rabinow (eds), *Michel Foucault: Beyond Structuralism and Hermeneutics*, 2nd edn (Chicago: University of Chicago Press, 1983), 220.

67   See Jean Baudrillard, *Jean Baudrillard: Selected Writings*, ed. Mark Poster (Cambridge: Polity Press, 1988).

68   Michel Foucault, "On the Genealogy of Ethics: An Overview of Work in Progress," in Dreyfus and Rabinow, *Michel Foucault*, 232.

69   See Stephen K. White, *Political Theory and Postmodernism* (Cambridge: Cambridge University Press, 1991).

70   B.F. Skinner, *Walden Two* (New York: Macmillan, 1948).

71   B.F. Skinner, *Beyond Freedom and Dignity* (New York: Vintage, 1971), 191, 205–6.

72   Michel Foucault, "On the Genealogy of Ethics: An Overview of Work in Progress," in Dreyfus and Rabinow, *Michel Foucault*, 232.

73   Michel Foucault, *Language, Counter-Memory, Practice*, ed. Donald Bouchard (Ithaca: Cornell University Press, 1977), 151.

74   Michael Walzer, "The Communitarian Critique of Liberalism," *Political Theory* 18 (February 1990): 21.

## CHAPTER 4

# THE POLITICS OF IDENTITY AND DIFFERENCE

Individual and collective identities are shaped and contested in the crucible of political life. This chapter investigates the development and political significance of racial and religious identities, gender identities and economic identities. To this end, it examines the conquest of America, the development of feminist thought, liberalism, communism and socialism. The chapter explores whether, how, and to what extent identities are social constructions and grapples with the political challenge of embracing both equality and difference.

## WE HOLD THESE TRUTHS...

Consider these famous words, penned in 1776 by Thomas Jefferson:

> We hold these truths to be self-evident, that all men are created equal, that they are endowed by their Creator with certain unalienable Rights, that among these are Life, Liberty and the pursuit of Happiness. That to secure these rights, Governments are instituted among Men, deriving their just powers from the consent of the governed. That whenever any Form of Government becomes destructive of these ends, it is the Right of the People to alter or to abolish it, and to institute new Government, laying its foundation on such principles, and organizing its powers in such form, as to them shall seem most likely to effect their Safety and Happiness.

Who is the "We" that Jefferson invokes? Clearly the pronoun is not limited to the 56 participants in the Continental Congress who signed the *Declaration of Independence*.

Commenting on this declaration, which inaugurated the American Revolution with as worthy a statement as has been written for a political founding, Jefferson wrote:

"Neither aiming at originality of principle or sentiment, nor yet copied from any particular and previous writing, it was intended to be an expression of the American mind, and to give to that expression the proper tone and spirit called for by the occasion."[1] Jefferson suggests that he has rendered into words the essence of an American way of thinking and acting, which subsequently came to be embodied in its system of government.

Jefferson employs an individualist framework for politics, which assumes that independent, autonomous individuals have stable values, beliefs, and interests which determine their actions. He subscribed to the "social contract" theory of the state which is the hallmark of modern political thought. Stemming from Hobbes, Locke and the French political theorist Jean-Jacques Rousseau (1712–78), social contract theories maintain that free, autonomous and independent individuals with distinct, preformed interests voluntarily join together to form a government that secures these interests.

Social contract theory was the coin of the realm for America's Founding Fathers. But every coin has two sides. Though the *Declaration of Independence* ostensibly celebrated the freedom, independence and equality of every individual, it obscured the patent lack of these cherished goods for well over half the population of America at the time.

In championing the status of the autonomous individual, the document valorized the experience of free white males while ignoring the status and experience of women, aboriginal people, and black slaves. In 1776, all thirteen colonies permitted slavery, and of the 56 signatories to the declaration, over half owned slaves, including Jefferson himself. To say that a truth is self-evident is to assert that it is patent to any rational individual. When the declaration's self-evident truths were given voice, however, women, native Americans and black slaves were not considered to be fully rational. Despite its rhetoric, Jefferson's proclamation does not reflect the status and experience of all or even most Americans. Rather, it reflects the status and experiences of free white male property owners, like Jefferson himself. Under the guise of universality, it invokes the parochial privileges of specific social and economic actors, while occluding the inequality and domination of others.

The *Constitution of the United States of America* likewise belies reality with rhetoric. It famously begins with the words "We the people of the United States." Again, who is this "We"? When the Constitution was adopted in 1789, it did not represent the interests of all the people of the United States. Constitutional guarantees applied only to "Free Persons." The *Constitution* expressly protected the institution of slavery and deemed a slave to constitute only "three-fifths" of a person for representational purposes. It denied both native people and African Americans the rights of citizenship. Women at the time were not begrudged all civil rights, but they could not vote or carry out many business transactions. In turn, property regulations restricted the political rights of white males.

By invoking a universally inclusive *We*, both the *Declaration* and the *Constitution* effectively perpetuated the exclusivity of power and privilege in America. In celebrating the autonomy and equality of the individual, the rights of the majority of people who did not share the status of free white (property owning) males were suppressed. As one social theorist observes, "In social contract theory, the individuals empowered by the opportunity to participate in the implicit contract were so many members of a set of equivalent citizens. . . . Thus individualism ironically repressed difference."[2] Words are powerful political forces of inclusion and exclusion, of identity and difference.

Yet words are also fickle. They may be put to many uses, including those unintended or unrealizable by their authors. Jefferson's language in particular has been employed by women, African Americans, native people, and other minorities to assert their political, civil and economic rights. Many of the differences suppressed or obscured by the Founding Fathers have been reclaimed and reaffirmed using their own words.

At the turn of the twentieth century, W.E.B. Du Bois wrote *The Souls of Black Folk*, decrying the prejudice of his times and looking toward the day when a black person might be fully recognized and embraced as "a co-worker in the kingdom of culture, to escape both death and isolation, to husband and use his best powers and his latent genius." To this end, Du Bois insists,

> By every civilized and peaceful method we must strive for the rights which the world accords to men, clinging unwaveringly to those great words which the sons of the Fathers would fain forget: "We hold these truths to be self-evident: That all men are created equal; that they are endowed by their Creator with certain unalienable rights; that among these are life, liberty, and the pursuit of happiness.[3]

A *We* that originally obscured and served to perpetuate privilege and domination was redeployed by Du Bois to promote democratic inclusivity.

This chapter addresses the struggles over identity and difference that animate political life, emphasizing the difficulty of recognizing, understanding, accepting and respecting that which is different from oneself, and that in oneself which is different. As employed here, the term *politics of identity and difference* is not to be equated with *identity politics*. The latter term generally refers to political movements (ethnically or racially defined organizations, for example) that base their power on the assumed uniformity of the interests and values of their participants. Identity politics suggests that social groups have essential characteristics shared by all their members. But minorities and other social groups are not collections of clones. They do not uniformly share the same traits. And the traits that they do share do not wholly isolate them from others. Horizons may always be fused, as Du Bois demonstrated.

Too often, identity politics serves to privilege certain groups while depreciating others. The tribe, and its uniformity, is celebrated. Consequently, identity politics often suppresses difference, stifles diversity of opinion, discourages critical thinking, and values dogmatic beliefs above the open exchange of ideas. In contrast, the *politics of identity and difference* addresses the way identities are generated and negotiated, and how difference can be acknowledged and respected. Culturally and socially no less than biologically, what we have in common with other human beings is much greater than what we have in contrast.

## RACE, RELIGION AND OTHERNESS

In the year 1492, the Spanish monarchs Ferdinand of Aragon and Isabella of Castille conquered Granada. In doing so, they put an end to the Moorish kingdom in Europe. That year, Ferdinand and Isabella also expelled all the Jews from Spain who would not convert to Christianity or who were suspected of retaining Jewish practices. A dozen years after the Spanish Inquisition began, Spain had been made homogeneously Christian. In this same year, when all non-Christians were forcefully driven from Spain, a separate effort was launched to lay the groundwork for the expulsion of Muslims from non-European cities and the conversion of Asians into Christians.

Funded by Ferdinand and Isabella after eight years of supplication, Christopher Columbus (1451–1506), a forty-one-year-old Genoan, set sail to the West from Palos, Spain. Columbus was an avid explorer and brilliant navigator. Embarking on the *Santa Maria* and accompanied by two other ships, Columbus sought a western route to India. His intent was twofold. He wanted to facilitate the conversion of the people of India to Christianity, and a more direct sea route would abet this project. Columbus also hoped to amass enough profit from the increased sea trade with India to fund yet another religious crusade to wrest Jerusalem from the Muslims. "Gold is most excellent," Columbus wrote in his journal, "he who possesses it, can do as he wishes in the world. It can even drive souls into Paradise."[4] The concern for wealth repeatedly appears in Columbus' journals. Religious goals justify its pursuit.[5]

A little over two months after setting sail, Columbus and his crew stumbled on what are now called the Bahamian Islands. After exploring the Caribbean for some time, Columbus sailed back to Spain. He was made admiral and governor general of all newly discovered Western lands. Columbus made return voyages in subsequent years that put him on the shores of South and Central America.

Upon his initial arrival, Columbus gave the name Indians to the inhabitants of the Caribbean. He did so because the people of India were those he set out to find. Indeed, he forced his entire crew to take oaths affirming that the island they had landed on one day—present-day Cuba—was the Indian subcontinent. In these and other matters, Columbus saw what he expected to see. What did not fit neatly within his own intellectual, cultural, and religious conceptual scheme was either forced to fit in a Procrustean fashion or was ignored and devalued.

In his book *The Conquest of America*, Tzvetan Todorov examines the relations that Columbus established with the inhabitants of the Americas, and those subsequently established by the Spanish conquistadors and missionaries. Todorov wrote his book to investigate the "discovery *self* makes of the *other*."[6] Despite being famous as an explorer, Columbus never explored the other. While venturing to the new world, Columbus never ventured beyond his Christian, European identity. He failed to understand or appreciate difference. As Todorov observes, though Columbus discovered America, he failed to discover the Americans.

Columbus saw the New World through European, Christian lenses that he could neither remove nor adjust. When he was confronted with the unfamiliar languages, customs, systems of exchange, religions, and moralities of aboriginal people, he frequently denied their existence. He falsely maintained, for example, that the natives had no religion of their own, and hence could easily be converted to Christianity.[7] The native peoples he encountered were taken to be unmolded pieces of inferior metals awaiting the masterful hands of European sculptors.

In 1519, years after Columbus had returned to Spain and had died in neglect, Hernán Cortés (1485–1547), a Spanish conquistador, left Cuba for Mexico with a few hundred soldiers. Within two years, Cortés managed to conquer and subdue the entire Aztec empire, which spread out across most of Mexico and numbered over 10 million people. At the time, the Aztecs were being decimated by smallpox and other diseases brought to the New World by the Spanish. Taking advantage of the Aztecs' misfortune, Cortés strategically planned their conquest. He forged military alliances with their enemies and with neighboring people who had been subjugated and forced to pay tribute to the Aztec empire. Upon learning that only Aztec generals had gold shields, he instructed his soldiers to kill first in battle all those warriors carrying gold shields. Once their easily identifiable leaders were eliminated, the Aztec army quickly fell into disarray. Cortés' amazing success was aided by the fact that Montezuma, the Aztec leader, mistook Cortés for Queztalcoatl, a mythical god that the Aztecs believed would one day return to rule their land. Cortés cunningly exploited this mistake. Allowed entrance into the Aztec capital under this misrepresentation, Cortés quickly took Montezuma hostage. After gaining control of the palace, the conquistadors pillaged the capital and ruthlessly suppressed resistance.

Columbus failed to understand the native Americans because he could not conceive of anything being markedly different yet somehow equal. Differences in language, culture, and race forever kept Columbus from recognizing a common humanity. He was blinded by the prejudice of superiority. In many respects, Montezuma resembles Columbus. In mistaking Cortés for a god, he, like Columbus, failed to understand difference. Where Columbus saw difference, he assumed inferiority. Where Montezuma saw difference, he assumed superiority. Neither could understand the other as different yet equal.

Cortés, in contrast, was very skilled at understanding and communicating with the native people. For Cortés, however, communication was a tool utilized to manipulate and exploit. Communication and conquest went hand in hand. Unlike Columbus,

Cortés came to know the native people quite well. Yet he sought to understand them only to master them.

Bartolomé de Las Casas (1474–1566), a Catholic priest who accompanied the conquistadors, was initially blinded not by the prejudice of superiority or inferiority, but by the prejudice of equivalence. Las Casas could not conceive that anything essentially equal could somehow still be different.

Columbus came to America, Las Casas wrote, to "open wide doors so that the divine doctrine and the Gospel of Christ might enter therein." By discovering the natives, Columbus ensured that "an infinite number of their souls . . . was saved."[8] Las Casas offered the natives equality, but it came at a price. Equality could be gained only at the cost of sacrificing much of their identity. The natives would have to abandon their religious beliefs and many of their cultural practices and convert to Christianity.

Eventually Las Casas, unlike Columbus, exchanged his Eurocentric lenses for less opaque ones. While he continued to encourage religious conversion, Las Casas no longer saw natives solely as potential Christians. Observing the atrocities committed by the conquistadors firsthand and witnessing the humanity of the native people in their daily lives, Las Casas learned to love and respect the aboriginals. He devoted his life to ending their abuse and slavery at the hands of the European settlers.[9] No longer was acceptance dependent upon the other serving as a mirror of the self. No longer was assimilation of the other the only solution to the uncomfortable perception of difference.

The story of the Spanish conquest of America is illustrative of the power of religious and racial identities to undermine opportunities to understand those who are different. Columbus, and for a time Las Casas, were so enclosed within their own cultural identities that they could not adequately open themselves to others. Cortés was sufficiently enclosed in his identity as a conquistador that his skills in communication were employed only to dominate and destroy the other.

Politics concerns the exercise of power that accommodates difference rather than destroying it. But violent domination is not the only threat to politics. The attempt to impose uniformity is also a danger. Politics is threatened whenever difference is suppressed in the name of equality, with no opportunity for resistance. Transforming individuals into identical images of the self, as Las Casas' original efforts illustrate, may create the illusion of equality. But the cost is high. The tragedy of the "discovery" of America is that the opportunity for political life—for sustaining individuality within community, and equality with difference—was lost.

## The Other in America

Aboriginal people had been living in the "New World" for tens of thousands of years prior to the Europeans' arrival. In the 1500s, more than 70 million native inhabitants may have occupied the Americas. Within a few centuries, fewer than 5 million remained. Tens of millions of human lives were lost to disease, mistreatment and outright slaughter.

We briefly examined some of the causes of this decline in what is now known as Central and South America. Genocide (destruction of a race or people) also took place in North America, though on a much smaller scale. At the time of the European incursion there were some 500 distinct nations of native people with a combined population north of the Rio Grande of 7 million. Five of those 7 million were in what is now the contermi-nous United States (the lower 48 states). Throughout the 1800s, these aboriginal people rapidly diminished in numbers, eventually dwindling to a few hundred thousand. Some speculated, and not without pleasure, that the natives might be exterminated altogether. Certain tribes, such as the Susquehanna, were destroyed; others, such as the Pequot, came very close to annihilation. Viewing the burning of a Pequot village in 1637, one colonist wrote:

> Those that escaped the fire were slain with the sword, some hewed to pieces, others run through with their rapiers, so as they were quickly dispatched and very few escaped. It was conceived they destroyed about 400 at this time. It was a fearful sight to see them thus frying in the fire and the streams of blood quenching the same, and horrible was the stink and scent thereof; but the victory seemed a sweet sacrifice, and they gave the praise thereof to God, who had wrought so wonderfully for them, thus to enclose their enemies in their hands and give them so speedy a victory over so proud and insulting an enemy.[10]

Pequots of other villages who were not killed or sold into slavery were, like many aborigi-nal tribes, forbidden to speak their language or practice their customs. The few hundred Pequots that survive today have had to rely on anthropologists to recover fragments of their lost heritage.

Alexis de Tocqueville wrote in the 1840s that

> the [Indian] nations I have mentioned formerly covered the country to the seacoast; but a traveler at the present day must penetrate more than a hundred leagues into the interior of the continent to find an Indian. Not only have these wild tribes receded, but they are de-stroyed; and as they give way or perish, an immense and increasing people fill their place. There is no instance upon record of so prodigious a growth or so rapid a destruction.[11]

The destruction was rapid indeed. At its nadir, between 1890 and 1900, the population of aboriginal people in the United States dwindled to between 4 and 5 percent of its former size. As one scholar writes, for native Americans, the "arrival of the Europeans marked the beginning of a long holocaust."[12] Indeed, Adolf Hitler claimed that his approach to genocide was inspired by his study of the American extermination of its aboriginal people.[13] The comparison of the American settlers' destruction of natives with the Nazis' destruction of European Jewry may seem harsh, particularly because many of America's aboriginal peoples perished from disease. Nevertheless, government officials did pay scalp bounties to Indian killers, and it is known that General Jeffrey Amherst, among others, supplied blankets infected with smallpox to tribes to hasten their demise.

Between 1600 and 1890, 200 major battles were fought between settlers and indigenous groups, and about three-quarters of the native population was destroyed. The infamous massacre of hundreds of Sioux Indians, mostly women and children, at Wounded Knee, South Dakota, in 1890, ended the so-called Indian Wars. Even when outright violence was checked, however, the autonomy, laws, and rights of native peoples were denied. They were forbidden to practice many of their customs and rituals and their means of livelihood were whittled away as land was settled by European immigrants.

Plains Indians, for example, depended on the vast herds of bison, also known as buffalo, for food, clothing, shelter, pouches, paints, fuel, utensils and religious worship. As many as 60 million bison roamed the plains at the beginning of the nineteenth century. By 1895, less than 500 of these great beasts survived. Many were simply shot for sport and left to rot in the sun. Calvary troops were given explicit orders to shoot all bison on sight to make way for cattle ranching. General George Crook's motto for his troops was "Kill a buffalo, starve an Indian." With the destruction of the plains bison, a rich aboriginal culture and a way of life also died.

Many esteemed statesmen voiced cruel opinions or established deplorable policies regarding the American Indian. President George Washington called for the "total destruction and devastation" of certain Indian settlements. Benjamin Franklin speculated that inducing alcoholism among native Americans might be the means "to extirpate these savages in order to make room for cultivators of the earth." President Andrew Jackson, who oversaw the deadly forced march of Choctaw, Cherokee and Creek Indians from the southeastern states to settlements west of the Mississippi, deemed native Americans to have "neither the intelligence, the industry, the moral habits, nor the desire of improvement" needed to survive competition with the "superior race" of white settlers. President Andrew Johnson told Congress in 1867 that "if the savage resists, civilization, with the Ten Commandments in one hand and the sword in the other, demands his immediate extermination." President Theodore Roosevelt believed that the settler and pioneer had "justice on their side" in their usurping and development of land that otherwise would have remained "but a game preserve for squalid savages." He advocated the extermination of the buffalo as a means of ensuring that Indians remained on reservations. Congress, in turn, violated hundreds of treaties that native Americans had signed in good faith.[14] In short, many of America's leading statesmen concurred with General Phil Sheridan's infamous remark that the only good Indian was a dead Indian.

Thomas Jefferson was one of the most compassionate and liberal of America's leaders regarding the native people (and black slaves). Yet the only encouragement Jefferson could find for the Indians was to suggest that they abandon their way of life and join ranks with the European settlers in subduing the land. To survive, Jefferson argues, the American Indians must cease to be what they always were: hunters and gatherers who lived off the bounty of the land with a rich cultural life but little in the way of commercial development. When his efforts "to save and to civilize" American natives were met with resistance, Jefferson announced that their actions "justified extermination."[15]

Writing in the early 1880s, Black Elk summarized the unhappy fate of his people:

> Once we were happy in our own country and we were seldom hungry, for then the two-leggeds and the four-leggeds lived together like relatives, and there was plenty for them and for us. But the Wasichus [white men] came, and they have made little islands for us and other little islands of the four-leggeds, and always these islands are becoming smaller, for around them surges the gnawing flood of the Waisichu; and it is dirty with lies and greed.[16]

At about the same time, Washakie of the Shoshone tribe protested to the governor of the Wyoming territory, saying

> What you proudly call America, not very long ago belonged to the red man.... [But] our fathers were steadily driven out, or killed, and we, their sons, but sorry remnants of tribes once mighty, are cornered in little spots of the earth.... Knowing all this, do you wonder, sir, that we have fits of desperation and think to be avenged?[17]

Certain native tribes did seek revenge and commit atrocities matched by those their people suffered. The resort to violence, however, only further ensured that the aboriginal people would fight a losing battle.

Beginning in the first half of the twentieth century, some of the demands made by native Americans for greater autonomy and economic improvement found more receptive ears. Still, their cultures remain severely threatened and they experience significantly higher rates of unemployment, poorer education, and greater poverty than the average American.[18]

## Identity and Difference

Throughout history and across the globe, people have been oppressed and destroyed owing to their racial or ethnic identities. Aboriginal Tasmanians were completely exterminated within less than two and a half centuries of their island's discovery by Europeans. The population of aboriginal Australians declined from 300,000 to 60,000 after the first 130 years of the continent's colonization. Over a million Armenians were killed by Turks in 1915. Over 10 million Jews, Gypsies, and Slavs were killed by Nazis between 1933 and 1945. This sordid chronicle could be extended extensively were it to include genocidal practices grounded not only in racial and ethnic bigotries but in religious, cultural and ideological beliefs.

In the face of countless brutalities committed against individuals owing to their identities, it is appropriate that we concern ourselves with the affirmation of difference. At the same time, such affirmations should not create unnecessary barriers to communication or become an apology for neglect, provincialism, or narrow partisanship. The affirmation of difference is not an apology for divisiveness.

Segregationists, for example, affirmed racial differences in their efforts to keep African Americans from becoming integrated in American society. Hundreds of years of black slavery were ended with the Civil War. After the end of hostilities, the *Constitution* dictated that no state could deny any person equal protection under the law. But this proviso was largely unenforced. A period known as Jim Crow developed, initiating semiformal acceptance of racial segregation. Almost a century would elapse before Chief Justice Earl Warren led the Supreme Court to rule in the 1954 case of *Brown* v. *Board of Education* that segregation in schools should be outlawed. The Court repudiated the "separate but equal" doctrine, arguing that the educational separation of minority children "generates a feeling of inferiority as to their status in the community that may affect their hearts and minds in a way unlikely ever to be undone." Yet the court did not require that segregation be brought to an immediate end. It simply called for "all deliberate speed" in ending segregation. This ambiguous formulation allowed for inaction.

The affirmation of difference becomes a defense of divisiveness when the members of specific groups are presumed to constitute a homogeneous body that is *essentially* different. Identity politics falls into this trap. In respecting "otherness," we want to avoid the mistake of assuming all "others" to be somehow the same. In turn, the affirmation of difference should not obscure what people have in common.

At the same time, the affirmation of what people have in common should not obscure important differences. It has been suggested, for example, that Westerners who "proclaim the equality of all mankind" are often the "staunchest upholders of the cultural superiority of the West." Upholding the principle of equality effectively means conferring the "right and duty of all mankind . . . to accept the ways of thinking of the Western societies."[19] Here egalitarianism amounts to a belief that others should be, and want to be, just like us. The problem is that "by failing to attend to the actual life situations and needs of certain groups, by glossing over and ignoring important and legitimate differences, we come to frame principles and norms that reflect partial, not generalizable interests."[20] While equal rights to life and liberty are universal goods, their pursuit and institutionalization will vary based on social, cultural and national contexts. That does not justify turning a blind eye to gross injustices in other lands or cultures. It does mean that our practical judgments should be informed by the beliefs and values of those for whom we seek justice.

Martin Luther King, Jr. famously stated at the 1963 March on Washington that the self-evident truth that all men are created equal does not mean that we cease to make judgments about each other. It simply means that people "will not be judged by the color of their skin but by the content of their character." That was the essence of the "dream" that King sought to share with the nation. Democracy demands that we judge others by their actions rather than their race, creed, sex, or any number of other personal attributes. The point is not simply to make judgments. The point is to have good reasons for one's judgments. By well exercising practical judgment we can acknowledge difference without neglecting what we have in common, and we can acknowledge what we have in common without imposing assimilation in the name of equality.

Why is difference important to democracy? "In the diversity of others," John Dewey (1859–1952) wrote, "we see the possibility of our own adaptations."[21] Democracy, Dewey argued, was an experiment in both statecraft and soulcraft. If one's own identity—one's most basic beliefs, values, and self-understandings—are generated within a diverse social environment, then there is cause to safeguard this diversity—if for no other reason than to facilitate one's further development.

In the same vein, Sheldon Wolin writes:

> A political being is not to be defined . . . as an abstract, disconnected bearer of rights, privileges and immunities, but as a person whose existence . . . draws its sustenance from circumscribed relationships: family, friends, church, neighborhood, workplace, community, town, city. These relationships are the sources from which political beings draw power—symbolic, material and psychological—and that enable them to act together. For true political power involves not only acting so as to effect decisive changes; it also means the capacity to receive power, to be acted upon, to change, and be changed.[22]

Politics entails mutual influence. The unique individual becomes an individual because she exists in community. As Seyla Benhabib writes: "The 'I' becomes an 'I' only among a 'we,' in a community of speech and action. Individuation does not precede association; rather it is the kinds of associations which we inhabit that define the kinds of individuals we will become."[23] Identity develops by way of interaction with others. It co-evolves with difference.

For Alasdair MacIntyre, answering the question "Who am I?" involves locating oneself in "a nexus of social relationships."[24] We understand who we are by way of the social relationships we form. We come to know the self by way of the other. Social theorist Craig Calhoun observes that "self-knowledge—always a construction no matter how much it feels like a discovery—is never altogether separable from claims to be known in specific ways by others."[25] Much self-knowledge is gained by observing our reflection in the eyes of others. In turn, we learn much about ourselves, and about different parts of ourselves, by understanding the diverse individuals with whom we share our world. Like Socrates, we ought to take to heart the Delphic oracle's dictum to "Know thyself." And like Socrates, who spent his days probing the hearts and minds of fellow citizens, we come to know ourselves best through open, critical exchanges with others.

To deny difference is to turn away from one's own heritage and impoverish, if not abandon, opportunities for self-development. Dewey observed that "We are free not because of what we statically are, but inasfar as we are becoming different from what we have been."[26] To be allergic to otherness—whether it be encountered in society or the self—is to forfeit political life.

## GENDER AND IDENTITY

In her book, *Sexual Politics*, Kate Millett states that "the personal is the political."[27] The phrase is something of a watchword for feminists but captures equally well the struggles of those who face discrimination on account of their sexual orientation. The point is that the public self that is the bearer of rights cannot truly exercise those rights if the private self is discriminated against and dominated within the home, workplace and society.

As Millet argued, psychological and social relations of domination inevitably translate into political inferiority, despite constitutional or legal recognitions of equality. By politicizing the personal, and challenging the distinction between public and private realms, feminist theorists expose how women throughout the ages and across the globe have been excluded from political life. The point is not that privacy should be abolished. Feminists want to maintain crucial distinctions between the public realm and the private realm.[28] Nonetheless, they contest the way the line separating these realms traditionally has been drawn. In turn, they argue that the line is not so thick, so straight, or so impermeable as is often assumed.

Feminist proponents of abortion rights, for instance, generally argue that the government should keep out of women's private lives. The "pro-choice" argument has mostly been based on a woman's right to make personal decisions about her body and life—whether to carry a pregnancy to term or to abort the fetus—without interference by the state. Indeed, it was on the fundamental right to privacy that the Supreme Court established a woman's right to abortion in its 1973 *Roe* v. *Wade* ruling. Invoking a similar argument about the right to privacy, a 1965 Supreme Court ruling, *Griswold* v. *Connecticut*, struck down laws in 29 states that held the use of contraception to be illegal.

Still, the distinction between the public and the private deserves interrogation and contestation. Politics occurs not only when people speak and vie for power in public. It also happens when people are kept powerless within a private realm. Silencing someone or keeping her from attaining a full and equal voice—or even gaining an audience—is a political act.[29] For some to speak and be heard, others must remain silent. For some to lead, others must follow. In an ideal democracy, each citizen would take her turn at speaking and listening, leading and following. Democratic politics, as Aristotle argued, is about ruling and being ruled in turn. When men are doing most of the speaking and acting, and some of that speaking and acting is designed to keep women silent and inactive, a form of politics known as patriarchy develops. Patriarchy is the rule of men—in and out of turn. It has a long history.

### Feminism and Gender Justice

In ancient Greece, women could neither own property nor vote. They were mostly kept at home, where they would weave, manage domestic slaves, and generally maintain the household. They were considered part of the domestic economy and were forbidden to participate in public affairs. Indeed, the word *economy* comes from the Greek words meaning private household and management (*oikos* + *nemein*). In ancient Greece, the economy was explicitly distinguished from the political realm, the affairs of the home (*oikos*) were separated from the affairs of the city-state (*polis*).

Democracy in ancient Greece was a democracy of a very restricted type. The *demos* or people who had political power consisted only of free-born male citizens. The time and leisure that these men found to engage in public affairs was largely gained through the privatized labor of women and slaves. The establishment of the Greek household as a private domain therefore served an explicitly political purpose and was maintained by explicitly political means.

The household was at the center of economic life in ancient Greece and continued to play an important role throughout much of the West over the next two millennia. Though disabled from political participation, women remained important to economic affairs. While generally denied the right to own property, they often exercised economic power as managers of the household.

The Industrial Revolution that began in Europe and America during the eighteenth century created job opportunities for women outside the home. In one respect, however, the Industrial Revolution diminished the economic power of women. As the locus of the economy shifted from the home to the factory, women's status as key players in the home economy was eroded. When husbands and brothers left the farm and household to work in factories, the wages they brought home underscored the economic powerlessness of their wives and sisters. Denied political equality in the public realm, and increasingly denied economic equality in the private realm, women were left with fewer means to control their lives or affect the lives of others, except perhaps the lives of dependent children.

Modern feminism arose in the eighteenth and nineteenth centuries, as women began to assert their rights to both economic and political equality. Mary Wollstonecraft (1759–97), one of the first modern feminists, wrote *Vindication of the Rights of Women* in 1792, a year after Thomas Paine published his popular *The Rights of Man*. Paine had attacked the privileges of the aristocracy in the wake of the French Revolution and gallantly defended the equality of all men. Despite all the grand talk of equality, Paine and the republican revolutionaries left women wholly out of the picture.

Meek wives make for foolish mothers, Wollstonecraft observes. Indeed, the oppression of women in the home undermines the development of many other facets of their lives and characters. If women are "educated for dependence," taught and trained to submit to the arbitrary will of brothers and husbands, then it is no surprise that the character of women will become corrupted, no less than the character of their male dominators. Women's exclusion from the public realm was justified by the claim that they exhibit a dearth of reason and glut of passion. To the extent that these traits are evident, Wollstonecraft observes, they are not natural to women. Rather, these traits are the "natural consequence of their education and station in society." If women "share the rights" of men, Wollstonecraft concludes, they will also exhibit their fair share of political capacities and virtues.[30]

Notwithstanding Wollstonecraft's effort, feminism had a slow and rocky start. It was close to a century later, in 1869, that the English liberal theorist John Stuart Mill would produce another important work in feminist theory. Strongly influenced by and often collaborating with his companion (and later wife) Harriet Taylor, Mill wrote *The Subjection of Women*. Here Mill argued for the equality of women, suggesting that such equality is the "surest test and most correct measure of the civilization of a people or an age."[31] Mill's effort, like Wollstonecraft's, was directed at ending oppression by gaining for women the rights already enjoyed by men.

Following English common law, the early legal system in the United States assigned women an inferior status. Women were denied certain forms of education, barred from certain professions and occupations, excluded from juries and public offices, and restricted in their ability to own property, sign contracts, go into business, or write wills. Women had few if any political rights and subsequently had little say when they were denied economic rights by all-male legislatures. In an early attempt to challenge this injustice, Abigail Adams pleaded with her husband, John Adams, who participated in the 1789 Constitutional Convention. "In the new code of laws," she wrote in a letter, "I desire you would remember the ladies and be more generous and favorable to them than your ancestors. Do not put such unlimited power in the hands of the husbands. . . . If particular care and attention is not paid to the ladies, we are determined to foment a rebellion, and will not hold ourselves bound by any laws in which we have no voice or representation."[32] Despite the warning, John Adams imitated his ancestors and ignored his wife. The other attendees of the convention followed suit.

Abigail Adams was ahead of her time. Only at the Women's Rights Convention at Seneca Falls, New York in 1848 was the American woman's movement set fully in motion. Here women gathered together to assert their rights in public. Paraphrasing the *Declaration of Independence*, the Seneca Falls attendees proclaimed: "We hold these truths to be self-evident: that all men and women are created equal. . . . " But these truths were neither self-evident nor acknowledged by the male legislators of the day.

Political equality for women was the goal of the women's suffrage movement, led by Elizabeth Cady Stanton and Susan B. Anthony.[33] The suffrage movement simmered for half a century before becoming well organized in the last decade of the nineteenth century. In 1917, the first woman member of Congress was elected. The mobilization of women was further enhanced owing to their greater integration in the workforce. During World War I, many women took on jobs outside the home. At the end of hostilities in 1918, they shifted back into the domestic realm as their industrial services were no longer needed with the return of the soldiers. But the ability of women to fill the nation's economic shoes had been demonstrated. When these efforts did not subsequently translate into political recognition, increasing numbers of women began to mobilize. After much popular protest and lobbying, legislators yielded to pressure in 1920, when the Nineteenth Amendment was added to the Constitution, giving American women the right to vote. (Suffrage had already been extended to women in New Zealand by 1893 and in Australia by 1902. It was established in most Western nations by the 1950s. Switzerland enfranchised women only in 1971).

The percentage of women who vote has steadily climbed since female suffrage was instituted and by the 1980s equaled the percentage of men voting. Since then, the percentage of women voting has consistently surpassed that of men. The larger number of women voters, however, has not translated into equal political power. Women remain significantly underrepresented in local, state, and national governments. Globally, only one in four elected representatives to national legislatures is a woman. In the US, that figure is one in five.

Leadership in the business world is even more inequitable. Less than one in six executive business officers are women worldwide, and less than one in twenty CEOs of Fortune 500 corporations are women. Disadvantages and discrimination that women experience in the business and professional world likely contribute to their political inequality. If women work in less prestigious and poorly remunerated professions, hit a "glass ceiling" that prevents their rising to top leadership positions, and disproportionately neglect or postpone professional development to care for children and maintain the household, then their opportunities to translate economic and professional achievement into political power will be diminished.[34]

The feminist struggle against economic discrimination did not truly begin until well after World War II, spurred on by the 1952 publication of *The Second Sex* by French feminist Simone de Beauvoir. Betty Friedan's *The Feminine Mystique*, written in 1963, had an even greater impact, challenging the notion that women find fulfillment only in childrearing and homemaking. In 1966, Friedan helped found the National Organization for Women (NOW), which brought pressure on government and business to end discrimination against women and initiated the "second wave" of feminism.

Women's groups lobbied, petitioned, and marched in demonstrations to ensure that equal rights for women would be safeguarded by the Constitution in the form of an

Equal Rights Amendment (ERA). The amendment stated that "equality of rights under the law shall not be denied or abridged by the United States or any state on account of sex." The ERA was not ratified by the required 38 states within ten years of its passage by Congress in 1972; consequently, it failed to become law. The Equal Pay Act of 1963, the Civil Rights Act of 1964, the Equal Employment Opportunity Act of 1972, and the political and legal recognition of sexual harassment as a form of sexual discrimination in the 1980s formally put an end to overt sexual discrimination in employment. Nonetheless, the "gender gap" in pay remains. Women in the United States earn only about 80 percent of what their male counterparts earn.

Discrimination against women, whether it is legal, political, economic, or social, constitutes the systematic denial of equal treatment. Feminist theorists decry it as a form of injustice. The exercise of power or force that denies justice to a specific group of people is called *oppression*. Oppression does not simply mean suffering or deprivation, as that may occur for all sorts of reasons, including natural catastrophes or illness. Oppression takes place only when suffering is systematically inflicted by some individuals or groups on others. Few would deny that historically women have been oppressed. Yet many believe that such oppression is a thing of the past, particularly in a country such as the United States where everyone has formal equality, that is, equality under the law. But as we have seen, equality under the law often does not translate into equality of opportunity.

For some feminists, even equality of opportunity is insufficient. Shulamith Firestone argues that the physical differences between the sexes will always lead to a "fundamental inequality" in the economic, social, and political arenas. She suggests that the solution lies with the development of technological procedures to overcome these physical differences. For Firestone, the only way for women to escape the "tyranny" of their biology is to do away with the "barbarism" of pregnancy. The answer to the problem of gender justice, it follows, is "artificial reproduction."[35] Only by unburdening themselves of biological demands can women finally achieve true equality with men in the workplace and the political realm. Equality under the law and equality of opportunity will never deliver justice, Firestone maintains. Only an equality of condition can do so. Men and women themselves, not simply the rules and opportunities they face, must be made the same.

Artificial wombs are now in development. Still, Firestone's radical solution to the problem of gender justice has been widely criticized by feminists. Such an egalitarian society, critics argue, would be gained at too high a price. Women's social, economic and political equality might indeed be achieved in such a world, but only by denying their unique capacity to give birth to children. Equality would be achieved by destroying difference.

Most feminists advocate equality under the law and equality of opportunity, and endorse political rather than technological means to their achievement. Gender justice also demands cultural change, as cultural mores structure our private lives, and the personal is the political. For instance, in *Beyond God the Father*, Mary Daly argues that women who worship a male deity are subject to a subtle form of psychological self-depreciation. They may come to believe that they are inferior to men in spiritual affairs. This religious inequality mutually reinforces women's economic, social and political subservience. The reverse, of course, holds for men, who may justify their domination of women by invoking the masculinity of God or the patriarchy upheld in religious scripture.

Daly advocates that women assert their equality in religious matters by abandoning patriarchal religion and adopting female deities. To combat patriarchy, which, Daly argues, is "the prevailing religion of the entire planet," women must adjust not only their relationship to the earth but their relationship to heaven.[36]

There are good data to buttress the claim that economic inequality translates into political inequality. Historically and across the globe, wealth and political power have gone hand in hand. Daly does not supply us with an adequate historical or comparative analysis to validate her thesis that religious inequality, defined as the worship of a male deity, leads to political inequality. Regardless, Daly's thesis deserves reflection and further study. It confronts us with the question of when and how cultural mores impact political life.

## Equality and Difference

Most feminists do not want women to gain equality by becoming more like men. Equality should not require masculinization. As Carole Pateman writes, "women's equal standing must be accepted as an expression of the freedom of women *as women*, and not treated as an indication that women can be just like men."[37] To achieve this goal, some argue, the world itself—its mores, institutions, and practices—would have to become more feminine, or at least more balanced in its feminine and masculine features.

What would a more feminine world look like? Are there distinctly feminine ways of thinking, feeling, or acting? Are there such things as a feminine epistemology and feminine ethics? Carol Gilligan maintains that there are. Gilligan observes that women do not easily fit within existing models of how children develop morally. Two possible explanations offer themselves: either there is something wrong with the morality of women or there is something wrong with the standard models of development. Gilligan suspects the latter. Viewing the world through masculine eyes, male theorists naturally produced models of moral development that reflected their own experiences.

Gilligan argues that women exhibit distinct social concerns and that these concerns lead them to employ different criteria to evaluate moral quandaries. The mores that structure men's and women's ethical choices differ. Judging women in terms of masculine morality leads to misunderstandings and unfair evaluations. "It all goes back, of course, to Adam and Eve," Gilligan states, reminding her readers of the biblical tale where God fashioned the first woman from a rib of the first man. Though left to prosper in the Garden of Eden, Adam and Eve were soon cast out of paradise for their misdeeds.

The moral of the story, Gilligan writes, is that "if you make a woman out of a man, you are bound to get in trouble."[38]

The differences Gilligan proposes between masculine and feminine moral orientations are relatively straightforward. Women tend to conceive the ethical realm as pertaining to the requirements and responsibilities of relationships. Morality concerns the duty to care for those within one's interpersonal network. Women arrive at solutions to moral dilemmas by increasing communication within their network so that mutual caring is sustained. Women develop what Gilligan calls a "morality of care." Here compassionate engagement, not adherence to abstract principles, fosters justice. Women feel a duty to ensure that no one is excluded from the network of connection and care. Those who are hurt owing to fractures in such networks should be quickly reintegrated. This puts a premium on the empathy required to discern the needs of others.

Men, in contrast, perceive the ethical realm to be circumscribed by the rules of fair play and the rights of autonomous individuals. One solves moral problems by consistently applying universally applicable rules in a neutral, objective manner. Moral problems are approached as logical puzzles. The task is to analyze and prioritize conflicting rights, standards, duties, and laws. In this way, the appropriate boundaries between individuals may be reestablished and safeguarded. Men develop what Gilligan calls a "morality of rights." One strives to view others abstractly, as representative bearers of rights. Equality under the law, reciprocity, fair play, and individual liberty are the goods to be achieved and protected. Impartial reasoning is the route to justice.

We might summarize Gilligan's thesis by saying that women's morality is primarily concerned with the maintenance and mending of relationships, while men's morality is concerned with the problems that arise when relationships overly constrain or encroach on the freedom and autonomy of individuals. Gilligan does not suggest that men never evidence a (feminine) morality of care and women never evidence a (masculine) morality of rights. She is speaking of tendencies. These tendencies do not necessarily reflect innate structures. They may be artifacts of culture. Indeed, the morality of care may have developed as a means for women to cope with life in a patriarchal world that demanded constant sacrifice from them as sisters, wives and mothers.

Gilligan acknowledges that both feminine and masculine moral orientations have their shortcomings. The morality of care may lead to self-sacrifice, particularly when exercised by women in relationships with men. The proclivity for self-sacrifice is best tempered, Gilligan suggests, by embracing aspects of a morality of rights, which stimulates a sense of independence and prompts women to stand up for what is their due.

In turn, the impartial justice promoted within a masculine morality is best tempered by a morality of care. The feminine orientation to the contextual nature of relationships may soften rigid rule-following and the focus on autonomy. A morality of care may help produce equity, moving beyond procedural justice (upholding the rules of fair play) to ensure substantive justice (achieving for each a fair share). We will further examine equity and its relationship to justice in Chapter 5.

Neither masculine nor feminine moralities are sufficient on their own. Justice is best attained, Gilligan argues, by balancing rights with care, law with equity, and independence with responsibility. Within each of us, the potential for masculine and feminine morality exists. The goal is for men and women to let both voices speak together.[39]

Arguably, not only ethics but also epistemology is gendered. Feminist theorists have claimed that knowledge in general, not only moral knowledge, is gained and employed in specific ways by women. There is not only feminine and masculine ways of acting but also feminine and masculine "ways of knowing."[40] Whereas men view knowledge as an objective representation of reality obtained through impartial observation, women view knowledge more contextually. For women, knowledge consists in the discovery of networks of relations. Knowledge is developed through mutual exchanges that reveal the intricacies of these networks.

If women's cultural mores, psychologies, and epistemologies are significantly different from men's, how and why might this arise? Nancy Chodorow, a feminist psychoanalyst, offers an explanation based on the early socialization of children. A girl's sexuality and sense of self, Chodorow theorizes, is "ascribed" to her through her relationship with her caretaker mother. It is experienced as given rather than earned. She naturally integrates herself into her world by identifying with her same-sex caretaker. A girl comes to understand her identity as expressive of her own nature rather than dependent on specific achievements.

In most societies, a boy grows up largely in his father's absence, as work roles supersede caretaker roles for adult men. Consequently, a boy's sexuality and sense of self are much less the product of his identification with a same-sex, nurturing parent. Instead, a boy's identity must be "achieved" in distinction, and perhaps in opposition, to his caretaker. Achieving a stable male identity becomes a matter of asserting independence from the mother. It is a product of the defensive demarcation of ego boundaries. The independent, aggressive nature of the male identity is further accentuated by the cultural emphasis on the active rather than receptive character of the male sexual act.

Feminine identity is socialized as a relational *being*, Chodorow observes, whereas masculine identity, constantly in need of demonstration, is socialized as an assertive and often competitive *doing*. Feminine identity is a discovery of one's place in the world, while masculine identity is an assertion of one's prerogative to act in the world. This difference in the development of feminine and masculine identities in early childhood produces a disjunctive and hierarchical social structure. Masculine values of independence and competitive achievement oppose, dominate, and are reinforced by feminine values of dependence, caretaking, and passivity.

The psychological development of children, in other words, has an important and potentially deleterious impact on public life. Chodorow maintains that "until masculine identity does not depend on men's proving themselves, their *doing* will be a reaction to insecurity rather than a creative exercise of their humanity, and woman's *being*, far from being an easy and positive acceptance of self, will be a resignation to inferiority."[41] The general recommendation is that fathers should take a greater role in childrearing. Were this to occur, men and women would develop more balanced moralities, epistemologies and identities.

Gender roles are largely a function of historical and cultural contexts. Simone de Beauvoir put the point succinctly in *The Second Sex*, writing, "one is not born, but rather becomes, a woman."[42] But one does not simply become a woman (or man) in some generic sense, one becomes a certain sort of woman (or man). Many feminists insist that any attempt to define the essence of womanhood would privilege the characteristics of a certain sort of women (e.g., women of a specific class, race, ethnic group, sexual orientation or ideology).[43] Carol Gilligan, for instance, has been criticized for speaking about a feminine morality in general when in fact the women she interviewed for her study were all college students in the United States. Perhaps, then, what Gilligan depicts as a feminine morality is really a privileged, white, middle-class morality. Gilligan's work ignores the potentially distinctive moralities of racial and ethnic minority women within the United States, who remain underrepresented in American colleges, as well as the moralities of women of color living in developing societies. With this in mind, Hester Eisenstein deplores the "false universalism" within certain feminist writings.[44]

John Stuart Mill anticipated Beauvoir's famous statement, writing that "what is now called the nature of women is an eminently artificial thing—the result of forced repression in some directions, unnatural stimulation in others." To the extent his assessment was accurate, Mill recognized, it applied not only to the construction of female identities but also to the construction of male identities. "I deny that any one knows, or can know, the nature of the two sexes," Mill holds, "as long as they have only been seen in their present relation to one another."[45] Gender identity is a fluid product of history and culture.

## Liberalism, Patriarchy and Power Feminism

John Stuart Mill was an early feminist, though the term was not current in his day. He was also a liberal. In the Western world, many, perhaps most, feminists consider themselves to be liberal feminists, as opposed to socialist feminists, conservative feminists, or radical feminists.[46] Yet most feminist theorists, including liberal feminists, are wary of traditional forms of liberal politics and theory. Liberals promote liberty by establishing (legal) boundaries that protect individuals from illegitimate interference by government or society. Consequently, liberalism is primarily concerned with securing individual rights through the rule of law.

In much liberal theory, law is promulgated by a limited government whose legitimacy derives from a social contract. The social contract establishes governmental rule through the agreement of independent and autonomous individuals who wish to escape the anarchy of a state of nature. Many feminists claim that liberalism's origins in social contract theory belie its masculinist tendencies. It focuses on the male concern for the protection of individual rights and independence while ignoring the feminine concern for the sustaining of relationships and community. Most starkly put, the charge is that "liberalism has no place for women *as women*."[47] Women must think and act like men to fit into a liberal world.

Social contract theorists assume the independent existence of autonomous (male) actors who confront the task of negotiating a fair means of establishing and maintaining a peaceful collective existence. John Rawls invokes this tradition. He asks us to imagine ourselves in an "original position" that serves a similar purpose as the imagined state of nature for social contract thinkers such as Hobbes, Locke and Rousseau.

The original position is not proposed as an actual or even imaginary historic event. It is an intellectual abstraction designed to aid theorizing. In the original position, one finds oneself situated behind a "veil of ignorance" that keeps one unaware of one's class position and social status, race and religion, gender, abilities, predispositions, and propensities, natural strengths and weaknesses, and future life prospects. The veil of ignorance prevents one from designing principles of justice that favor one's idiosyncratic conditions or attributes. Not knowing what place in society one occupies, one would adopt a social contract that is as fair as possible to everyone, safeguarding individual rights and liberties, maintaining equality of opportunity, fairly distributing primary goods, and ensuring that those inequalities that do arise in society are arranged so that they benefit the least advantaged.[48]

Rawls' theory of justice is a masterpiece of contemporary liberal political theory. From a feminist perspective, however, it has serious shortcomings. Like all liberal social contract theories, Rawls' work is primarily concerned with maintaining the greatest autonomy possible for individuals who negotiate with each other from positions of potential rivalry. A feminist thinker explains the problem with such assumptions:

> Giving theoretical primacy to contract relationships and the choices made by independent individuals is possible only by imagining a "state of nature" made up of unrelated adults. But no one is born that way. Our first and most fundamental human relationships are those of trust and dependence as infants, and any society that will reproduce itself has to create the conditions under which such diffuse obligations will be satisfied. If mother-and-child, rather than adult male, is seen as the basic human unit, creating community does not seem so fraught with difficulty, nor does competition seem the archetypal human emotion.[49]

The way we theorize ourselves—from a masculinist perspective of competitive, autonomous individuals in a state of nature or from a feminist perspective of community members held together by naturalized obligations—may play a significant role in how we organize political life. Rawls invokes justice, understood as the rules of fairness negotiated by autonomous individuals, as the "first virtue" of any society. Feminists encourage us to reflect upon different social and political histories, and imagine different social and political futures.

Inspired by these feminist concerns, Owen Flanagan writes that

> There is in the end something misleading in the widely held view that justice is the first virtue of society.... [F]rom the point of view of one very natural perspective, there is no incoherence in thinking of care as at least as fundamental as justice—for it is care between children and their caretakers that creates the possibility conditions for identity, individual character, family, and wider community in the first place.[50]

Feminist theorists seek to reconstruct the mores that ground both conceptions of the self and politics so that women's voices might be heard and feminine points of view embraced.

In many countries, women bear the largest share of the daily workload both in the field and at home.[51] Yet they languish with lower levels of nutrition, education, health care, social status, economic opportunity, and political power. These facts may be interpreted in different ways. Many feminists focus on the oppression. Others resist depicting women as victims. There is a danger, they argue, in always portraying women as the sufferers of oppression and men as perpetrators of injustice. The danger is that such portrayals will reinforce these roles. To view women as casualties of a patriarchal world is to promote a debilitating "victim feminism." To focus on the strength and resourcefulness that have allowed women to prevail under oppressive conditions—managing households, caring for children, carrying on work outside the home, succeeding in professions, and becoming politically active—is to promote a more invigorating "power feminism."[52] Power feminists insist that the description of women as passive depositories and victims of the mores of a patriarchal culture is neither historically accurate nor psychologically helpful. The assumption that oppression—whether based on gender, race, ethnicity, sexual orientation or other identities—provides the dominated group with the ethical high ground, Wendy Brown argues, may lead the oppressed to become attached to the wounds of their victimization.[53] Such attachments may reinforce identity boundaries that should be met with critical inquiry and practical contestation.

The differences between men and women, when coupled with the exercise of power, often lead to inequality and injustice. Feminists carry out the dual task of exposing this oppression while celebrating and furthering the development and flourishing of women. They assert that the boundary between private and public realms is permeable and politically maintained. They take on the challenge of balancing the struggle for equality with the celebration of difference. The pursuit of gender justice is grounded in this balance.

## THE POLITICS OF CLASS

François Fourier (1772–1837), a French socialist with a utopian project for agricultural communes, observed that the degree of women's emancipation is the natural measure of the general emancipation of a society. Friedrich Engels (1820–95), a German thinker who moved to England to manage his father's textile factory, agreed. Engels was following a long tradition among socialist and communist thinkers in advocating the equality of women. This tradition extends back 2,500 years. In the *Republic*, Plato proposes the creation of a communistic society in which women are fully emancipated and treated as equals. One suspects that Plato's proposal might have been ironic. Engels was very serious.

Engels believed that the oppression of women would cease only after other forms of oppression had ended. Long after the slaves had lost their chains, the serfs had won their freedom, and wage laborers had gained full economic rights, women in society would still remain second-class citizens. The end of women's oppression would mark the end of oppression in general.

Karl Marx, a German philosopher who became the most important theorist of communism, was the long-time collaborator and friend of Engels. Apart from a few of Engels' later writings, notably *The Origin of the Family, Private Property and the State*, and even fewer statements from Marx, the question of gender had no part in the work of these thinkers. Marx and Engels were preoccupied with other issues. Their concern was not the emancipation of women but the emancipation of the working class.

Marx's career as a journalist led him to confront the plight of the impoverished grape growers of the Moselle region of his native Germany and the plight of peasant wood gatherers who were forbidden to make use of the forests of the nobility. Steeped in German philosophy during his days as a student at the University of Berlin, Marx theorized broadly about the nature of labor, class interests, and class conflict in capitalistic society and of the potential for a communist revolution.

In an early work written in 1843 called "On the Jewish Question," Marx analyzed religious freedom, an issue of much interest in his day. He addresses the question of whether the Jewish people of Germany should be granted full political rights. Hitherto religion had kept Jews from becoming political (and professional) equals in the Christian German state. (Marx's father had converted to Christianity, for example, as a Prussian edict made it impossible for him to practice law as a Jew.) Liberal thinkers at the time argued that the remedy for this injustice entailed a separation of church and state. Religious belief should become a wholly private affair. With state religion abolished, liberals believed, the traditional religious rationale for excluding Jews from politics would no longer be valid. Jewish people, like any other religious group, would gain full political rights.

Marx acknowledged that this liberal solution constituted an advance over the Christianized German state, which was a remnant of theocratic feudal times. Yet he insisted that the liberal proposal did not go far enough. It is here that we first glimpse Marx's genius and the kernel of his radicalism. Marx argues that making religion a private affair would not fully emancipate the Jews. Nor, for that matter, would it further the emancipation of Christian Germans. Political emancipation, Marx argues, is not a final emancipation. In the liberal state, one gains "religious liberty," but one is not therefore "liberated from religion." Full emancipation would entail the end of religious belief.

Why should Marx care whether people believe in God? What possible political significance could one's private religious beliefs have, assuming the state and the church have been adequately separated?

Religion, Marx holds, is a symptom of a political life stripped of its full potential. Following the argument of Ludwig Feuerbach, Marx maintains that religious belief is rooted in dissatisfaction with the conditions of worldly existence. Religious scripture promises that suffering on earth will be compensated for by heavenly happiness. But scripture is not written by the hand of God, Marx observes. It is written, and believed, by human beings who, unable to fulfill their needs and desires in this life, imagine a God who will reward them in an afterlife. In a now-famous passage, Marx wrote: "Religion is the sigh of the oppressed creature, the sentiment of a heartless world, and the soul of soulless conditions. It is the *opium* of the people."[54] For Marx, religion is an anesthetic that dulls people's sense of earthly pain and oppression and produces delusions of a blissful beyond. The problem with such a drug is that it saps the drive for revolutionary change.

### Alienation and Revolution

By obscuring the true nature of present conditions and preventing action to improve them, Marx holds, religion fosters alienation (the German word is *Entfremdung*, literally "estrangement"). Alienation keeps us strangers from ourselves, from our world, and from our full potential as human beings. It marks the extensive gap between humanity's present condition and its potential. Marx writes:

> The abolition of religion as the *illusory* happiness of men, is a demand for their *real* happiness. The call to abandon their illusions about their condition is a *call to abandon a condition which requires illusions*. The criticism of religion is, therefore, the *embryonic criticism of this vale of tears* of which religion is the *halo*. . . . The immediate *task of philosophy*, which is in the service of history, is to unmask human self-alienation in its *secular form* now that it has been unmasked in its *sacred form*. Thus the criticism of heaven is transformed into the criticism of earth, the *criticism of religion* into the *criticism of law*, and the *criticism of theology* into the *criticism of politics*.[55]

For Marx, religion is a symptom of a social disease whose cure is communism.

The impoverished conditions under which people suffer in this world stimulate the need for the opiate of religion. Poverty, however, is not the only problem. If it were, wealthy individuals would never become religious. Being satisfied is not simply a matter of having enough money and not suffering from material want. To be truly satisfied in life entails achieving one's full potential as a human being—and human beings do not live by bread alone. We are primarily social and political animals, Marx insists, and we need to live as integral parts of communities. Social alienation is the ultimate cause of dissatisfaction. The alienation that results from poverty is effectively the by-product of a deeper estrangement from human community.

Marx's concern with social alienation stems from his assessment of human nature. He holds that humanity is inherently collective or communal in nature. It is a "species being." Throughout history, fear and greed have pitted people against one another. A world of scarce resources made one person's gain another person's loss. Consequently, the world became populated by egoistic individuals who dominate and exploit one another in the pursuit of wealth and power. In failing to live collectively harmonious lives, human beings become alienated from their species being. This alienation is suffered by rich and poor alike. For the poor scraping out a living in the sweat of their brows, however, the suffering is compounded by material deprivation.

The chief concern for Marx was not *"naturally existing* poverty," which he believed had all but disappeared in the industrial nations of his time. The chief concern was "poverty *artificially produced*." This artificial poverty was the direct consequence of the *"disintegration* of society."[56] In modern times, Marx argues, poverty is a product of the way society is organized into distinct economic classes. A class society is chiefly defined by its economic inequalities and the resulting injustice. Such a society is filled with antagonisms, torn by conflicts, and saturated with alienation.

Marx suggests that the working poor are alienated in multiple ways. First, workers are alienated from the products of their labor. What factory workers produce does not constitute a lasting tribute to their capacities, as a painting testifies to the skill of the artist. Instead, the goods produced by workers belong to the capitalist. They are mere commodities to be bought and sold in the marketplace, with no intrinsic value for the workers and only an instrumental, economic value for the capitalist. Second, workers are alienated from the processes of labor. The division of labor in society forces them to perform menial and uninteresting work, such as assembly-line production. They cannot realize their full potential as creative individuals. Third, workers are alienated from fellow human beings. Always threatened by poverty and the loss of their means of subsistence, workers view capitalists as their exploiters and fellow workers as competitors for scarce jobs. Fourth, workers are alienated from nature. Caught up in the system of capitalist production, they cease to cherish the earth as a home. It becomes instead a storehouse of resources to be ruthlessly exploited and transformed into merchandise. Finally, Marx observes, workers become alienated from themselves. Viewed as labor power by the capitalists, workers eventually come to think of themselves as commodities to be bought and sold in the market for the price of wages.

The solution to the problem of alienation is social revolution. Only revolution, Marx believed, could wipe out class distinctions, economic injustice, and alienation. To succeed in this endeavor, a social revolution would have to abolish private property because the right to acquire private property fosters the unequal accumulation of wealth, the unequal accumulation of wealth fosters the unequal exercise of power based on wealth, and the unequal exercise of power based on wealth leads to the development of a hierarchical and alienated society. The theory of communism, Marx wrote, "may be summed up in the single sentence: Abolition of private property."[57]

For Marx, rights to private property, along with other liberal rights, which he calls "bourgeois rights," effectively constitute a "right of inequality." Because bourgeois rights recognize and accept the inequality of individual endowments, those individuals with the greatest intelligence and strength, or the greatest ruthlessness and inherited wealth, rise to the top of society. In contrast, concrete needs, not abstract rights, determine social relations in a communist society.

In a society without class divisions, where property is held in common and equally shared, human beings can realize the fullness of human life unsullied by want, greed, or exploitation. Here labor ceases to be a burden to life. It becomes instead life's "prime want," a means of self-fulfillment. Marx writes that in "communist society, where nobody has one exclusive sphere of activity but each can become accomplished in any branch he wishes, society regulates the general production and thus makes it possible for me to do one thing today and another tomorrow, to hunt in the morning, fish in the afternoon, rear cattle in the evening, criticize after dinner, just as I have a mind, without ever becoming hunter, fisherman, shepherd or critic."[58] In capitalist society we are burdened with narrow economic identities, rigidly circumscribed by an unjust division of labor. We are what we do (for a living) and little else. In communist society, our identities are neither rigid nor static. We would be free to change them at will.

In a communist society, Marx suggests, everyone would joyfully contribute to the common good and none would go without. The banner hanging over this utopian world would read, "From each according to his ability, to each according to his needs!"[59] With the arrival of the highest phase of communistic society, Marx proposes, humanity would end alienation in all its forms. No longer would individuals be estranged from the products or processes of their labor, from one another, from nature, or from themselves. Life after the revolution would not only be free of economic conflict; it would be free of all social conflicts.

## Materialism and Idealism

Marx's theory was grounded in his rejection of idealism, particularly the philosophic idealism of the German philosopher G.W.F. Hegel (1770–1831). Idealists argue that action follows from thought, and that thought is fundamentally free. They maintain that the realm of ideas (thought and understanding) constitutes the true engine of history. The world we construct around us, ultimately, is a reflection of our minds.

Marx held that idealism inverts reality. Ideas are the effect, not the cause, of the material conditions in which we live. Human beings are distinguished from other animals, Marx states, not because they have ideas but because they produce their own means of subsistence by way of organized labor.[60] In turn, the way people collectively produce their means of subsistence determines the ideas they have. As Marx states, "life is not determined by consciousness, but consciousness by life."[61] What one thinks, values, and believes, in other words, is a function of one's economic and social environment. The type of society one lives in and the class of which one is a member largely determine one's identity.

History, Hegel argued, is the systematic unfolding of the *Idea* in time. As a materialist, Marx rejected Hegelian idealism. But he retained Hegel's belief in progressive historical development, melding it with Feuerbach's thought. The result was a labor-based theory of history. Society, Marx argued, developed progressively through periods of revolutionary upheaval and adjustment. All history is the history of class conflict, Marx states, and class conflict had progressed to the point of requiring a final, transformative revolution.

While criticizing the idealist tradition, Marx also attempted to explain how and why it arose. The idealist conviction that innate freedom allows us to determine our beliefs, values and identities, he argues, is itself a product of the social and economic conditions under which we live. Specifically, idealism is the product of a society that has, through the division of labor, separated those whose work is primarily mental from those whose work is primarily manual. Those who engage in mental labor generally exercise most of the power in a society because they control the means of production or are strategically aligned with those who do. By internalizing the effects of their social power, those who engage primarily in mental labor come to believe that the realm of ideas is independent from, and constitutes a greater historical force than, the material conditions of life. Owing to the preponderant social power of idealists, their belief in the independence of thought becomes accepted as a universal truth. The ideas of the ruling class in a society, Marx observes, become the ruling ideas of that society.

As we have seen, Marx calls these ruling ideas *ideology*—a system of thought that distorts or inverts reality but becomes widely accepted as true owing to the power of those whose interests it serves. Marx describes the victims of ideology as having a *false consciousness* that keeps them from understanding and pursuing their true interests. By justifying economic inequalities and social hierarchy, ideology provides the ruling class with a rationale for its power and privilege while making the working class complacent with their hardships. Industrial workers with false consciousness believe that they have freely contracted with employers to give a fair day's labor for a fair wage. In fact, Marx argues, these workers are being systematically exploited by a parasitic economic system.

131

While the capitalists get rich owing to their workers' hard labors, the workers, who are the actual producers of wealth, remain oppressed and impoverished. Ideology keeps workers from recognizing this injustice.

Ideology is important to Marx because it explains how an exploited class of people can be kept in submission when it would be in its interest to engage in revolutionary struggle. Nevertheless, Marx maintains that revolution cannot be staved off forever. Regardless of the power of the ruling class and its ideology, social upheaval is inevitable. The reason has little to do with the power of revolutionary ideas, including those Marx himself propagated. In this regard, Marx was consistent in his materialism. Not changes in thinking and beliefs, but changes in material conditions are what really matters. The further development of technology under capitalism, he speculated, would allow for a vast production of wealth sufficient to eliminate poverty. To the extent poverty continued to exist, it could only be understood as artificially produced by the class divisions in society. Eventually, the large working class, or proletariat, would realize that the cause of its suffering was its exploitation by a much smaller capitalist class, the bourgeoisie. Casting aside their ideological blinders, the proletariat would engage in revolutionary activity. The capitalistic economic system would be overturned, ending the privileges of the bourgeoisie and putting an end to all class distinctions. A communist society would be born.

Though collaborating with Engels extensively, Marx was the more formidable thinker as well as the chief writer. Engels recognized this, and provides a summary of those ideas that belong "solely and exclusively to Marx" and constitute the core of Marxism:

> [E]conomic production and the structure of society of every historical epoch necessarily arising therefrom constitute the foundations for the political and intellectual history of that epoch; that consequently (ever since the dissolution of the primeval communal ownership of land) all history has been a history of class struggles, of struggles between exploited and exploiting, between dominated and dominating classes at various stages of social development; that this struggle, however, has now reached a state where the exploited and oppressed class (the proletariat) can no longer emancipate itself from the class which exploits and oppresses it (the bourgeoisie), without at the same time forever freeing the whole of society from exploitation, oppression and class struggles.[62]

Because all history is the history of class struggle, history effectively ends with the communist revolution. That is not to say that all technological and human development ceases. Nonetheless, the book of history written with the ink of blood and strife can finally be closed because the engine of class struggle disintegrates once its source—economic want and injustice—is abolished.

Marx believed that anything that helped bring about the end of alienation and class conflict was a good thing. He therefore considered capitalism beneficial. It generated

132

vast amounts of wealth, abolishing the "natural" state of poverty. In turn, capitalism created the "artificial" poverty that would foment revolution. Though he praises its historical role in bringing about the communist revolution, Marx sharply criticizes capitalism on all other counts. In capitalistic society, he believed, the scourge of alienation becomes pandemic.

Theories of communism are to be found in the works of Plato, the early and medieval millenarian Christians, Thomas More (1478–1535), the Diggers and Levellers during the English Civil War and the Puritan Revolution (1642–48), Claude Henri de Saint Simon (1760–1825), Robert Owen (1771–1888), Charles Fourier (1772–1837, who provided inspiration for the communistically organized Brook Farm in Massachusetts), and Auguste Comte (1789–1857). Marx was critical of these thinkers for their idealism. He insisted that communist society could be born only out of specific historical conditions and revolutionary struggle. It would not emerge from wishful thinking or isolated acts of altruism based on idealist premises. Marx criticized his socialist and communist predecessors for being utopian.

Yet Marx's own thought is surely utopian. Can the greed, selfishness, and lust for power that have stained the pages of history with so much blood ever be fully eliminated from the human heart? Can what Marx called the "muck of the ages" be wiped away for good by means of revolutionary struggle? Certainly there is no empirical evidence for such hopes. And as we have seen, revolutions often eat their children.

There is, as well, good reason to worry that such a world as Marx envisions would not be desirable. Social and governmental power would have to be very extensive to ensure that individuals are nowhere exploited and that inequalities never arise. Those wielding such power would not always employ it virtuously, one suspects, or give it up without a struggle when called to do so. One might be particularly wary of the "vanguard" of revolutionaries that Marx believed would take control during the transitional period between the dissolution of the bourgeois state and the formation of the communist society.

The anarchist Mikhail Bakunin, like Marx, hoped that exploited workers would rise up against the bourgeois state. Unlike Marx, Bakunin was suspicious of the dictatorship of the proletariat, however temporary its proposed tenure. Any revolutionary elites acceding to power, Bakunin warns, "will no longer represent the people, but only themselves and their claims to rulership over the people." Bakunin concludes that "those who doubt this know very little about human nature."[63] The revolutionary ideals of an elite vanguard, Bakunin held, mask a lust for power that will never exit history's stage. Marx, taking this criticism rather personally, counseled Bakunin to "send all his nightmares about authority to the devil."[64] Apparently, a nerve had been struck. As we reflect on the totalitarian regimes of the twentieth century that claimed Marx as their inspiration, Bakunin's understanding of human nature and his worries about power appear vindicated.

We can nonetheless appreciate Marx's many theoretical insights. Although he exaggerates the role played by the division of labor and shortchanges many other social relationships that impact us, he does illuminate how our economic position in society substantially shapes our identities. He also illustrates how ideology legitimates unjust social and economic structures. By reading Marx, we may better understand how we are blinded or constrained by the identities we adopt, whether as women or men, laborers or business people, students or teachers, religious believers or atheists, rulers or ruled.

This is not to suggest that we are complete prisoners of social circumstances or material conditions. It would be taking on the worst and foregoing the best in Marx to believe so. Marx was a materialist, but he was not a fatalist or a strict economic determinist. He did not hold, or at least did not consistently hold, that our material conditions completely determine what we value and believe, and what we struggle to protect or overturn. Marx wrote that "circumstances make men just as much as men make circumstances."[65] The latter half of this phrase should not be ignored. He argued that "men are products of circumstances and upbringing, and that, therefore, changed men are products of other circumstances and changed upbringing." At the same time, he encouraged us not to forget "that it is men who change circumstances."[66] In other words, while Marx argues that we are products of our technological, economic and social environment, he also insists that we have the opportunity—and responsibility—to transform this environment. Many employ Marx as a guide in their efforts to effect such change.[67]

### Communism versus Socialism

Marx advocated the abolition of private property. Yet Marx himself began his career not as a revolutionary communist but as a reform-oriented socialist, and his work has contributed greatly to socialist thought.

Socialists do not advocate the abolition of private property. They prefer governmental regulations that restrict the sorts of private property that can be owned, the means by which wealth may be produced and obtained, and the amount of wealth one can produce and obtain relative to fellow citizens. As a means of tempering class distinctions without abolishing private property, socialists advocate highly progressive systems of taxation. This taxation limits the rate at which wealth may be accumulated and redistributes it to alleviate poverty and ensure equality of opportunity. Many socialists argue that the government should own the means of production by which certain basic goods and services are produced. Public ownership of key means of production, they argue, will ensure that society is never held hostage by capitalists for the provision of its basic needs.

Socialists do not endorse violent revolution. Gradual reform is preferred. They hold that incremental change can produce a just society. It has been said that communists are simply socialists in a hurry. But there is more to the distinction between communism and socialism than patience. Like liberals, socialists worry that many important individual rights and freedoms would be quashed in a violent revolution. These rights and freedoms, once sacrificed to revolutionary zeal, might never be fully resuscitated. To safeguard individual liberties, socialists accept private property and tolerate certain social inequities.

For many contemporary socialists, the goal is less to overthrow liberalism than transform it through greater democratic participation and social equality. For instance, Ernesto Laclau and Chantal Mouffe, socialists of a postmodern temperament, maintain that "the task of the Left therefore cannot be to renounce liberal-democratic ideology, but on the contrary, to deepen and expand it in the direction of a radical and plural democracy."[68] Laclau and Mouffe seek to move "beyond the theoretical and political horizon of Marxism" in order to locate the socialist pursuit of economic equality within a struggle for deeper democracy. [69]

Likewise, Ralph Miliband suggests that the promotion and safeguarding of certain liberal rights goes hand in hand with greater social equality. Because economic life cannot be separated from political life, political equality can never be achieved or maintained in a capitalist state. Miliband writes that "Unequal economic power, on the scale and of the kind encountered in advanced capitalist societies, inherently *produces* political inequality, on a more or less commensurate scale, whatever the constitution may say." In capitalistic societies, therefore, civil and political liberties are often "a mere cloak for class domination."[70] Miliband acknowledges nonetheless that "the civic freedoms which, however inadequately and precariously, form part of bourgeois democracy are the product of centuries of unremitting popular struggles. The task of Marxist politics is to defend these freedoms; and to make possible their extension and enlargement by the removal of their class boundaries."[71] The question, then, is whether these class boundaries are to be removed by means of revolution or by the slower processes of democratically-based reform.

If the latter course is taken, then Miliband's neo-Marxism amounts to socialism. Indeed, it may even approach a highly egalitarian form of liberalism, as the struggle for greater social equality is grounded in an overarching concern for individual rights and well-being. Indeed, many liberal theorists endorse a "democratic welfare state" that has socialist attributes. Here the market is regulated "to reduce or ameliorate the socially adverse effects of essentially self-interested exchanges" while the state provides both free education and "a level of material well-being that is sufficient to enable [all] people to live at least minimally 'respectable' lives." These economic reforms are deemed necessary to provide the "means for everyone to attain full membership in society."[72] Economic equality is not the primary goal for liberals and socialists. Rather, meeting basic economic needs is a means toward realizing greater political equality.

At his best, Marx offers a sustained argument for increased human equality and a cogent explanation of why it has not yet been realized. At his worst, Marx plays into the hands of those who, under the guise of pursuing equality, destroy freedom, shackle individuality, and stifle difference. The totalitarian communist regimes of the twentieth century exemplified this threat, as absolute rulers presided over powerless subjects.

R.H. Tawney (1880–1962), a British historian and social theorist, offers one of the most incisive statements about equality and its limits:

> To criticize inequality and to desire equality is not, as is sometimes suggested, to cherish the romantic illusion that men are equal in character and intelligence. It is to hold that, while their natural endowments differ profoundly, it is the mark of a civilized society to aim at eliminating such inequalities as have their source, not in individual differences, but in its own organization, and that individual differences, which are a source of social energy, are more likely to ripen and find expression if social inequalities are, as far as practicable, diminished.[73]

Marx predicted a final resolution to the politics of class through the revolutionary creation of a communist society. But there are no final resolutions to the problems posed by collective human existence. To determine what diminishment of social inequalities is beneficial and practicable, our aspirations for justice must be translated into well-functioning institutions. In turn, we must navigate the politics of identity while safeguarding difference. These are not puzzles to be solved once and for all. They are perennial tasks.

## REFERENCES

1   Thomas Jefferson, *Thomas Jefferson on Democracy* (New York: Mentor, 1939), 13.
2   Craig Calhoun, "Social Theory and the Politics of Identity," in *Social Theory and the Politics of Identity*, ed. Craig Calhoun (Cambridge: Blackwell, 1994), 3.
3   W.E. Burghardt Du Bois, *The Souls of Black Folk* (Chicago: A.C. McClurg, 1909), 4, 59.
4   Quoted in Anthony Pagden, *European Encounters with the New World* (New Haven: Yale University Press, 1993), 19.
5   See *Journals and Other Documents on the Life and Voyages of Christopher Columbus*, trans. and ed. Samuel Eliot Morison (New York: Heritage Press, 1963).
6   Tzvetan Todorov, *The Conquest of America*, trans. Richard Howard (New York: Harper & Row, 1984), 3.
7   Christopher Columbus, *Journal of First Voyage to America* (New York: Albert and Charles Boni, 1924), 26, 36.
8   Quoted in Pagden, *European Encounters with the New World*, 20, 97.
9   See Bartolomé de Las Casas, *The Devastation of the Indies: A Brief Account*, trans. Herma Briffault (Baltimore: The Johns Hopkins University Press, 1992) and Bartolomé de Las Casas, *History of the Indies*, trans. Andrée Collard (New York: Harper and Row, 1971).
10  Wayne Moquin and Charles Van Doren, eds, *Great Documents in American Indian History* (New York: Praeger, 1973), 104–5.
11  Alexis de Tocqueville, *Democracy in America* (New York: Vintage Books, 1959), 349.
12  Russell Thornton, *American Indian Holocaust and Survival: A Population History since 1492* (Norman: University of Oklahoma Press, 1987), xv–xvi.

13  Cited in Wub-e-ke-niew, *We Have the Right to Exist: A Translation of Aboriginal Indigenous Thought* (New York: Black Thistle Press, 1995), 130.

14  Clark Wissler, *Indians of the United States*, rev. edn (New York: Doubleday, 1966). See also Daniel G. Payne, *Voices in the Wilderness: American Nature Writing and Environmental Ethics* (Hanover: University Press of New England, 1996).

15  Jefferson, *Thomas Jefferson on Democracy*, 106–7.

16  Quoted in Robert McHenry and Charles Van Doren, eds, *A Documentary History of Conservation in America* (New York: Praeger, 1972), 186.

17  Moquin and Van Doren, eds, *Great Documents in American Indian History*, 236–37.

18  See https://www.epi.org/publication/bp370-native-americans-jobs/

19  Marcel Griaule, quoted in Marimba Ani, *Yurugu: An African-Centered Critique of European Cultural Thought and Behavior* (Trenton: African World Press, 1994), 532.

20  J. Donald Moon, *Constructing Community: Moral Pluralism and Tragic Conflicts* (Princeton: Princeton University Press, 1993), 185.

21  John Dewey, *The Later Works of John Dewey, Volume 14* (Carbondale, IL: Southern Illinois University Press, 2008), 101.

22  Sheldon Wolin, "What Revolutionary Action Means Today," in Chantal Mouffe, ed., *Dimensions of Radical Democracy: Pluralism, Citizenship, Community* (London: Verson, 1992), 251–52.

23  Seyla Benhabib, *Situating the Self* (New York: Routledge, 1992), 71.

24  Alasdair MacIntyre, *A Short History of Ethics* (New York: Macmillan, 1966), 187.

25  Calhoun, "Social Theory and the Politics of Identity," 10.

26  John Dewey, *The Political Writings* (Indianapolis: Hackett, 1993), 136.

27  Kate Millett, *Sexual Politics* (Garden City, N.Y.: Doubleday, 1970).

28  Jean Bethke Elshtain, *Public Man, Private Woman: Women in Social and Political Thought*, 2nd edn (Princeton: Princeton University Press, 1993), 357–58.

29  See Peter Bachrach and Morton S. Baratz, "Two Faces of Power," *American Political Science Review* 56 (1962): 947–52.

30  Mary Wollstonecraft, *A Vindication of the Rights of Woman* (New York: A.J. Matsell, 1833), 50, 165, 214.

31  John Stuart Mill, *Three Essays* (Oxford: Oxford University Press, 1975), 451.

32  Quoted in Nancy McGlen and Karen O'Connor, *Women's Rights: The Struggle for Equality in the Nineteenth and Twentieth Centuries* (New York: Praeger, 1983), 1.

33  See Elizabeth Cady Stanton, Susan Anthony, and Matilda Gage, eds, *History of Woman Suffrage*, 3 vols. (Rochester: Charles Mann, 1881–91); and Susan Anthony and Ida Harper, eds, *History of Woman Suffrage*, vol. 4 (Indianapolis: Hollenbeck Press, 1902). See also Jean Bethke Elshtain, "Moral Woman and Immoral Man: A Consideration of the Public-Private Split and its Political Ramifications," *Politics and Society*, 4 (1974): 453–73.

34  See Nancy Hartsack, *Money, Sex, and Power: Toward a Feminist Historical Materialism* (Boston: Northeastern University Press, 1983). Jody Newman, "Perception and Reality: A Study Comparing the Success of Men and Women Candidates" (Executive Summary). National Women's Political Caucus, 1994. Claire Cain Miller, Kevin Quealy and Margot Sanger-Katz, "The Top Jobs Where Women Are Outnumbered by Men Named John," *New York Times*, April 24, 2018. Accessed April 2018 at https://www.nytimes.com/interactive/2018/04/24/upshot/women-and-men-named-john.html?nl=top-stories&nlid=71023177ries&ref=cta

35  Shulamith Firestone, *The Dialectic of Sex* (New York: Bantam Books, 1970), 198–99.

36  Mary Daly, *Gyn/Ecology: The Meta-Ethics of Radical Feminism* (Boston: Beacon Press, 1978), 39.

37  Carole Pateman, *The Sexual Contract* (Stanford: Stanford University Press, 1988), 231.

38  Carol Gilligan, *In a Different Voice: Psychological Theory and Women's Development* (Cambridge: Harvard University Press, 1982), 6.

39  See Seyla Benhabib, "The Generalized and the Concrete Other: The Kohlberg-Gilligan Controversy and Feminist Theory," in Seyla Benhabib and Drucilla Cornell, eds, *Feminism as Critique: On the Politics of Gender* (Minneapolis: University of Minnesota Press, 1987), 77–95.

40  Mary Belenky et al., *Women's Ways of Knowing: The Development of Self, Voice, and Mind* (New York: Basic Books, 1986).

41  Nancy Chodorow, *Feminism and Psychoanalytic Theory* (New Haven: Yale University Press, 1989), 44. See also Nancy Chodorow, *The Reproduction of Mothering: Psychoanalysis and the Sociology of Gender* (Berkeley: University of California Press, 1978); Dorothy Dinnerstein, *The Mermaid and the Minotaur* (New York: Harper Colophon, 1976).

42  Simone de Beauvoir, *The Second Sex* (New York: Vintage Press, 1973), 301.

43  See Alison Jaggar, *Feminist Politics and Human Nature* (Totowa, N.J.: Rowman and Allanheld, 1983).

44  Hester Eisenstein, *Contemporary Feminist Thought* (Boston: G. Hall, 1983), 132.

45  Mill, *Three Essays*, 451.

46  See Alison Jagger and Paula Rothenberg, *Feminist Frameworks: Alternative Theoretical Accounts of the Relations between Women and Men* (New York: McGraw-Hill, 1978).

47  Carole Pateman, *The Problem of Political Obligation: A Critique of Liberal Theory* (Cambridge, England: Polity Press, 1985), 189.

48  John Rawls, *A Theory of Justice* (Cambridge: Harvard University Press, 1971).

49  Myra Marx Ferree, "The Political Context of Rationality," in Aldon Morris and Carol McClurg Mueller, eds, *Frontiers of Social Movement Theory* (New Haven: Yale University Press, 1992), 36.

50  Owen Flanagan, *Varieties of Moral Personality: Ethics and Psychological Realism* (Cambridge: Harvard University Press, 1991), 225.

51  Susan Moller Okin, "Gender Inequality and Cultural Differences," *Political Theory* 22 (February 1994): 5–24.

52  Allison Pearson, "Feminism with a Friendly Face," *World Press Review* (February 1994): 38–39.

53  Wendy Brown, *States of Injury: Power and Freedom in Late Modernity* (Princeton: Princeton University Press, 1995).

54  Karl Marx, "Contribution to the Critique of Hegel's *Philosophy of Right*: Introduction," in Robert C. Tucker, ed. *The Marx-Engels Reader*, 2nd edn (New York: Norton, 1978), 54.

55  Marx, "Contribution to the Critique of Hegel's *Philosophy of Right*: Introduction."

56  Marx, "Contribution to the Critique of Hegel's *Philosophy of Right*: Introduction," 64.

57  Karl Marx and Friedrich Engels, "Manifesto of the Communist Party," in *The Marx-Engels Reader*, 484.

58  Marx, "The German Ideology," 160.

59  Karl Marx, "Critique of the Gotha Program," in *The Marx-Engels Reader*, 530–31.

60  Karl Marx, "The German Ideology," in *The Marx-Engels Reader*, 150.

61  Marx, "The German Ideology," 155.

62  Friedrich Engels, "Preface to the German Edition [of the Communist Manifesto] of 1883," in *The Marx-Engels Reader*, 472.

63  Michael Bakunin, *Bakunin on Anarchism*, ed. Sam Dolgoff (Montreal: Black Rose Books, 1980), 331.

64  Karl Marx, *Selected Writings*, ed. David McLellan (Oxford: Oxford University Press, 1977), 563.

65  Marx, "The German Ideology," 165.

66  Karl Marx, "Theses on Feuerbach," in *The Marx-Engels Reader*, 144.

67  See, for example, Michael Ryan, *Marxism and Deconstruction: A Critical Articulation* (Baltimore: Johns Hopkins University Press, 1982), and *Politics and Culture: Working Hypotheses for a Post-Revolutionary Society* (Baltimore: Johns Hopkins University Press, 1989).

68  Ernesto Laclau and Chantal Mouffe, *Hegemony and Socialist Strategy: Towards a Radical Democratic Politics* (London: Verso, 1985), 176.

69   Ernesto Laclau and Chantal Mouffe, "Post-Marxism without Apologies," *New Left Review* 166 (November/December 1987): 79–106.
70   Ralph Miliband, *The State in Capitalist Society* (New York: Basic Books, 1969), 265–66.
71   Ralph Miliband, *Marxism and Politics* (Oxford: Oxford University Press, 1977), 189–90.
72   J. Donald Moon, *Constructing Community: Moral Pluralism and Tragic Conflicts* (Princeton: Princeton University Press, 1993), 69–70.
73   R.H. Tawney, *Equality*, 4th edn (London: Unwin, 1964), 57.

## CHAPTER 5

# ENDURING CHALLENGES IN A CHANGING WORLD

Across the millennia, political theorists have expounded and contested the enduring ideals of liberty, reason and justice. This chapter investigates these crucial political concepts in the context of a changing world. It examines the exercise and limits of freedom in terms of the relationship of positive liberty to negative liberty; the differences between economic, political and ecological forms of reason and their worldly impacts; and the meaning of justice, the danger of its immoderate pursuit, and the challenge of employing practical judgment to discern what is equitable.

## THE LIFE OF LIBERTY

In the history of the Western world, few aspirations have fostered more philosophical meditations, social struggles, revolutions and wars than the quest for freedom. Patrick Henry gave voice to the American revolutionary sentiment with his famous declaration, "Give me liberty or give me death." For Henry, liberty made life worth living, and was worthy of the ultimate sacrifice. President John F. Kennedy concurred, announcing in his inaugural address: "Let every nation know, whether it wishes us well or ill, that we shall pay any price, bear any burden, meet any hardship, support any friend, oppose any foe to assure the survival and the success of liberty." In the modern world, freedom is primary value.

After surveying the origins and development of the Western philosophic tradition, Hegel concluded that "the history of the world is none other than the progress of the consciousness of freedom."[1] Likewise, the theorist of medieval thought, A.J. Carlyle, wrote "it seems evident that the history of civilization during the last two thousand years is primarily the history of the development of liberty."[2] Indeed, the pursuit of liberty goes back at least two and a half millennia, to the time when the Greeks first developed democracy—a political regime grounded in the principle of freedom.

The extensive dependence on slaves in ancient Greece made freedom doubly significant. Liberty became a palpable good for some and an unattainable ideal for others. Throughout history, liberty has been celebrated in uneasy tension with the oppression of those lacking the power to secure it. "At its best, the valorization of personal liberty is the noblest achievement of Western civilization," sociologist Orlando Patterson writes, adding: "at its worst, no value has been more evil and socially corrosive in its consequences, inducing selfishness, alienation, the celebration of greed, and the dehumanizing disregard for the 'losers,' the little people who fail to make it."[3] Is the championing of liberty always a testimonial to a double standard? And what limits, if any, should be placed on its pursuit?

Edmund Burke (1729–97), a conservative British political thinker, believed freedom to be "a blessing and a benefit" for the individual no less than for the community. Liberty, he states in his "Letter to the Sheriffs of Bristol," is "a good to be improved, and not an evil to be lessened. It is not only a private blessing of the first order, but the vital spring and energy of the state itself, which has just so much life and vigor as there is liberty in it." Yet liberty, Burke acknowledges, is dangerous if taken too far.

Burke warns that political values such as liberty are not like "propositions in geometry and metaphysics which admit no medium, but must be true or false in all their latitude." With the pursuit of liberty as in most political affairs, Burke observes, compromises are in order:

> The *extreme* of liberty (which is its abstract perfection, but its real fault) obtains nowhere, nor ought to obtain anywhere; because extremes, as we all know, in every point which relates either to our duties or satisfactions in life, are destructive both to virtue and enjoyment. Liberty, too, must be limited in order to be possessed.[4]

We are qualified to exercise liberty, Burke holds, in proportion to our disposition and capacity for its restraint.

In cautioning his British compatriots against the excesses of the French Revolution, Burke wrote that "the effect of liberty to individuals is that they may do what they please. We ought to see what it will please them to do before we risk congratulations." When the French revolutionaries emblazoned *Liberté* at the top of their banners, Burke feared that their passionate pursuit would not be sufficiently moderated to preserve collective welfare or to safeguard the basic rights of individuals. Burke was right. The revolution became quite murderous. Yet revolutionary zeal developed in response to monarchical excess. The French revolutionaries believed themselves to be following Jefferson's dictum of refreshing the tree of liberty with the blood of tyrants. The tyrants in question were King Louis XVI and the French aristocrats. The king of France and much of the nobility eventually paid for their despotic power and excessive privilege with their heads. The revolutionaries' unmoderated pursuit of liberty was a response to the deprivations suffered by the common people under a regime that, in an equally unmoderated fashion, had monopolized liberty for a king and his court.

The idea that liberty must be limited to be possessed is perhaps most easily illustrated by the issue of free speech. Freedom of speech is one of the most fundamental and most cherished liberties in modern democracies. Without freedom of speech, democracy could not exist. Yet even in the case of this fundamental liberty, some restrictions necessarily apply. Freedom of speech must be limited when it immediately harms others. As Justice Oliver Wendell Holmes argued in the 1919 case of *Shenck* v. *United States*, "the most stringent protection of free speech would not protect a man in falsely shouting 'fire' in a theater and causing a panic." Such an irresponsible exercise of free speech would create a "clear and present danger" to the lives of individuals who might become injured in the panicked scramble of theatergoers to vacate the premises. Freedom of speech is not a freedom to say anything to anyone at any time in any place.

What is said here of freedom of speech applies to other liberties. All require limits. Often those limits are enforced by law. As Montesquieu writes, "liberty is a right of doing whatever the laws permit, and if a citizen could do what they forbid he would be no longer possessed of liberty, because all his fellow-citizens would have the same power."[5] To define liberty as the right to do whatever one pleases heedless of law or its impact on others would have no feasible political application, as it would be a form of liberty impossible for people to share. "To be free one must become a slave to the law," Cicero insisted. "Where there is no law," John Locke concurred, "there is no freedom."[6] *Libertas* is achieved by *civitas*: freedom is gained by citizenship and the laws that bind citizens together. Political liberty is not freedom from law, but freedom through law.

Across the ages, political theorists, attentive to the restrictions on freedom that make it viable, have examined how much liberty is beneficial, and when, how, and where it should be limited. The problem is made particularly troublesome because the word liberty means different things to different people at different times. As Hegel observed, the concept of liberty is "indefinite, ambiguous, and open to the greatest misconceptions."[7] Indeed, historians of ideas have gathered hundreds of meanings for the words liberty and freedom. We will explore the two most prominent formulations, and note their implications for politics.

### Positive and Negative Liberty

In Western political thought, two distinct meanings of liberty have attained preeminence: positive liberty and negative liberty. Kant was perhaps the first to differentiate "positive" and "negative" senses of the word freedom in *The Metaphysics of Morals*. T.H. Green, a nineteenth-century British political theorist, popularized the distinction. Subsequently, the twentieth century British political theorist Isaiah Berlin revitalized discussion and brought the terms into the mainstream with his lecture "Two Concepts of Liberty."

Negative liberty is freedom from interference, coercion or confinement. Positive liberty is a form of empowerment, a freedom to do or achieve something. Berlin wished to distinguish positive liberty from negative liberty because he thought the former to be treacherous. Making clear distinctions between the two concepts, he hoped, would prevent their meanings from becoming conflated. When misunderstood and misused, Berlin warned, words like liberty and freedom may acquire an "unchecked momentum and an irresistible power over multitudes of men that may grow too violent to be affected by rational criticism."[8] Berlin, like Burke, was thinking about the relationship between the liberty advocated by Rousseau and the bloody events of the French Revolution carried out in his name. Berlin was also thinking about the liberty advocated by Marxists in the then still powerful empire of the Soviet Union. Berlin's criticism of positive liberty was meant to militate against such extremes. Negative liberty was less dangerous than positive liberty, Berlin believed. It also served as a corrective to the excesses of its counterpart.

By adopting the label *negative* for a form of liberty, Berlin does not mean to suggest that it is in any sense bad or injurious. Negative liberty refers to something pernicious that is prevented rather than to something beneficial that is achieved. One is negatively free if one is neither physically restricted nor violently coerced (say, at gunpoint) from speaking or acting. Negative liberty denotes an *absence* of constraint, an open space within which an individual may pursue his desires unhindered by the impositions of others.

Negative liberty signifies a realm over which the individual exercises complete jurisdiction. This private realm is shielded from all external interference, whether that of the church, state, or society. In this vein, John Stuart Mill, one of the foremost advocates of negative liberty, argues that individual freedom requires protection not only from the reach of monarchs and oligarchs but from democratic majorities as well. Freedom is threatened not only by the prerogatives of the few but by the power of the many.

In modern society, Mill worried, individual freedom was in danger of being undermined by coercive social mores. Employing the famous phrase of Alexis de Tocqueville, Mill wrote of the impingement of freedom caused by the "tyranny of the majority." Against this threat, Mill penned his famous essay *On Liberty*. Its purpose was to establish a

> very simple principle, as entitled to govern absolutely the dealings of society with the individual in the way of compulsion and control, whether the means used be physical force in the form of legal penalties or the moral coercion of public opinion. That principle is that the sole end for which mankind are warranted, individually or collectively, in interfering with the liberty of action of any of their number is self-protection. That the only purpose for which power can be rightfully exercised over any member of a civilized community, against his will, is to prevent harm to others. His own good, either physical or moral, is not a sufficient warrant.[9]

Mill's defense of negative liberty is grounded, as A.V. Dicey later suggested, on the notion that "every person is in the main and as a general rule the best judge of his own happiness. Hence legislation should aim at the removal of all those restrictions on the free action of an individual which are not necessary for securing the like freedom on the part of his neighbors."[10] The only justification for constraining an individual, for Mill, is that he is inflicting some harm or deprivation on another. In all other matters, freedom ought to prevail. Notably, Mill thought this principle applied only to "civilized" societies. He believed that compulsion might still be warranted and justified when advanced nations governed less developed ones. Here Mill was effectively justifying British rule over India. While ahead of his time in his defense of women's rights, Mill proved subject to common biases and mores regarding imperial prerogatives.

For Mill, liberty is evident whenever "over himself, over his own body and mind, the individual is sovereign."[11] Negative liberty generally includes an individual's rule not only over his body and mind, but also over his personal possessions. Negative libertarians often consider private property as an extension of the self. The argument for this claim was first made by John Locke in his "labor theory of property." Locke suggests that private property arose within a state of nature even before the formation of political society. Everything was originally held in common. Once effort was exerted by an individual to gather, hunt, cultivate, or appropriate land or the things that grow or are found on it, however, this land or these things became the property of the laboring individual. Property exists because individuals invest their labor into natural resources.

Through labor, Locke argues in his *Second Treatise of Government*, the self may effectively extend its sovereignty beyond the reach of its own limbs, establishing dominion over those resources which previously had been ownerless.[12] Following Locke, negative libertarians maintain that to be free means that no one may trespass on, appropriate, or otherwise interfere with one's body or property. Indeed, negative liberty, which Benjamin Constant called the "liberty of moderns," is identified with the right "to dispose of property, and even to abuse it."[13]

Positive liberty, in contrast, is not a freedom *from* but a freedom *to*. It signifies not the absence of interference but an enablement. To be positively free is to be empowered, to possess the means to achieve a good. The negative freedom to do something does not mean that one *can* do it. Monkeys supplied with paper and pen, for instance, are negatively free to write commentaries on Shakespeare's poetry. No one physically prevents their doing so. Pen-bearing monkeys are not positively free to engage in literary criticism, however, for they lack the intellectual means with which to accomplish the task. Likewise, a person is negatively free to repair an automobile if no one prevents his doing so. He is only positively free to repair an automobile if he has the knowledge, skill, and tools necessary to accomplish the task. Positive liberty requires more than the absence of constraint. It entails capacity.

To be positively free is to be capable of realizing one's will. Positive liberty entails pursuing a goal of one's own choosing or abiding by a law of one's own making. Obstacles to this self-direction or self-legislation may come from other people and the external world or from one's own intellectual, emotional, or psychological shortcomings. The acrophobic person (who is intensely fearful of heights) is not free to walk across a high bridge, even though no one bars his way. While he may truly want to walk across the bridge, his fear disempowers him. The freedom to cross high bridges is only truly gained once this debilitating fear is overcome.

For the negative libertarian, deciding whether freedom exists is a relatively straightforward affair. One simply observes if there are any physical constraints that prevent a person's speaking, acting, or enjoying his private property. In the absence of such constraints, people are free. For the positive libertarian, deciding whether freedom exists is more complex. First, the question of what is desired must be answered. Then, one must determine if the person is capable of fulfilling this desire. The problem is further complicated if one holds, as most positive libertarians do, that what someone says he needs or wants is not always what he *really* needs or wants.

Imagine a person who, under the pernicious control of a hypnotist, furiously rubs his eyes every time the word "freedom" is uttered. If asked why he is rubbing his eyes on such occasions, the person would respond, as per instructions given under trance, that his eyes itch and it feels good to rub them. Now if this person happens to attend a lecture on Berlin's two concepts of liberty, his eye-rubbing might become so intense as to cause physical injury. Clearly this would not be in his best interest. Is this person truly free in such circumstances? Negative libertarians would answer yes, as no one is physically constraining him. For the positive libertarian, the answer is clearly no, as the victim of hypnosis cannot keep from rubbing his eyes, and doing so is not in his best interests.

Suppose the cause of self-destructive action is not a hypnotist but an internal weakness. It is commonly said, for example, that people become slaves to their passions or slaves to alcohol, tobacco or other addictive drugs. The idea is that positive freedom can be lost because one loses self-control. In the *Republic*, Plato speaks of those who are ruled by, rather than rule over, their appetites and passions. Those who are ruled by their appetites and passions believe themselves to be free because they do whatever they please. Plato thinks them slaves because they do not know how to pursue their own best interests. Indeed, they do not know what their best interests really are. Rousseau, who had a more charitable opinion of natural impulses and passions than Plato, also held that one only truly achieves liberty by mastering oneself. The "mere impulse of appetite," Rousseau stipulates, "is slavery."[14] Likewise, Durkheim observed that "to be free is not to do what one pleases; it is to be master of oneself."[15]

The political relevance of the relationship between freedom and self-mastery is addressed by Karl Marx. For Marx, the most critical loss of freedom occurs not for the victim of his own appetites or addictions, but for the victim of ideology. An exploited worker who strongly supports the laws that protect private property and the accumulation of capital, Marx insists, is not truly free. Rather, he suffers from false consciousness. Effectively, he has been duped by ideological means to support a political and legal system that violates his interests. False consciousness is like a pernicious hypnotic trance. It causes the victim to partake of a system designed to exploit him. And like the libertines criticized by Plato, the victims of ideology are particularly resistant to liberation because they believe themselves already free.

### Forced to be Free

To be positively free one must face no external constraints or internal impediments that prevent the pursuit of one's best interests. Internal impediments may consist of beliefs, attitudes, values, predispositions, and deficiencies in aptitude. Examples of such impediments would be posthypnotic suggestions, irrational impulses, appetites, passions and phobias, weaknesses of character, false consciousness, ignorance, apathy, lack of knowledge or skill, and shortsighted judgment.

For the most part, positive libertarians are not interested in our freedom to fix cars, traverse high bridges, or escape malicious hypnotists. They are interested in politics. More specifically, they are interested in the freedom to exercise one's fair share of power. Negative liberty is primarily a private liberty grounded in individual rights. Positive liberty, in contrast, is fundamentally a public liberty. It is historically identified with civic virtue and popular self-rule, values that developed within the republican tradition, first in ancient Rome and subsequently in the city-states of the Italian Renaissance.

Negative liberty primarily pertains to the protection of citizens *from* government. Positive liberty pertains to the involvement of citizens *in* government. Positive liberty is a disposition for civic virtue coupled with the opportunity to put this disposition into practice by means of self-rule.

For positive libertarians, negative liberty is a necessary but not a sufficient condition for the exercise of political freedom. Jean-Jacques Rousseau, one of the early modern advocates of positive liberty, insists that freedom is only ever obtained when people take their collective lives into their own hands. As Rousseau states, "obedience to a law which we prescribe to ourselves is liberty."[16] Criticizing representative systems of government, Rousseau writes in *The Social Contract* that

> the people of England regards itself as free; but it is grossly mistaken; it is free only during the elections of members of parliament. As soon as they are elected, slavery overtakes it, and it is nothing. The use it makes of the short moments of liberty it enjoys shows indeed that it deserves to lose them.[17]

Freedom, Rousseau insists, is a form of sovereignty, and sovereignty cannot be represented. It must be exercised directly. Far from minding one's own business and staying at home, everyone in a truly free society "flies to the assemblies" to let his voice be heard and to take part in the legislative affairs of the commonwealth. Those who do not participate in making laws forgo the opportunity for self-legislation and hence the opportunity for freedom.

Rousseau, like Hobbes, posits a social contract that effectively politicizes a prior state of nature and puts an end to anarchy. For Rousseau, this social contract constitutes a real loss of freedom. He conceives the anarchical state of natural man—that is, man prior to the advent of private property and government—in much better terms than Hobbes. He criticizes Hobbes for equating the state of nature with a state of war. This equation is made possible, Rousseau states, because Hobbes projects onto natural man all the degenerate traits, such as the lust for power, that are developed in society. In the original state of nature, Rousseau insists, the instincts of primitive humans were largely benign. Consequently, their world remained mostly free of hostility. Only "civilized" man becomes prideful, acquisitive and power-hungry.

Primitive man, Rousseau states, had few worries and, except for purposes of mating, lived in isolation. He could be found "satisfying his hunger at the first oak, and slaking his thirst at the first brook; finding his bed at the foot of the tree which afforded him a repast; and, with that, all his wants supplied."[18] Not caring much about others, and not caring at all what others think of him, primitive man experiences freedom in the absence of external constraints and rests content with the satisfaction of a few basic needs. A stranger to envy or pride, he has no cause to covet his neighbors' goods and finds no quarrel with anyone he meets. The state of nature is a state of peace and liberty.

Civilization changes all that. The freedoms gained by entry into social life, that is, the freedom from fear of violent death and the freedom to own property, mark the end of a greater "natural liberty." Social life in general, and property relations specifically, entail a panoply of rules and regulations. "Man is born free; and everywhere he is in chains," Rousseau famously observes.[19] The newborn child, like the primitive in the state of nature, is unburdened by the legal restrictions and social mores that constrain the behavior of his civilized elders. But childhood freedom cannot last. Society necessarily burdens its members with rules that dictate much of what they can and cannot say, where they can and cannot go, how they can and cannot act.

Absolute negative liberty is impossible for social man. With the natural liberty of the primitive forever lost, Rousseau believes that social man must develop a worthy substitute, namely, positive liberty. To achieve positive liberty, however, one's integration in society must become more, not less, extensive. The alternatives for Rousseau were stark and clear. "The source of human misery is the contradiction between man and citizen," he writes. "Give him wholly to the state or to himself . . . if you divide his heart you tear him apart."[20] Having developed the egoism endemic to social life, what Rousseau called *amour-propre*, man can never again be given wholly to himself. Rousseau proposes that we therefore give ourselves wholly to the state, transforming our individual egoism into a collective egoism. Ideally, *amour de la patrie*, love of one's country, would replace *amour-propre*, or prideful self-love, and all the envy and greed that accompanies it. Rousseau urges us to cultivate positive liberty within a highly politicized and unified society. To forgo this opportunity by not participating in the democratic process, he warns, leaves us with no freedom whatsoever.

The prospects for this transformation, Rousseau laments, are not very good. The negative liberty exercised in society has largely been reduced to the freedom to own and amass property and wealth. If positive, political liberty is to redeem this sordid state, it must first turn self-interested, economically egoistic individuals into a community of patriots who experience their greatest freedom and fulfillment when acting for the common good. Positive liberty is manifest in the desire and ability to adopt the interests of society, expressed as the "general will" of the people, as one's own. Rousseau famously states that we may justly be compelled to abide by the general will, in which case we are effectively "forced to be free."

Having the capacity for and engaging in self-rule is a good thing. It seems obvious, for instance, that the acrophobic person who cannot get himself to walk over high bridges is not as free or fortunate as someone who does not bear the burden of an obsessive fear of heights. The problem arises when we examine positive liberty in social and political life, where conflicting interests and ideas frequently prevent consensus. Historically, Berlin notes, positive libertarians have assumed that the selves being ruled in the public realm are identical in their interests, desires, and needs, with catastrophic results. The quest for positive liberty, Berlin observes, has often led to a "prescribed form of life" that often served as "a specious disguise for brutal tyranny."[21]

### Freedom in the Balance

In 1958, when Berlin lectured on the two concepts of liberty, he was concerned with the actual and potential abuses of positive liberty. At that time, he observed, the view of those who reject negative liberty and favor its positive counterpart "rules over half our world."[22] He was thinking about the Soviet empire and "the great clash of ideologies" that dominated his time. In the communist world, behind the "iron curtain," negative liberty and personal freedom was trampled underfoot in the ostensible effort to secure positive liberty for citizens. Political leaders whose power was largely unchecked determined what citizens' true interests were, and how they would collectively be pursued.

In contrast, negative libertarians maintain that participation in politics is less an end in itself than the only tried-and-true means of protecting negative liberties. Samuel Johnson advocated this position in its starkest form, claiming that "political liberty is good only so far as it produces private liberty."[23] John Locke held a similar view.[24]

Democratic participation, by this account, simply serves the goal of ensuring that despots who would threaten private liberties do not come to power. To extend Thomas Jefferson's famous adage, the tree of liberty must occasionally be fertilized with the blood of tyrants and patriots, and continuously watered with the sweat of active citizens.

History has effectively rechanneled many of the Marxist yearnings for positive liberty, and swept away their institutional perversions. At the same time, the pursuit of positive liberty remains very much alive, chiefly manifested in efforts to develop more participatory democracies. It animates, as well, the work of "communitarian" political theorists. Communitarians seek to balance individual rights and liberties with the sense of ethical and political responsibility that individuals and groups (such as families) can cultivate to strengthen the moral fiber of society and sustain community.[25] Communitarians argue that justice cannot be served if the pursuit of individual freedom is not balanced with the pursuit of equity.

Consider the fact that poverty has a deleterious effect on intellectual and emotional development. Lower IQs and greater fear and anxiety are evident in children who chronically or even occasionally live in poverty.[26] Poverty and lack of education also correlate with lower levels of integration and participation in the political system. Equality under the law, as we earlier observed, does not always translate into equality of opportunity. Although the rules of the game may be the same for all, a political system grounded solely in negative liberty is unlikely to create a level playing field. If history is any guide, the children of the disadvantaged will face a markedly uphill climb during their own life journeys.[27]

Positive libertarians need not advocate social and political programs as radical as those of Rousseau or Marx. They may hold positive liberty to be one among many goods, including negative liberty, that ought to be realized. In turn, many positive libertarians insist that other goods much prized by negative libertarians, such as civil rights, need not be sacrificed. Indeed, we can fully take advantage of our individual political rights—our right to free speech or freedom of association and assembly, for example—only once we have sufficiently developed and expressed our capacity for political participation. Advocating the increased citizen activity of a "strong democracy," Benjamin Barber writes: "To be free we must be self-governing; to have rights we must be citizens. In the end, only citizens can be free. The argument for strong democracy, though at times deeply critical of liberalism, is thus an argument on behalf of liberty."[28] Positive liberty, in this instance, is both an end in itself and a means by which negative liberties may become more fully realized and more vigilantly protected.

Likewise, negative libertarians appreciate a diversity of goods. Achieving some of these goods, such as justice, may require a diminution of (negative) liberty. Still, negative libertarians want to make clear conceptual distinctions between liberty and other goods. Once these distinctions are made, one may better judge which goods are to be realized at the (partial) expense of others. To underline this point, Berlin observes that we force children to go to school. In so doing, we constrain their negative liberty to elevate another value, namely, the growth of knowledge and the diminution of ignorance. Berlin believes we should acknowledge and accept this sacrifice of liberty.

A society grounded solely on negative liberty would be a pretty harsh place. The negative liberty to go one's own way under one's own steam also entails the danger of falling between the cracks and being left behind. In the jungle, the fate of those less fortunate or less favored is sealed. They become lunch for the strong. In society, most believe that those who stumble and fall deserve aid. In turn, equality of opportunity is a worthy goal. For Berlin, positive liberty *is* a good, but a dangerous one when taken to extremes. He writes:

> The only reason for which I have been suspected of defending negative liberty against positive and saying that it is more civilized is that I do think that the concept of positive liberty, which is of course essential to a decent existence, has been more often abused or perverted than that of negative liberty. . . . Certainly the weak must be protected against the strong. . . . Negative liberty must be curtailed if positive liberty is to be sufficiently realized; there must be a balance between the two.[29]

Absent this balance, only the very powerful would have the wherewithal to make use of their liberty. There would be freedom to accumulate wealth but no freedom from poverty. There would be freedom to pursue power but no freedom from domination. Negative liberty, like positive liberty, is certainly not immune to abuse. A balanced pursuit of positive liberty and negative liberty mitigates the susceptibility of each to excess.

## RULE WITHIN REASON

Plato defined law as the embodiment of reason. Like Plato, Aristotle believed that reason should legislate the appetites and passions of the soul just as it should legislate the citizens of the polis. Unlike Plato, Aristotle believed that reason was exercised not only by philosophers but by a wide range of the citizenry.

Aristotle acknowledged that the best possible regime would be a monarchy (or aristocracy) in which the philosopher king(s) ruled supreme. This would also be a very precarious regime, however, unlikely to arise and easily corrupted once established. The best practicable regime, both easier to achieve and more stable once in place, Aristotle called a polity. A polity is a mixed regime that incorporates both aristocratic and democratic principles. Here citizens learn to rule and be ruled in turn. In the polity, a large segment of the population actively exercises reason in the day-to-day affairs of managing the ship of state. Upholding the prejudices of his day, however, Aristotle maintained that women and slaves should be excluded from politics along with children because they were naturally deficient in reason.

At the onset of modernity, systems of authority and tradition—religious, monarchical and aristocratic in nature—began to crumble. Reason was no longer assumed to be a faculty of the privileged few. Extolling Enlightenment values, Kant argued that humankind's maturity and progress depended upon the "freedom to make public use of one's reason in all matters."[30] The language of reason became the *lingua franca*, the vernacular of an increasingly scientific and secular age.

The political preeminence of reason has continued to this day. "If we had to choose a single normative standard for the understanding and evaluation of liberal democratic political systems," Thomas Spragens observes, "the one that would get the farthest would be neither liberty, nor fairness, nor neutrality, nor utility, nor pluralist bargaining, but instead would be the ideal of rational practice."[31] What makes for good public policy, morality, and law within the modern state, Stephen Macedo writes, is its grounding in reason, which is to say its "capacity to gain widespread agreement among reasonable people moved by a desire for reasonable consensus."[32] In modern times, reason rules.

What, then, is this thing called reason? Its meaning is hotly debated. Feminists challenge the universal claims of "masculine rationality" in an effort to establish the groundwork for the "situated knowledge" of a "feminist rationality."[33] African-centered theorists challenge Western forms of rationality that attempt to "explain all of reality as though it had been created by the European mind for the purposes of control."[34] Western theorists equally wary of the identification of reason with the instrumental pursuit of self-interest, endorse a "communicative rationality" that promotes social change and political community through free, competent and informed dialogue conducted in the absence of deceit, strategizing, self-deception and domination.[35] And other theorists doubt whether reason can or should aspire to such lofty goals, maintaining that "the opposition between rationality and irrationality is simply the opposition between words and blows."[36] The meanings of reason are myriad, and there is no end in sight to their contestation.

Foucault set himself the task of investigating reason, asking: "What are its historical effects? What are its limits, and what are its dangers? How can we exist as rational beings, fortunately committed to practicing a rationality that is unfortunately crisscrossed by intrinsic dangers."[37] Attentive to historical effects, limits and dangers, three prominent conceptions of reason are examined below. We start by exploring economic rationality, which is widely considered "the dominant form of reason in contemporary industrial society—and, arguably, the defining feature of those societies."[38] In turn, we examine how economic reason is contested by advocates of political reason and ecological reason.

## Economic Reason

Max Weber's chief concern was the investigation of "rationalism" in the Western world.[39] Yet he refused to give reason or rationality a single definition. Over a dozen distinct meanings for the terms have been charted in his writings.[40] Weber writes that "a thing is never irrational in itself, but only from a particular rational point of view."[41] Likewise, a thing is never rational in itself. The meaning of rationality is contextual.

Despite the multiple forms that modern rationality assumes in different historical and cultural settings, Weber suggests they all share a unifying essence. The process of rationalization, Weber writes, is always a function of the "striving for order."[42] To rationalize is to seek control. Rationality constitutes an attempt to gain either a "theoretical mastery of reality" or a "practical mastery of the world."[43]

Rationality systematizes and routinizes, putting the unpredictable or chaotic into order. Weber was intrigued by the capacity of religion to systematize and routinize. He argued that Calvinism, a form of Protestantism developed by the French (and later Swiss) theologian John Calvin (1509-64), marks the apogee of religious rationalization. Calvinists believe in predestination, the idea that God decides for each man and woman, even before birth, whether he or she will go to heaven or hell. What an individual does in life can neither win salvation nor ensure damnation. Only the hand of the Almighty can tip the scales. Salvation is attained by the grace of God. What one does in earthly life—the performance of rituals, the offering of sacraments, or the doing of good deeds—cannot alter one's fate.

Calvinists originally adopted the doctrine of predestination because they thought it prideful for a person to believe eternal salvation could be gained by personal effort, effectively tying God's hands. Ironically, the Calvinists' belief in predestination did not lead to fatalism or passivity. If a person was "chosen" for salvation, Calvinists maintained, he would give evidence of this enviable status by way of his devotion. He could not help but display his "calling." Of course, no one *really* knew who was chosen for salvation. But this uncertainty only strengthened the Calvinists' resolve. In the effort to prove to themselves, and others, that they were among the chosen few, Weber theorized, Calvinists embraced a strict life of duty. They fervently devoted themselves to a vocation so they were never left idle. Were a person truly among the chosen few, he would always be occupied doing good deeds. Even brief periods of idleness would suggest that one was not predestined for a heavenly afterlife, or at least it would give one pause to consider the horrific possibility.

For the Calvinists, Weber writes, good works became "technical means, not of purchasing salvation, but of getting rid of the fear of damnation."[44] Devotion to work was a way of convincing oneself and others that personal salvation had been secured. The key was always to remain in full control of one's time and actions. The enemy of this religious rationalism was not so much the *enjoyment* of life as its *spontaneity*. For impulsiveness, not pleasure per se, suggests a life untethered to the mandate of duty. Calvinism turned "with all its force against one thing: the spontaneous enjoyment of life and all it had to offer."[45] The Protestant ethic, Weber argued, developed out of a need to display a steadfast and calculated devotion to duty.

The great irony is that an attempt to heighten religious devotion produced an increasingly secular work ethic. The deprecation of spontaneity and the celebration of duty led to a preoccupation with work for its own sake, which was quickly translated into a preoccupation with the accumulation of wealth, regardless of the pleasures it could afford. This preoccupation, Weber suggests, was the impetus for capital accumulation.

Weber's thesis has been criticized by historians who point out that capitalism began to develop centuries before the Protestant Reformation occurred. The fact that capitalism also developed in non-Protestant countries, such as Italy, further undermines Weber's thesis.[46] Despite its historical and cultural inaccuracies, Weber's work is much celebrated for its originality and tantalizing twists of logic.

Weber rightly rejected the notion that the vast diversity of modern individuals could somehow be described as having a unitary "group mind" that operated in accordance with "a single formula."[47] Nonetheless, he maintained that economic rationality was indeed a predominant feature of modern life. Indeed, Weber believed the world was becoming increasingly rationalized. The pursuit of mastery—the efficient control of both the natural and social world—was experienced as the exercise of reason.

Adopting this Weberian understanding, certain social scientists propose that all human thought and behavior, to the extent that it is 'rational,' is amenable to economic analysis. Rationality allows one to secure the best means to given ends by systematically measuring the costs and benefits of available options. Social science becomes a matter of explaining the decisions and choices people make in the rational effort to minimize costs and maximize benefits.[48] From this point of view, any thought or behavior that is rational may be reduced to an economic calculation.

To analyze behavior in terms of economic rationality is not to assume that everyone always acts selfishly or attempts to accumulate wealth. As Weber demonstrated, economic rationality arose in the service of God, not mammon. Likewise, contemporary theories of economic rationality are not built on the assumption that all actors are driven by narrow self-interest. The goals of the economically rational person need not be egoistic, venal, or even financially oriented. The economic actor, as Anthony Downs writes, is simply interested in "maximizing output for a given input, or minimizing input for a given output."[49] The ends served by the "cost–benefit" analyses may be egoistic, altruistic or a mix of both. Rather than assume individuals to be selfish, theorists of economic rationality assume they behave in ways that are "wholly determined by the endeavor to relate means to ends as efficiently as possible."[50] Not *selfishness* but *efficiency* is the key feature of a rational action.

The rational actor's effort to relate means to ends efficiently is often neither easy nor completely successful owing to the complexities and confusions of life. Herbert Simon, an organizational theorist, introduced the notion of "bounded rationality." The rational actor seldom if ever selects the most efficient means to achieve given ends. Instead, he selects those means found satisfactory given his cognitive limitations, the availability of information, and the constraints placed on his time and resources. The rational actor is engaged not in maximizing but in "satisficing" values, that is to say, in achieving satisfactory rather than optimal results. The rational actor satisfices, Simon bluntly states, because he does not have "the wits to maximize."[51] Likewise, Anthony Downs considers an actor to be rational not because he always achieves his goals with the least expenditure of effort, but because he "moves toward his goals in a way which, *to the best of his knowledge*, uses the least possible input of scarce resources per unit of valued output."[52]

The "glory" and "power" of economic rationalist theory is its parsimony, its "ability to imply a great range of testable hypotheses from few assumptions."[53] But this parsimony declines notably once the boundedness of its actors' rationality is taken into account. Simon insists that there is no alternative to sacrificing some parsimony to better grasp actual human behavior in a complex world.[54] James March, who collaborated with Simon, goes beyond exposing the cognitive limitations of the rational actor.[55] The rational actor not only frequently fails to employ the most efficient means; he also fails to pursue stable goals. Actors, March observes, may exhibit an "ambiguity of preferences."[56] If preferences or goals are ambiguous or unstable, then efficiency in attaining them is impossible. The most direct route cannot be chosen if the destination remains unknown. This brings us to the concept of political reason.

## Political Reason

The unstable nature of preferences or goals is particularly notable in political life. Politics is an activity that goes well beyond the efficient pursuit of preconceived individual interests. It involves the shaping and reshaping of interests and the formation and transformation of identities. Political life makes us as much as we make it. Our life experiences (what we do in life and what is done to us by life) heavily influences what values and commitments we hold. Behavior shapes attitudes and interests. Often we cannot efficiently pursue our goals through instrumental action because our goals only become formulated in the midst of taking action.

"The preferences of citizens vary not only or even mainly with the amount of information they receive and absorb, but also with how they receive and absorb it—including how their preferences are influenced by participating in politics," Amy Gutmann and Dennis Thompson observe. "Aggregating what citizens want individually . . . does not necessarily produce the same result as asking citizens to consider together what they want collectively."[57] Political participation shapes preferences and goals. Political reason involves the formation of preferences, goals and values not simply their efficient pursuit.

Modern economic rationality is instrumental. It stands in marked contrast to classical (Platonic and Aristotelian) and medieval (scholastic) understandings of substantive reason. Substantive reason is not restricted to devising efficient means to serve given ends. Substantive reason determines what the ends of action ought to be. Plato, we remember, held that reason should rule over the passions, determining what the nature of the good life was and setting us on its path. Here reason determines the *goals* of life as well as the *means* to secure them. The rise of economic rationality in the modern era left reason only the latter, instrumental task.

David Hume (1711–76), the Scottish philosopher, famously reversed Plato. Hume writes in his *Treatise of Human Nature* that "reason is, and ought only to be, the slave of the passions, and can never pretend to any other office than to serve and obey them."[58] Following Hume, Bertrand Russell insisted that "reason has a perfectly clear and precise meaning. It signifies the choice of the right means to an end that you wish to achieve. It has nothing whatever to do with the choice of ends."[59] Herbert Simon, in developing his theory of bounded rationality, accepted this understanding. He maintains that "reason is wholly instrumental. It cannot tell us where to go; at best it can tell us how to get there. It is a gun for hire that can be employed in the service of any goals we have, good or bad."[60] Plato, Aristotle and the medieval scholastics acknowledged that reason had an instrumental function. Unlike many modern theorists, however, the ancients did not think that instrumental rationality was the only form of rationality or even the most important form.

Jean-Pierre Vernant, a classical scholar, writes that "when Aristotle defined man as a 'political animal,' he emphasized what differentiates Greek reason from today's reason. If in his eyes *Homo sapiens* was *Homo politicus*, it was because Reason itself was in essence political."[61] The *polis* or city-state, Aristotle writes, originally arose as a means of satisfying basic human needs, such as the provision of food, shelter and safety, needs that are only possible, or at least easier, to secure in a community. Nevertheless, the *polis* exists, Aristotle reminds us, not simply to make life possible but to make the *good* life possible. The good life, for Aristotle, is an active life of reason.

The ancient Greek philosopher and biographer Plutarch (A.D. 46–120) wrote that

> they are wrong who think that politics is like an ocean voyage or a military campaign, something to be done with some end in view, something which levels off as soon as that end is reached. It is not a public chore to be got over with; it is a way of life.[62]

Politics, for the ancients, is not simply an instrumental endeavor. It is a practice that allows for the exercise of reason and other virtues.[63] Reason is a virtue, for Aristotle, and like other virtues constitutes its own reward.

There is a difference, for Aristotle, between a craftsperson who *makes* something and a citizen who *does* something. *Poiesis*, or craft production, is not the same as *praxis*, or political action. Aristotle stipulates that "doing and making are different in kind, since the maker of a thing has a different end in view than just making it, whereas in doing something the end can only be the doing of it well."[64] Like a participant in a dialogue, the political actor involves himself with others in the cooperative determination of a course of action and a destination through the exercise of reason.[65] Jürgen Habermas maintains that rationality in political life is achieved by "removing restrictions on communication" so that all may participate in "public, unrestricted discussion, free from domination."[66] This political communication is at one and the same time an instrumental means of achieving ends, a means of determining the substance of these ends, and an end in itself, that is to say, an intrinsic aspect of the good life. *Praxis* is performative rather than merely instrumental. It is a self-fulfilling activity that incorporates reason into the world.

Following in the footsteps of Anthony Downs and Joseph Schumpeter, many theorists of economic rationality assume that politics is best described as the aggregate effects of instrumental voting and office seeking.[67] Votes are analogous to dollars that citizens spend efficiently to reap the biggest electoral rewards. Politics is reduced to a marketplace where rational buyers (voters) and sellers (candidates) strike their bargains. The elegance of this economic theory of politics is appealing. It may serve admirably as a tool for analysis. But economic rationalist theory ignores the performative aspect of politics and the substantive aspect of rationality.

An analogy may clarify the point. Cats will patiently wait for hours in front of mouse holes, ostensibly having decided that the chance of satiating their hunger with a capture justifies the time invested in motionless loitering. After observing this phenomenon for some time and charting these observations, one might construct an elegant theory that illustrates the respective value cats place on their time and the satiation of their appetites. One could then predict how long cats will wait in front of a mouse hole before moving on, employing a cost-benefit analysis that accounts for the relative scarcity of mice, mouse holes, and hours in a day. Yet any such theory would distort the nature of cats and the activity of mouse hunting. Cats value the stalking of prey regardless of its value as food. Placed in a room teeming with mice, cats will initially kill and eat their fill. Then they will kill a few more but forgo their consumption. Finally, they will spend their time stalking mice across the room while ignoring those that scamper over their forepaws.[68]

The point is not that people are genetically programmed to engage in politics for its own sake, as cats are presumably programmed to engage in stalking and hunting. Still, politics cannot be reduced to instrumental pursuits. Albert O. Hirschman's likening of public action to a pilgrimage is illuminating in this regard:

> The implication of the confusion between striving and attaining is that the neat distinction between costs and benefits of action in the public interest vanishes, since striving, which should be entered on the cost side, turns out to be part of the benefit.... The best illustration is perhaps the phenomenon of *pilgrimage*.... Obviously, it would make no sense to categorize the travel as the cost of the pilgrimage, and the sojourn and prayers at the holy site as benefit. The discomforts suffered and perils confronted during the trip were part and parcel of the

total "liminal" experience sought by the pilgrim, and the distance from the site often acted as a stimulant to the decision to go forth rather than as a brake.[69]

Hirschman's point is that political action is not reducible to economic analysis. Crucial to politics is the lived experience of reasoning together and its capacity for value and identity formation and transformation. The instrumental pursuit of self-interest is an intrinsic part of political life because it is an intrinsic part of human nature. Humans, like all other animals, systematically seek their own welfare. But the instrumental pursuit of self-interest is not the whole of politics. Political life entails the self-fulfilling exercise of reasoning together.

### Ecological Reason

Environmental issues consistently rank near the top of people's concerns and a "strong environmental ethic" is evident within the public at large. Nonetheless, opposition to specific efforts to protect the environment arise when such measures involve "personal sacrifice" or specific costs to the individual. Theorists of economic rationality explain that public environmental goods, such as clean air or water, are "nonexcludable." People will accrue the benefits of a healthier environment regardless of whether they personally make a contribution to its protection. Faced with this fact, economically rational actors will opt to "free ride" on the efforts of others. The general attitude is that "someone else should bear the burden."[70]

Letting someone else bear the burden is rational from an economic perspective. It allows one to gain benefits at no cost. As such, it constitutes the height of economic rationality. Competition within the marketplace ensures that those who behave in an economically rational manner will succeed and those who are less efficient, eventually, will fail.[71] The conclusion follows that economic survival depends on shunning personal responsibility for environmental care.

Environmental theorists observe that modern society in general and American society specifically "was conceived, born, and bred on the principles of economic rationality."[72] Yet they strongly disagree with the assumption that self-interested economic behavior is always rational. They insist that our ecological viability and survival as a species rests squarely on our escaping narrowly conceived self-interest and the rationality that serves it.

In addressing the root causes of our environmental woes, Al Gore laments that "the future whispers while the present shouts."[73] With similar concerns, Robert Heilbroner speaks of the "inverted telescope through which humanity looks to the future."[74] The metaphors are apt. The impression the future makes on us is faint. Indeed, under the guidance of economic rationality we would maximize our pleasures and profits today and let tomorrow take care of itself. In the language of economics, the future becomes "discounted." The farther something is in the future, the more it is discounted, the weaker its whisper.

Discounting the future is good economics. But it is bad ecology. If the goods and services we consume today are cheap because there is no account taken for the environmental harms caused by their production, delivery and disposal, then our present savings are effectively gained at the expense of future generations whose resources will be depleted and natural environment degraded. The so-called invisible hand that the Scottish classical economist Adam Smith (1723–90) said was guiding the free market decidedly lacks a green thumb. Freedom in today's market often commits future generations to paying ecological reparations. As Theodore Roszak observes: "Our habit has been to regard the future as the carpet under which environmental degradation gets swept. It is called 'externalizing' the costs, meaning writing them off to our children's, children's, children's. . . . Out of sight, out of mind."[75] Environmental theorists reject rationality that legitimates securing present benefits at the expense of future generations. A popular environmental slogan stipulates that "We have not inherited the earth from our parents, we borrow it from our children." Implicit in these words is a form of rationality animated by a future focus.

Those who deny the severity of the ecological crisis have charged that "much of the modern environmental movement is a broad-based assault on reason."[76] Yet environmentalists do not so much denigrate reason as challenge the hegemony of a specific form of reason. Environmental theorist David Orr writes that "a humane version of sustainability will [not] come about solely as the result of 'economically rational' behavior. It will only come about as the result of a higher and more thorough rationality."[77] John Dryzek sketches out the features of a higher and more thorough ecological rationality grounded in sustainable practices. He argues that "The pursuit of all . . . values is predicated upon the avoidance of ecological catastrophe. Hence the preservation and promotion of the integrity of the ecological and material underpinning of society—ecological rationality—should take priority over competing forms of reason in collective choices with an impact upon that integrity."[78] Ecological rationality, Dryzek argues, has priority because it is sustainable.

Individuals may accrue economic benefits at a relatively low price by fobbing off environmental costs on those living "downstream." Regardless of whether people live downstream in time and downstream in space, environmental theorists argue, they should not have to pay the costs for the benefits we receive. They reject any concept of rationality that pertains only or primarily to securing individual interests at the expense of future generations or neighbors. And as there is but one earth shared by all, neighbors may live on the other side of the globe.

A global orientation logically complements a future focus, as the justification for the rights of future generations is difficult to separate from the justification for the rights of those who live beyond national borders.[79] Once we acknowledge an obligation to those incapable of actively representing their ecological interests for temporal reasons (i.e., they will live in the future), we are hard pressed to justify excluding from consideration those who are incapable of actively representing their ecological interests for

158

geographical reasons (i.e., they live in another country). In both instances, obligations exist to preserve the environment for people who do not have the present capacity to demand that we live more sustainably.

With an orientation toward sustainability, environmental theorists emphasize the interdependence of interests across generations and across the globe. Climate change provides the most striking example. The environmental benefits we seek for ourselves, or for our compatriots and progeny, are becoming increasingly difficult to accrue without also ensuring global environmental protection. One country's effort to restrict its production of greenhouse gases will not secure the health and welfare of its citizens if other countries are not similarly committed. Ensuring a healthy environment within national borders increasingly entails the extension of ecological care and the promotion of ecological mores beyond national borders.

Lester Milbrath observes that "a central axiom of environmentalism is, 'We can never do merely one thing. We must learn to ask, for every action, And then what?'"[80] The question "And then what?" pertains to the effects of our actions on those who are distant in time and space. The geographically nonlocalizable nature of many environmental problems (e.g. climate change) and the temporally nonlocalizable nature of other environmental concerns (e.g. the depletion of biological diversity, as the extinction of a species robs all future generations of that species) have spatially and temporally expanded our political obligations.

One of the "flaws in mainstream economics," David Orr writes, is that "it lacks an ecologically and morally defensible model of the 'reasonable person,' helping to create the behavior it purports only to describe."[81] If we reduce all human action to the product of instrumental economic calculations, we are both misrepresenting reality and stifling the development of more sustainable ways of thinking and acting.

Environmental theorists argue that reason, a core political concept, must become transformed to account for our changing relationship to space and time. Rationality must become increasingly farsighted and foresighted to adequately reflect the interdependencies of contemporary life.

R.H. Tawney once observed that economic ambitions may be good servants, but they make very bad masters. One might say the same thing about economic rationality. It may serve our purposes admirably, when our purposes are well known and narrowly defined. Yet it cannot sustain political community and global welfare on an ecologically precarious planet. There is much at stake. The future of civilization may depend on our understanding and exercise of reason.

## THE SCALES OF JUSTICE

Justice always has been and remains today a central concern of political thought. It is a paramount political virtue and defining feature of political community. But what is the nature of justice? How is it achieved? And can the too-forceful pursuit of this virtue transform it into a vice?

## The Primacy of Justice

Plato's *Republic* is the *locus classicus* of the theoretical effort to comprehend justice as a social order and virtue. Plato believed that the justice displayed in well-ordered societies reflected the virtue of justice in well-ordered souls. It is always in one's interest to be just, Plato insists. No real harm can come to the just person, or at least no harm greater than that suffered by acting unjustly. To act unjustly is to pitch one's soul into disarray. The pursuit of justice, therefore, trumps all other concerns.

Aristotle follows Plato in giving justice no lesser task than producing happiness for the political community. Justice is the good for which the state aims. For Aristotle, as for his mentor, justice is a "complete" and "perfect" virtue. Indeed, it is held to be "the whole of virtue." [82] With justice, Aristotle maintains, humans are the best of all animals. Without justice, they are the worst.

In ancient Rome, justice remained a central concern of political thought. The most important thing for theorists and philosophers to understand, Cicero insists, is that human beings are born for justice. Of all the obligations assumed by political leaders, he states, the most important is to provide justice. The centrality of justice for theorists and philosophers was further underlined during the decline of the Roman Empire. "Remove justice," Augustine writes having observed the sack of Rome by the Goths, "and what are kingdoms but gangs of criminals on a large scale."[83] Justice is the defining feature of civilization.

In medieval times, Thomas Aquinas maintained the classical understanding that justice was the foremost moral virtue and the keystone of social order. This valorization of justice was carried into modernity. David Hume argued that historically it was not uncommon for collective life to arise and persevere in the absence of formal government. Justice, however, was indispensable: "though it be possible for men to maintain a small uncultivated society without government, it is impossible they should maintain a society of any kind without justice."[84] Justice, for Hume, is the *sine qua non* of collective human existence.

"Let justice be done though the earth perish," (*fiat justitia et pereat mundus*) is the ancient Roman admonition that underlines the unique status of justice. Indeed, there are few other ideals, if any, for which people have been as willing to forgo so many earthly goods. It has been observed that "No other value than justice can legitimize the intentional sacrifice of all other human ends and values, including liberty and human life."[85] Though liberty, particularly in modern times, has been celebrated as a supreme value, justice remains the ultimate, if not the most immediate political good. In the late eighteenth century, with intent to ensure the healthy birth and infancy of a nation,

James Madison announced that "Justice is the end of government. It is the end of civil society. It ever has been and ever will be pursued until it be obtained, or until liberty be lost in its pursuit."[86] In the struggle for justice, life and liberty may well be sacrificed to a greater end.

In practice, relatively few people prove eager to sacrifice life and liberty, let alone allow the earth to perish, for the sake of justice. The cause of justice is often overwhelmed by the mundane pursuit of self-interest and security. Yet self-sacrificial struggles for justice offer an inspiring—if sporadic—testimony to the enduring power of this ideal. Less heroic but perhaps no less significant quests for justice pervade social and political life. People often make decisions and choices contrary to their (economic) self-interest in deference to the demands of justice. Empirical experiments demonstrate that most people allocate resources in ways that they consider fair, such that each receives what he or she is believed to deserve. Even when self-serving opportunities arise, people demonstrate a commitment to justice.[87]

In Plato's *Republic*, Thrasymachus observes that people censure injustice not because they shrink from committing it, but because they fear becoming its victims. In a similar vein, François La Rochefoucauld, the seventeenth century French aphorist, observed that "The love of justice is simply, in the majority of men, the fear of suffering injustice."[88] Whether justice or self-interest lies deeper in the heart of humankind is a question that theorists have debated for millennia. Certainly Thrasymachus and La Rochefoucauld are not alone in their pessimistic assessments. But neither are they unopposed.

Those who exhort us to uphold justice as an end in itself, rather than as a pragmatic means to gain security or other goods, are known as *deontologists*. Deontology is the study of duty or obligation. For deontologists, justice is a duty that should never be shirked or compromised. It must be pursued for its own sake, regardless of the benefits or costs it brings. A deontological understanding of justice was first systematically formulated by Kant. Justice demands that we act in accord with a "universal law" such that one's free action is compatible with a reciprocal freedom for others.[89] Defending this Kantian understanding of justice, John Rawls maintains that

> Justice is the first virtue of social institutions, as truth is of systems of thought. A theory however elegant and economical must be rejected or revised if it is untrue; likewise laws and institutions no matter how efficient and well-arranged must be reformed or abolished if they are unjust. Each person possesses an inviolability founded on justice that even the welfare of society as a whole cannot override. . . . Being first virtues, truth and justice are uncompromising.[90]

For Rawls, as for Kant, the concept of right is prior to that of the good. We should uphold justice not only or primarily because of the goods we thereby gain or evils we avoid. We should uphold justice because it is our most fundamental obligation.

For Rawls, justice is, quite literally, definitive of human being. "The desire to express our nature as a free and equal rational being," Rawls insists,

> can be fulfilled only by acting on the principles of right and justice as having first priority. . . . Therefore in order to realize our nature we have no alternative but to plan to preserve our sense of justice as governing our other aims. This sentiment cannot be fulfilled if it is compromised and balanced against other ends as but one desire among the rest.[91]

Here Rawls answers the question of why one might wager life and liberty, or let the earth perish, in the pursuit of justice. To do anything less would be to forfeit one's very humanity.

In contrast to deontologists, utilitarians argue that justice is a means to secure a more important end: the greatest good for the greatest number of people. The consequences of action, understood in terms of the goods achieved or maximized, become the focus of concern. Allowing the earth to perish to fulfill the dictates of justice is illegitimate. Utilitarians are consequentialists. The ends must always justify the means. It is not enough to act from a firm sense of duty. To act justly is to yield the most good for the most people. For utilitarians, the good is prior to the right.

While justice is not uncompromising for utilitarians, it remains a first virtue. John Stuart Mill writes that justice constitutes "the chief part, and incomparably the most sacred and binding part, of all morality." Mill believed that justice was the sum of all moral duty. He explains that "Justice is a name for certain moral requirements, which, regarded collectively, stand higher in the scale of social utility, and are therefore of more paramount obligation, than any others."[92] Justice is the paramount virtue because it is the most useful of the virtues. It provides for social order and protects individual liberties, fostering the greatest happiness for the greatest number.

### Equity and Practical Judgment

The French philosopher Michel de Montaigne (1533-92), stated that "we can grasp virtue in such a way that it will become vicious, if we embrace it with too sharp and violent a desire."[93] That truth applies to the virtue of justice. When immoderately pursued, justice undermines itself. Unbounded justice, indeed, is no justice at all.

As a form of "moral goodness," Aristotle writes, justice consists in feeling and acting "at the right times on the right occasions towards the right people for the right motive and in the right way . . . that is, somewhere between the extremes."[94] Justice is a "permanent attitude of the soul towards the mean." Aristotle contrasted his understanding of justice as a mean to the absolute justice advocated by Plato. Indeed, Aristotle had his former teacher in mind when he observed that the best often becomes the enemy of the good. In the *Republic*, it seemed to Aristotle, the pursuit of an ideal form of justice (the best) prevents a free and fair but inevitably imperfect society (the good) from being achieved. In Plato's regime, the rule of philosopher-kings renders a strict justice. But this justice is achieved at the expense of human freedom and plurality. Plato's idealism yields an absolute form of justice, but its costs are prohibitive. Aristotelean justice is moderate, a midpoint between extremes that attempts to balance social order with freedom.

Moderation has been championed by political theorists throughout the ages, as a cautionary note accompanying the celebratory discourse on justice. Cicero argues that the implementation of extreme forms of justice often produces extreme injustice. In *The Spirit of the Laws* (1748), Montesquieu insists that justice, when taken too far, undermines the very liberties it is designed to protect.[95] Even Kant, uncompromising as he was, acknowledged that "The strictest justice is the greatest injustice."[96] When justice spurns all limits, it self-destructs. In the absence of appropriate boundaries to the its application and exercise, justice is transformed into its opposite.

The miscarriages of law well exhibit the dangers of an unbounded pursuit of justice. The poet Alexander Pope put the point most eloquently when he wrote:

Mark what unvaried laws preserve each state,
Laws wise as nature, and as fixed as fate.
In vain thy reason finer webs shall draw,
Entangle justice in her net of law,
And right, too rigid, harden into wrong.[97]

Justice can only thrive under the rule of law. Indeed, in the absence of law, justice could not survive. But justice withers when the rigidity of the rule of law overpowers its animating spirit. Law is, of necessity, unvarying and enduring. In democratic societies, it is to be applied equally to all. Yet the human condition is characterized by diversity and change. Something given to variability and growth cannot easily be forced into a rigid container. When law becomes Procrustean, justice is ill-served.

Plato himself recognized this truth. In his dialogue *The Statesman*, we read that

Law can never issue an injunction binding on all which really embodies what is best for each. . . . The differences of human personality, the variety of men's activities, and the inevitable unsettlement attending all human experience make it impossible for any art whatsoever to issue unqualified rules holding good on all questions at all times. . . . It is impossible, then, for something invariable and unqualified to deal satisfactorily with what is never uniform and constant.[98]

Drawing the appropriate conclusions from this line of thinking, Aristotle maintains that the strict enforcement of law must be supplemented with a concern for equity. In pursuing justice, one ought to balance the lawful with the equitable.

163

Equity pertains to the achievement of substantive justice above and beyond the narrow dictates of procedural justice. Equity is concerned with respecting the spirit of the law, not simply enforcing the letter of the law. Aristotle writes that "Equity, though just, is not the justice of the law courts but a method of restoring the balance of justice when it has been tilted by the law.... Equity essentially is just this rectification of the law."[99] Because equity achieves a balance between the undesirable extremes of lawless anarchy and rigid, unyielding rules, Aristotle deems equity "the highest form of justice."[100]

How does one determine what is equitable? Aristotle's answer was practical judgment, *phronesis* in Greek. Practical judgment, also known as prudence or practical wisdom, blends abstract thought with sound and useful assessments about the world. It integrates knowledge of the way things should be, attending to ideals and principles, with practical assessments of the way things are, grounded in experience.[101]

One might think of justice as a well-built house. Law corresponds to the blueprints for the house, its architectural design. Without blueprints, the house could not be built. For a house to be built well, however, one needs more than a good set of plans. One needs a carpenter who can interpret the plans and amend them as the situation requires. The variability of building materials and environmental conditions makes the carpenter's practical judgment indispensable. Likewise, owing to the variability of the human condition and the particularities of context, practical judgment is needed to discern the equitable.

That does not mean that law may be wantonly ignored or dismissed arbitrarily. Just as a blueprint is required to construct a good house, so law is required to maintain a just state. To pursue justice in the absence of law—through practical judgment alone—would demand too much of citizens and statespeople. Aristotle defined law as the incarnation of reason minus the fickle passions that often influence decisions. An individual's judgments inevitably will be biased by affiliations, led astray by passions, such as love or revenge, hampered by insufficient information and flawed by faulty reasoning. To exercise practical judgment is not to ignore law. One should begin with established rules and principles, Aristotle holds, and employ practical judgment to determine how they should be applied in particular situations and when departures are warranted.

The inability of law on its own to achieve justice prompts Plato to advocate the rule of philosopher-kings. In this fashion, Plato believed, practical judgment could be best applied to the affairs of the state.[102] Aristotle, more democratically and realistically, observed that citizens, not only philosopher-kings, must exercise good judgment on a regular basis. Indeed, the distinguishing mark of a citizen, Aristotle held, is "participation in judgment and authority."[103] Examining the most venerated definition of justice will demonstrate how law and practical judgment prove complementary.

### Giving to Each What is Due

From ancient times through the present day, justice has been defined as "giving to each what is due." To achieve justice, Aristotle asserted, is to ensure that one neither has "more than one ought . . . [nor] less than one ought." To mete out justice is "to give each his proportionately equal share."[104] The Roman Emperor Justinian (482–565 A.D.) reiterated this understanding as did Thomas Aquinas, who wrote in his *Summa Theologica*: "Justice is a habit whereby a man renders to each one his due by a constant and perpetual will."[105] Justice, then, is the virtue of acting lawfully and navigating prudently between the extremes of giving more or less than what is due to others and receiving more or less than what is due to oneself.

J.S. Mill argues that justice arises from a rule of conduct supposed common to all and from a natural desire to punish those who violate this rule.[106] Coupled with the desire to requite evil with evil is the impulse to repay good with good. This latter impulse is also born of powerful natural sentiments, namely, the disappointment, resentment, and sense of betrayal that comes when good deeds are not reciprocated. Humans are psychologically predisposed to mete out justice, to give each what is deserved, be it reward or punishment, even when doing so is neither easy nor cost free. Mill writes:

> The principle, therefore, of giving to each what they deserve, that is, good for good as well as evil for evil, is not only included within the idea of Justice as we have defined it, but is a proper object of that intensity of sentiment, which places the Just, in human estimation, above the simply Expedient.[107]

The desire to give to each what is due, Mill suggests, goes beyond considerations of utility or practicality. It lies deep within the human heart.

In days gone by, giving to each what is due was associated with personal revenge. While justice today often entails inflicting punishment on wrongdoers, we do not condone people "taking the law into their own hands" to requite evil with evil. Acts of revenge are seldom fair and may quickly escalate. In modern times, only the state has the prerogative to enforce law and punish criminals. Dueling and feuding are proscribed.

In ancient times, the justice meted out by authorities was often little more than acts of state-sanctioned revenge. Aristotle observed that Rhadamanthus, the Greek god of the underworld, had established his own form of vengeful justice by inflicting on the perpetrator of any evil deed a like evil.[108] This form of justice, also found in ancient Judaism, was first codified into law by the Babylonian king, Hammurabi (1792–1750 B.C.), who famously insisted upon exacting "an eye for an eye, and a tooth for a tooth." The point of punishment was retaliation. Most modern governments insist that the punishment of criminals be oriented toward deterrence and the safety of society rather than retaliation and revenge, and that all punishment be humanely conducted, regardless of how inhumane the crime. Historically, however, justice was often barbaric.

Giving to each his or her due entails meting out of punishment (retributive justice), compensation for harms suffered (commutative justice), and the proper allotment of social goods (distributive justice). Retributive justice (e.g. criminal law) is concerned with the punishment an individual is due owing to his crimes against other individuals or against society at large. Commutative justice (e.g. contract and tort law) pertains to what an individual is due in compensation for a personal (economic, physical, mental or status-oriented) injury, with the goal of reestablishing something like the *status quo ante*. Distributive justice (e.g. welfare policy and other laws that reallocate resources) addresses what each is due according to criteria of need, merit, desert or status. Each of these three forms of justice is concerned with giving and receiving what is due.

Retributive, commutative and distributive forms of justice all consist in like cases being treated alike and unlike cases being treated unlike. As Aristotle (and Aquinas) observed, justice allocates to each what is due according to the rules of proportionality. The individual who has stolen more, for instance, deserves a greater punishment. Today we acknowledge this proportionality in the difference between milder penalties for misdemeanors and harsher punishments for felonies.

What we are due, and what we receive, also depends upon our membership in specific groups. Basic human rights, we presume, are due to all individuals owing to their being members of the human race. People are also due specific legal and political rights based on their national citizenships and residencies. In turn, people gain particular rights based on their memberships in the diverse associations that compose civil society. We live our lives within intersecting "spheres of justice" according to Michael Walzer. "The principles of justice are themselves pluralistic in form," he writes: "different social goods ought to be distributed for different reasons, in accordance with different procedures, by different agents."[109] In a similar vein, Alasdair MacIntyre insists that "There is no place for appeals to . . . a justice-as-such to which all rational persons would by their very rationality be compelled to give their allegiance. There is instead only the . . . justice-of-this-or-that-tradition."[110] Disregarding the cultural traditions of minorities and other disadvantaged groups under the guise of "treating people as individuals," Will Kymlicka writes, "is itself just a cover for ethnic and national injustice."[111] The pursuit of a timeless and universal of justice, many fear, would undermine efforts to give context and pluralism its due. The broad claim is that justice can only be achieved and preserved by "assuring the multiplicity of justices."[112]

What each is due, given the uniqueness of individuals, the variability of historical circumstances, and the characteristics of specific cultures, is neither static nor uniform. Whether it is punishment or reward, burden or benefit that is being allocated, what is due is always, in part, contextually specific and subject to change. One might worry with philosopher Hans Kelson that defining justice so contextually, as giving to each what is due, constitutes "an empty formula."[113] Indeed, the definition begs many questions.

How is one to determine, both in the abstract and in concrete situations, what each person is due? What criteria should be employed to make this determination? Should it be based on the fulfillment of fundamental duties (as deontologists insist), on an overarching concern for individual or collective happiness (as utilitarians argue), on the pursuit of equality of economic condition (as Marxists maintain), or on equality of opportunity and the maximization of individual freedom (as liberals contend)? How, in turn, is one to assess which individual attributes ought to be taken into account when meting out justice? Should one focus on ability, merit, effort, virtue, need, status, rank, or personal history? Without some means of sorting through these criteria, "giving to each what is due" may indeed merit the designation of an empty formula.

The benefit of law is that it offers (partial) answers to these puzzles. Justice, from a legalistic standpoint, is achieved through the impartial enforcement of law. Justice is done when law is applied equally to all. As such, justice is a form of impartiality. What each is due, first and foremost, is impartial treatment, which is to say, the consistent and universal application of the same rules. So understood, justice requires that law be enforced without prejudice or favoritism. Courts of law are often adorned with the figure of a woman who holds in her hands the scales of justice. The woman is blindfolded to indicate that she will not be swayed by biases: the law will apply equally to all. Justice is not supposed to play favorites.

Sometimes, however, impartiality serves less as a blindfold than a mask. For Marx, legal relations and concepts, such as principles of justice, are derived from the economic structure of a society.[114] Justice as impartiality is the ideological mask of a capitalistic economy. Wearing this mask allows the state to perpetuate class interests under the guise of legality. To be impartial is to see everyone as fundamentally the same, as having the same basic identity. To the extent that a capitalist state assesses its citizens impartially, it does so under the assumption that they all share one fundamental identity—that of independent property owners exercising their economic rationality. Here impartial justice primarily safeguards an individual's right to buy, sell and exchange property (including the property of their own labor power) in an open market. Impartial justice allows the unrestricted accumulation of wealth, but fails to address the inequality and alienation that arises in market economies.

Iris Marion Young explores the cultural and political ramifications of a "blind" justice. She writes that "The ideal of impartiality serves ideological functions. It masks the ways in which the particular perspectives of dominant groups claim universality, and helps justify hierarchical decisionmaking structures."[115] Like Marx, Young believes that impartiality is not really a blind form of justice. It is, rather, a form of justice that sees only one side of things: "Blindness to difference perpetuates cultural imperialism by allowing norms expressing the point of view and experience of privileged groups to appear neutral and universal."[116] The pursuit of impartiality secures the interests of the dominant in the name of justice. An impartial justice, in this regard, is an ideological means of allocating resources and meting out punishment such that privilege is both perpetuated and camouflaged. At best, impartial justice maintains the status quo in the name of fairness. At worst, it become a weapon of the strong against the weak, reinforcing social, cultural and political forms of domination.

In the same vein, Susan Moller Okin criticizes the "false gender neutrality" of Rawls' theory of justice. Rawls fails to account for the very different roles and status of men and women in contemporary society, particularly within the family where inequalities in power and labor generally exist. Justice as fairness is defined by Rawls as the "voluntary scheme" reached between "mutually disinterested," free and rational individuals operating behind a veil of ignorance in an original position, that is to say, where "none are known to be advantaged or disadvantaged by social and natural contingencies."[117] The veil of ignorance is a means of ensuring that the rules of justice are devised and applied impartially. But the public contract endorsed by equal, autonomous agents behind the veil of ignorance, like commercial deals struck in the free market, is premised on a private household and family where equality and autonomy are often absent.

The problem with understanding justice as impartiality or fairness, Okin argues, is that it is a theory "about men with wives at home."[118] Typically, wives assume most of the household obligations and mothers serve as the primary caretakers of children. Men are free to evaluate the criteria of fairness in the public realm because their wives maintain the private sanctuary of home—often under very inegalitarian conditions. While the rules of *fair play* are being determined in the public realm by men, within the family and household women are often prevented, or culturally discouraged, from claiming their *fair share*.

To have a just society, Okin argues, one must first have a just family, which provides the soil for moral development. "Unless the first and most formative example of adult interaction usually experienced by children is one of justice and reciprocity, rather than one of domination and manipulation or of unequal altruism and one-sided self-sacrifice, and unless they themselves are treated with concern and respect," Okin argues, "they are likely to be considerably hindered in becoming people who are guided by principles of justice."[119] In more concrete terms and at a minimum, Okin suggests, a just society would have to provide high-quality, subsidized childcare facilities and other incentives to encourage more equal parenting. In the absence of such justice in the family, an impartial justice in society will serve as a mask for patriarchal power.

Rawls has acknowledged the merits of Okin's critique, but believes his political conception of justice as fairness can adequately achieve liberty and equality for women.[120] Carole Pateman and many other feminists are skeptical that Rawls' theory, and contract theory more generally, can succeed in rendering gender justice. The claim is that the impartial justice celebrated in social contract theory typically aligns itself with the prevailing winds of dominant cultures or groups. Other critics of Rawls, such as Charles Mills, believe that the ideal of impartiality may significantly contribute to racial justice, notwithstanding the racial domination historically perpetuated in its name.[121]

If one rejects impartiality, what should be substituted for the ideal of universal standards applied equally to all? Feminist Donna Harraway advocates "partiality."[122] Likewise, Iris Young promotes "partial discourse," though she stipulates that this should not be equated with simple bias. "Moral reason certainly does require reflection," Young writes, "an ability to take some distance from one's immediate impulses, intuitions, desires, and interests in order to consider their relation to the demands of others, their consequences if acted upon, and so on."[123] To the extent that we are concerned with equity, with giving to each what is his or her due, justice will indeed be attuned to particularities. But the promotion of partiality requires qualification. Clearly one does not want to celebrate all forms of partiality, such as patriarchy or racial bigotry. Such partial discourses maintain that certain types of people are due much less than impartial justice would accord them.

To avoid pernicious partialities, we must first acknowledge our own biases and subsequently strive to gain some distance from them. That distance is gained by way of critical thinking and open encounters with others whose impulses, intuitions, desires, and interests differ from ours. Such encounters, the stuff of democratic experience, may challenge our beliefs and values. Navigating these informative but disconcerting encounters fosters the development of practical judgment.

Justice is a mean, Aristotle states, but no formula can locate it. That is why, for Aristotle, the just person, not an abstract, unchanging rule, constitutes the only "standard and yardstick" of justice.[124] To determine what is due in any particular situation, one must ponder what a just person would do, that is to say, someone informed by law, inclined to equity, attentive to context, and capable of practical judgment.[125] Equity, the highest form of justice, will always be a moving target for the political theorist, one that only ever becomes visible in a fusion of horizons. Only practical judgment observant of law and attentive to context allows us to keep the scales of justice in balance.

## References

1   G.W.F. Hegel, *The Philosophy of History*, trans. J. Sibree (New York: Dover, 1956), 19.

2   A.J. Carlyle, *Political Liberty: A History of the Conception in the Middle Ages and Modern Times* (Westport, Conn.: Greenwood Press, 1941), vii.

3   Orlando Patterson, *Freedom: Freedom in the Making of Western Culture*, vol. 1 (New York: Basic Books, 1991), 402–3.

4   Edmund Burke, *Selected Writings of Edmund Burke*, ed. W.J. Bate (Westport, Conn.: Greenwood Press, 1960), 211.

5   Baron de Montesquieu, *The Spirit of the Laws*, trans. Thomas Nugent (New York: Hafner Press, 1949), 150.

6   John Locke, *Two Treatises of Government*, ed. Peter Laslett (New York: Cambridge University Press, 1960), 348.

7   G.W.F. Hegel, *Hegel's Philosophy of Mind*, trans. William Wallace and A.V. Miller (Oxford: Clarendon Press, 1971), 239.

8   Isaiah Berlin, "Two Concepts of Liberty," in *Four Essays on Liberty* (Oxford: Oxford University Press, 1969), 119.

9   John Stuart Mill, *On Liberty* (Indianapolis: Bobbs-Merrill, 1956), 13.

10  A.V. Dicey, *Law and Public Opinion in England during the Nineteenth Century* (London: Macmillan, 1962), 146. Quoted in Vernon Van Dyke, *Ideology and Political Choice: The Search for Freedom, Justice, and Virtue* (Chatham, N.J.: Chatham House, 1995), 24.

11  Mill, *On Liberty*, 13.

12  Locke, *Two Treatises of Government*, 336–37.

13  Benjamin Constant, "The Liberty of the Ancients Compared with That of the Moderns: Speech Given at the Athènée Royal in Paris," in *Political Writings*, ed. Biancamaria Fontana (Cambridge, 1988), 310–11, quoted in Stephen Macedo, *Liberal Virtues: Citizenship, Virtue, and Community in Liberal Constitutionalism* (Oxford: Clarendon Press, 1990), 9.

14  Jean-Jacques Rousseau, *The Social Contract and Discourses*, trans. G.D.H. Cole (London: J.M. Dent and Sons, 1973), 178.

15  Quoted in Anthony Giddens, *Capitalism and Modern Social Theory: An Analysis of the Writings of Marx, Durkheim, and Weber* (Cambridge: Cambridge University Press, 1971), 117.

16  Rousseau, *The Social Contract and Discourses*, 178.

17  Rousseau, *The Social Contract and Discourses*, 240.

18  Rousseau, *The Social Contract and Discourses*, 47.

19  Rousseau, *The Social Contract and Discourses*, 165.

20  Jean-Jacques Rousseau, "On Public Happiness," *Oeuvres Complètes* 3 (Pleide, 1964): 510, 881.

21  Berlin, "Two Concepts of Liberty," 131.

22  Berlin, *Four Essays on Liberty*, 138, 141.

23  Quoted in James Boswell, *The Life of Samuel Johnson* (New York: Penguin Books, 1979), 140.

24  John Locke, *A Letter Concerning Toleration*, 2nd edn (Indianapolis: Bobbs-Merrill, 1955), 17.

25  See Amitai Etzioni, *Rights and the Common Good: The Communitarian Perspective* (New York: St. Martin's Press, 1995).

26  Bruce Bower, "Growing up Poor," *Science News* 146 (9 July 1994): 24–25.

27  See Robert D. Putnam, *Our Kids: The American Dream in Crisis* (New York: Simon and Shuster, 2015).

28  Benjamin Barber, *Strong Democracy: Participatory Politics for a New Age* (Berkeley: University of California Press, 1984), xvi.

29  Isaiah Berlin, "Philosophy and Life: An Interview," *New York Review of Books* (28 May 1992): 52–53.

30  Immanuel Kant, *Political Writings*, 2nd edn, ed. Hans Reiss (Cambridge: Cambridge University Press, 1991), 55.

31  Thomas A. Spragens, *Reason and Democracy* (Durham: Duke University Press, 1990), 255.

32  Macedo, *Liberal Virtues*, 46, 50.

33  See, for instance, Sara Ruddick, "Remarks on the Sexual Politics of Reason," in *Women and Moral Theory*, eds Eva Kittay and Kian Meyers (Savage, Md.: Rowman and Littlefield, 1987), and *Maternal Thinking* (Boston: Beacon Press, 1989); Roslyn Bologh, *Love or Greatness: Max Weber and Masculine Thinking—A Feminist Inquiry* (London: Unwin Hyman, 1990), esp. 240–65; Susan Moller Okin, *Justice, Gender, and the Family* (New York: Basic Books, 1989), esp. 41–73; and Donna Harraway, "Situated Knowledges: The Science Question in Feminism as a Site of Discourse on the Privilege of Partial Perspective," *Feminist Studies* 14 (1988): 575–99.

34  Marimba Ani, *Yurugu: An African-Centered Critique of European Cultural Thought and Behavior* (Trenton: African World Press, 1994), 107.

35  See Jürgen Habermas, *Theory of Communicative Action*, vol. 1: *Reason and the Rationalization of Society*, and vol. 2: *Lifeworld and System: A Critique of Functionalist Reason*, trans. Thomas McCarthy (Boston: Beacon Press, 1984 and 1987).

36  Richard Rorty, "Emancipating our Culture," in *Debating the State of Philosophy: Habermas, Rorty, and Kolakowski*, eds Josef Niznik and John T. Sanders (Westport: Praeger, 1996), 28.

37  Michel Foucault, *The Foucault Reader*, ed. Paul Rabinow (New York: Pantheon Books, 1984).

38  John S. Dryzek, *Rational Ecology: Environment and Political Economy* (New York: Basil Blackwell, 1987), 55.

39  Max Weber, *The Protestant Ethic and the Spirit of Capitalism*, trans. Talcott Parsons (New York: Scribner's, 1958), 26.

40  See Rogers Brubaker, *The Limits of Rationality: An Essay on the Social and Moral Thought of Max Weber* (London: George Allen and Unwin, 1984).

41  Weber, *The Protestant Ethic*, 194.

42  Max Weber, *The Sociology of Religion*, trans. Ephraim Fishcoff (Boston: Beacon Press, 1963), 22.

43  Max Weber, *From Max Weber: Essays in Sociology*, trans. H.H. Gerth and C. Wright Mills (New York: Oxford University Press, 1958), 293.

44  Weber, *The Protestant Ethic*, 115.

45  Weber, *The Protestant Ethic*, 166.

46  See Lewis Mumford, *The Myth of the Machine: Technics and Human Development* (San Diego: Harcourt Brace Jovanovich, 1967), 270–81.

47  Weber, *The Protestant Ethic*, 284.

48  Brian Barry, *Sociologists, Economists, and Democracy* (Chicago: University of Chicago Press, 1978), 31.

49  Anthony Downs, *An Economic Theory of Democracy* (New York: Harper, 1957), 5.

50  Ron Rogowski, "Rationalist Theories of Politics: A Midterm Report," *World Politics* 30 (1978): 299. See also Todd Sandler, *Collective Action: Theory and Applications* (Ann Arbor: University of Michigan Press, 1992), 4.

51  Herbert Simon, *Administrative Behavior*, 3rd edn (New York: Free Press, 1976), xxviii.

52  Downs, *Economic Theory of Democracy*, 5; italics added.

53  Rogowski, "Rationalist Theories of Politics," 300.

54  Herbert Simon, "Human Nature in Politics: The Dialogue of Psychology with Political Science," *American Political Science Review* 79 (1985): 297.

55  James March and Herbert Simon, *Organizations* (New York: Wiley, 1958), 21.

56  James March, "Bounded Rationality and the Engineering of Choice," *Bell Journal of Economics*, 1978; also see James March and J. Olson, *Ambiguity and Choice in Organizations* (Bergen: Universitätsforlaget, 1976).

57  Amy Gutmann and Dennis Thompson, *Democracy and Disagreement* (Cambridge: Harvard University Press, 1996), 173-74. See also David Gauthier, "The Social Contract as Ideology," *Philosophy and Public Affairs,* 6 (1977): 130-64.

58  David Hume, *Hume's Moral and Political Philosophy*, ed. Henry Aiken (New York: Macmillan, 1948), 25.

59  Bertrand Russell, *Human Society in Ethics and Politics* (London: Allen and Unwin, 1954), viii.

60  Herbert Simon, *Reason in Human Affairs* (Stanford: Stanford University Press, 1983), 7-8.

61  Jean-Pierre Vernant, *The Origins of Greek Thought* (Ithaca: Cornell University Press, 1982), 130.

62  Quoted in Jonathan Schell, *The Fate of the Earth* (New York: Avon, 1982), 109.

63  J. Peter Euben, *The Tragedy of Political Theory* (Princeton: Princeton University Press, 1990), 9. See also Joseph Dunne, *Back to the Rough Ground: "Phronesis" and "Techne" in Modern Philosophy and in Aristotle* (Notre Dame: University of Notre Dame, 1993), 263. Hannah Arendt, *The Human Condition* (Chicago: University of Chicago Press, 1958), 184, 206.

64  Aristotle, *Nichomachean Ethics,* Book 6:5, (London: Penguin, 1953), 177.

65  See Hans-Georg Gadamer, *Truth and Method* (New York: Crossroad Publishing, 1985); and M.M. Bakhtin, *The Dialogic Imagination* (Austin: University of Texas Press, 1981).

66  Jürgen Habermas, *Toward a Rational Society*, trans. Jeremy Shapiro (Boston: Beacon Press, 1970), 118.

67  Joseph Schumpeter, *Capitalism, Socialism, and Democracy*, 2nd edn (New York: Harper & Row, 1950).

68  See Bruce Mayhew, "Structuralism vs. Individualism," *Social Forces* 59 (1980): 335-75.

69    Albert O. Hirschman, *Shifting Involvements: Private Interest and Public Action* (Princeton: Princeton University Press, 1982), 85–88.

70    Frederick W. Allen and Roy Popkin, "Environmental Polls: What They Tell Us," *EPA Journal* 14, no. 6 (July/August 1988): 10. See also John Gillroy and Robert Shapiro, "The Polls: Environmental Protection," *Public Opinion Quarterly* 50 (1986): 270–79.

71    See Douglass North, *Institutions, Institutional Change, and Economic Performance* (Cambridge: Cambridge University Press, 1990).

72    Joseph M. Petulla, *American Environmentalism: Values, Tactics, Priorities* (College Station: Texas A & M University Press, 1980), 91.

73    Al Gore, *Earth in the Balance: Ecology and the Human Spirit* (Boston: Houghton Mifflin, 1992), 170.

74    Robert L. Heilbroner, *An Inquiry into the Human Prospect: Looked at Again for the 1990s* (New York: Norton, 1991), 138.

75    Theodore Roszak, *The Voice of the Earth* (New York: Simon and Schuster, 1992), 249–50.

76    Ben Bolch and Harold Lyons, *Apocalypse Not: Science, Economics, and Environmentalism* (Washington, D.C.: Cato Institute, 1993), viii.

77    David W. Orr, *Ecological Literacy: Education and the Transition to a Postmodern World* (Albany: SUNY Press, 1992), 181–82.

78    Dryzek, *Rational Ecology*, 58–59.

79    See Clive L. Spash, "Economics, Ethics, and Long-Term Environmental Damages," *Environmental Ethics* 15 (Summer 1993): 118, 127, 128.

80    Lester Milbrath, "Environmental Understanding: A New Concern for Political Socialization," in *Political Socialization: Citizenship, Education, and Democracy*, ed. Orit Ichilov (New York: Teachers College Press, 1990), 292. See Barry Commoner, *The Closing Circle* (New York: Bantam, 1972), 29.

81    Orr, *Ecological Literacy*, 10–11.

82    Aristotle, *Nichomachean Ethics*, trans. J.A.K. Thomson (New York: Penguin Books, 1953), 141–42. Aristotle, *The Politics*, trans. T.A. Sinclair (New York: Penguin, 1962), 29, 128.

83    Augustine, *City of God*, trans. Henry Bettenson (New York: Penguin, 1972), 139.

84    David Hume, A Treatise of Human Nature in Hume's Moral and Political Philosophy, ed. Henry D. Aiken (New York: Hafner Press, 1948), 103.

85    Melvin Lerner, "The Justice Motive in Human Relations," in *The Justice Motive in Social Behavior*, eds Melvin J. and Sally C. Lerner (New York: Plenum Press, 1981), 20.

86    James Madison, *The Federalist Papers*, eds Alexander Hamilton, James Madison and John Jay (New York: Mentor, 1961), 324.

87    Barbara A. Mellers and Jonathan Baron, eds, *Psychological Perspectives on Justice: Theory and Applications* (New York: Cambridge University Press, 1993), 102; Jane Mansbridge, ed., *Beyond Self-Interest* (Chicago: University of Chicago Press, 1990), 17. Lerner "The Justice Motive in Human Relations," 21–22; Daniel Kahneman, Jack L. Knetsch and Richard Thaler, "Fairness and the Assumptions of Economics," *Journal of Business*, 59 (1986): 299.

88    Francoise, Duc de la Rochefoucauld, *Reflections, or Sentences and Moral Maxims* (# 78).

89    Immanuel Kant, *The Metaphysical Elements of Justice*: Part I of the *Metaphysics of Morals*, trans. John Ladd (Indianapolis: Bobbs-Merrill, 1965), 35.

90    John Rawls, *A Theory of Justice* (Cambridge: Harvard University Press, 1971), 3–4.

91    Rawls, *A Theory of Justice*, 574. And see John Rawls, *Political Liberalism* (New York: Columbia University Press, 1993).

92    J.S. Mill, *Utilitarianism*, in *The Essential Works of J.S. Mill*, ed. Max Lerner (New York: Bantham Books, 1961), 244, 248.

93    Michel de Montaigne, "Of Moderation," in *The Complete Essays of Montaigne*, trans. Donald Frame (Stanford: Stanford University Press, 1985), 146.

94   Aristotle, *Nichomachean Ethics*, 154, 65.

95   Baron de Montesquieu, *The Spirit of the Laws*, two volumes, trans. Thomas Nugent (New York: Hafner Press, 1949), 2: 156.

96   Kant, *The Metaphysical Elements of Justice*, 40.

97   Alexander Pope, *An Essay on Man*, vol. 2 of *The Works of Alexander Pope* (London: John Murray, 1871), 415.

98   Plato, *Statesman* (294b), in *The Collected Dialogues of Plato*, eds Edith Hamilton and Huntington Cairns (Princeton: Princeton University Press, 1961), 1063.

99   Aristotle, *Nichomachean Ethics*, 166–67.

100  Aristotle, *Nichomachean Ethics*, 228.

101  See Leslie Paul Thiele, *The Heart of Judgment: Practical Wisdom, Neuroscience, and Narrative* (Cambridge: Cambridge University Press, 2006).

102  See Zdravko Planinc, *Plato's Political Philosophy: Prudence in the Republic and the Laws* (Columbia: University of Missouri Press, 1991).

103  Aristotle, *The Politics*, 102.

104  Aristotle, *Nichomachean Ethics*, 154–55.

105  Thomas Aquinas, "Of Justice," *Summa Theologica*, trans. Fathers of the Dominican Province (Burns, Oates and Washburn), First Article, in Jonathan Westphal, ed. *Justice* (Indianapolis: Hackett, 1996), 96–97.

106  Mill, *Utilitarianism*, 236–37.

107  Mill, *Utilitarianism*, 245.

108  Aristotle, *Nichomachean Ethics*, 151.

109  Michael Walzer, *Spheres of Justice: A Defense of Pluralism and Equality* (New York: Basic Books, 1983), 6.

110  Alasdair MacIntyre, *Whose Justice? Which Rationality* (Notre Dame: University of Notre Dame Press, 1988), 346.

111  Rawls, *Theory of Justice*, 13, 19.

112  James P. Clarke, "A Kantian Theory of Political Judgment: Arendt and Lyotard," *Philosophy Today* (Summer 1994): 146. See also Jean-François Lyotard, *Just Gaming*, trans. Wlad Godzich (Minneapolis: University of Minnesota Press, 1985), 100.

113  Hans Kelson, *What is Justice?* (Berkeley: University of California Press, 1957), in Jonathan Westphal, ed. *Justice* (Indianapolis: Hackett, 1996), 194.

114  See Karl Marx, "Critique of the Gotha Program," in Robert C. Tucker, ed., *The Marx-Engels Reader*, 2nd edn, (New York: W.W. Norton, 1978).

115  Iris Marion Young, *Justice and the Politics of Difference* (Princeton: Princeton University Press, 1990), 97.

116  Young, *Justice and the Politics of Difference*, 165.

117  Will Kymlicka, *Multicultural Citizenship: A Liberal Theory of Minority Rights* (Oxford: Clarendon Press, 1995), 194.

118  Susan Moller Okin, *Justice, Gender, and the Family* (New York: Basic Books, 1989), 13.

119  Okin, *Justice, Gender, and the Family*, 17.

120  John Rawls, *Justice as Fairness: A Restatement* (Harvard: Harvard University Press, 2001), 167–68.

121  See Carole Pateman and Charles Mills, *Contract and Domination* (Cambridge: Polity Press, 2007).

122  Donna Harraway, "Situated Knowledges: The Science Question in Feminism as a Site of Discourse on the Privilege of Partial Perspective," *Feminist Studies* 14 (1988): 575–99.

123  Young, *Justice and the Politics of Difference*, 105, 112.

124  Aristotle, *I Nichomachean Ethics*, 89.

125  See Richard Sorabji, "Aristotle on the Role of Intellect in Virtue," in Amelie Oksenberg Rorty, ed. *Essays on Aristotle's Ethics* (Berkeley: University of California Press, 1980), 201–19.

## CHAPTER 6

# TECHNOLOGY AND THE HUMAN PROSPECT

The scope and power of technology are ever expanding. Virtually every aspect of life, including politics, is affected. This chapter investigates the opportunities and dangers technology presents to political life in the twenty-first century. It addresses the machinery of government, information technology, automation, artificial intelligence and other emerging technologies. An expansive understanding of technology is proposed that accounts for its impact on human development. The art and craft of political theory is reframed in the light of this inquiry, highlighting the crucial mission for theorists in a technological age.

### Promethean Origins

In ancient Greek mythology, a titan named Prometheus was given the task of distributing to all the beasts of creation their unique capacities. Prometheus invited his brother, Epimetheus, to help. Epimetheus duly gave the lion its powerful jaws, the bear its brawn, the birds their feathered wings, and the snake its venom. Unfortunately, Epimetheus neglected one species, humankind.

Upon learning of the mistake, Prometheus returned to Mount Olympus, the home of the gods, to secure something of merit. He lit a torch from the sacred fire of the sun, and, stealthily placing a burning ember in a fennel stalk, slipped back down the mountain to bestow the purloined gift to the deprived race. And so humankind received the boon of fire, which, as the ancient Greek playwright Aeschylus observed, constitutes the source of all human arts and crafts. Aeschylus employs the word *techne* to designate the legacy of Prometheus. *Techne*, typically translated as *art* or *craft*, lifts humanity out of barbarism and sets it on the path to civilization. But Zeus, king of the gods, was angry that the sacred fire had been stolen. In retribution, he gave Epimetheus and his

174

bride-to-be, Pandora, a gift. When Pandora opened the box, a whole host of evils were loosed upon humankind.

For some, the myth of Prometheus identifies our species as uniquely blessed with technology, which brought us out of barbarism and into civilization. For others, the moral of the story is that technological innovation—stealing fire from the gods—opens a Pandora's box of unintended, and often catastrophic consequences. To be sure, humanity profited greatly from the pottery and tools that emerged from the hot kilns and forges alight with Promethean fire. But the great boon of fire would also make warfare more deadly and likely, as cumbersome wooden clubs gave way to metal spears and swords, cannons and rifles, and eventually bombs and missiles. In turn, kilns and forges were replaced by coal-fired power plants and internal combustion engines, producing the bane of climate change which, many worry, may destroy civilization and pitch humankind back into barbarism.

Technology has seldom been the explicit focus of political theorists, though it has been a longstanding interest and arguably a central concern since the early modern age.[1] The reason is clear. "Power and technology grow together; they co-evolve," Daniel Sarewitz observes: "Politically and militarily dominant societies have almost always been those that have chosen to take seriously the pursuit of technological advantage. Indeed, history can be told as a story of evolving technology applied to the exercise of power."[2] In the ancient civilizations of the Far East, Mesopotamia, Egypt, Greece and Rome, states intent on expanding their power fostered the development of military technology, fortifications, water supply and delivery systems, agriculture, mining, transportation and commerce. By the eighteenth century, nation-states were investing in technical schools. The launch of Sputnik by the Soviet Union in 1957, the first satellite to orbit the earth, initiated a "space race" and other state-sponsored research and development programs, which accompanied the nuclear arms race of the Cold War. Today technological capabilities continue to feature prominently in the military, industrial, economic and cultural power of states.

Political leaders are often evaluated based on their development and deployment of technology in the arenas of security and war, the economy and infrastructure, administration and government, media and culture. The Italian fascist leader Benito Mussolini famously took credit for "making the trains run on time." While Mussolini did somewhat improve the state-run railway system in Italy during the 1920s, particularly in showcase investments designed to be impressive, it is a myth that he made the trains run on time. But it was a myth Mussolini happily exploited. Likewise, contemporary political leaders present themselves as capable managers of the technologies upon which their people's security and welfare depend.

Technology has also transformed the ways in which leaders communicate. There has been a longstanding concern that electronic media encourage those seeking public office to focus more on image than substance, while fostering "single interest" politics

175

and intensifying inequalities of representation.[3] With the rise of social media, the impact of information technology (IT) on political life has grown. For these and other reasons to be explored, no political theory today can afford to neglect the meaning and impact of technology.

## THE MACHINERY OF GOVERNMENT AND SYMBOLIC TOOLS

What comes to mind when you hear the word *technology*? Perhaps you think of tools such as hammers and saws, or smart phones, self-driving cars, jet airplanes and other sophisticated gadgets and machines. But technology is not limited to hand-held implements, electronic devices, and machines. Candles and campfires are no less technological artifacts than cameras and computers. And a bureaucracy is as much a work of technology as a brick, bicycle, ballpoint pen, bulldozer, bikini, or barcode. Memoranda, memes, and mores are also technological artifacts. So are habits and skills, as John Dewey recognized.[4]

Technology may be understood to include anything—simple or complex, concrete or conceptual—that is designed and constructed for a specific purpose. Since language serves as a tool—to instruct, inquire, educate, entertain, inspire and mislead—it, too, is a form of technology, notwithstanding its generation from mental rather than material resources. A political theory, like an optical lens, is also a work of technology. It is an artifact constructed to focus vision in order to achieve (conceptual) clarity and gain (historical and normative) perspective.

We do not design or construct most of the concepts, memes, mores, theories, processes, institutions, tools and devices that we use every day. Rather, we inherit, borrow, or buy them. Still, they were created with a purpose in mind, whether it be transportation, in the case of a wagon and spaceship; communication, in the case of a poem and smart phone; economic gain, in the case of a farmer's market and a transnational corporation; physical or mental well-being, in the case of medical procedures and pharmaceutical drugs; or collective order, in the case of queueing lines at grocery stores, ideologies, and national constitutions.

A political state is also a technological artifact. In the *Laws*, Plato compares the lawgiver to the shipwright who constructs a sturdy sea vessel.[5] In the *Republic*, Plato employed the metaphor of the "ship of state," comparing governing to the technical skill of steering a ship and charting its course by the stars. Indeed, the word *government* derives from the Latin *gubernare*, meaning to govern or rule, which in turn stems from the Greek *kybernan*, meaning to steer or pilot a ship. Government, the steering of the ship of state, is a political technology.

Hobbes also described the state as an artifact. Observing that all "*Automata* (Engines that move themselves by springs and wheeles as doth a watch) have an artificial life," Hobbes likens the human body to a machine given life by God, the great "Artificer." Humans, in turn, use their own creative arts and crafts to give life to the commonwealth, which Hobbes likens to "an Artificial Man."[6] The state, Hobbes argues, is a machine modeled on the mechanics of the human body, much as Plato modeled the polity on the human soul. Likewise, Rousseau writes that "The lawgiver is the engineer who invents the machine." And the prince is "the mechanic who sets it up and operates it."[7] The contemporary phrase "machinery of government" reflects the fact that state structures and processes are understood to be technological artifacts.

Human beings are the sole creatures on the planet to form governments. But many other animals employ tools. Elephants use branches to scratch themselves and birds use twigs to acquire grubs. Chimpanzees throw stones at antagonists. They also employ twigs to extract termites from their mounds. Shells lying upon the seabed are utilized by octopuses as shields for protection. Egyptian vultures employ rocks to break open ostrich eggs. Ants domesticate and exploit certain plants and animals to produce food, excelling in the crafts of cultivating yeasts and fungi and "milking" aphids. While other species use tools, they do not make complex machines. The sophistication of human technology is unparalleled. More importantly, human beings are shaped and transformed by the technologies they create.

The word *technology* brings two Greek words together: *techne*, an art or craft, and *logos*, language or reason. The Greeks never joined these words to make *technologos*, but they did have a *techne* of *logos*, an art of speaking, which they called rhetoric. And Aristotle defined human beings as the animal with speech. Indeed, the most powerful tool that humans invented is not fire, the wheel, an agricultural implement, a military weapon, a machine, or an electronic device. The most powerful human invention is the symbol, and more specifically, symbolic language. This invention allowed for the political arts and crafts, making the *zoon logon echon*, the rational, speaking animal, a *zoon politikon*, a political animal.

Lewis Mumford, the most prolific twentieth century scholar of technology, rejected the common notion that the fabrication of physical tools was the best indicator of human uniqueness. Not the creation and mastery of implements but the development of individual and cultural self-expression, Mumford insists, best accounts for humanity's odyssey from bestiality to civilization.[8] Symbolic tools, rather than physical ones—namely those involved in play, ritual, and most importantly, language—are the crowning achievement of our species and the primary cause of its accelerated development. Language changed human behavior, and these behavioral adaptations impacted human evolution. The medium is the message, the Canadian communications theorist Marshall McLuhan famously observed. And in the case of symbolic language, the medium shaped the messenger.

The Roman politician, Appius Claudius Caecus (c. 340–273 B.C.) wrote "*Homo faber suae quisque fortunae*," which means, man is the maker of his own destiny. Unaware of Caecus' phrase, Hannah Arendt employed the term *Homo faber* to designate the equally aged notion that humans utilize the earth's resources to make useful things. In so doing, Arendt observes, "man the maker" aspires to becoming "lord and master of the whole earth."[9] In Promethean fashion, humankind controls its destiny by way of its arts and crafts.

*Homo faber* is a tool maker. It might be more accurate, however, to describe our species as *Homo fabricatus* rather than *Homo faber*: humans the made (by their own tools) rather than humans the makers (of tools). Our uniqueness among the countless species occupying the planet is less that we are tool users or tool makers, than that we have become shaped by the tools we have made. And this technological self-transformation is accelerating.

## BECOMING THE TOOLS OF OUR TOOLS

It has been understood for centuries that human biology, by way of its crowning achievement, the neocortex, is responsible for the development of human culture. More recently, evolutionary scientists have confirmed that human culture has significantly shaped human biology. Our genes made possible the creation of powerful cultural memes, including language and other artifacts. And these diverse artifacts, in turn, impacted the development of our genes.[10]

"Stone and symbolic tools, which were initially acquired with the aid of flexible ape-learning abilities," anthropologist Terrence Deacon explains, "ultimately turned the tables on their users and forced them to adapt to a new niche opened by these technologies.... The origin of 'humanness' can be defined as that point in our evolution where these tools became the principal source of selection on our bodies and brains."[11] We are, Deacon states, the "symbolic species." *Homo faber*, man the tool-maker, greatly transformed himself by way of his tools, including the tool of symbolic language. The memes created with symbolic language are the primary units of cultural transmission. They propagate through social interaction, leaping from brain to brain. Over evolutionary time scales, these linguistic memes transformed the human brain, and the behavior it stimulated and constrained.

"The haven all memes depend on reaching is the human mind," philosopher Daniel Dennett observes, "but a human mind is itself an artifact created when memes restructure a human brain in order to make it a better habitat for memes."[12] Our minds in important respects are the evolutionary product of cultural life, of the replication and transmission of memes. Cultural learning happens when memes pass from one human brain to another. Hominins better equipped for such learning gained an advantage in the struggle for survival, and produced more progeny. Consequently, our ancestors became ever more efficient at and ever more impacted by the replication of memes. The human mind is an artifact of this evolutionary process.

While the role of genes in human development often secures the headlines and the research funding, the contribution of memes is less well recognized. But the human species is the product of gene-culture co-evolution, the interaction of nature and nurture. The impact of symbolic language on our species' evolutionary history is the subject of challenging scholarship in the anthropological, archeological, psychological, neurological, genetic and biological sciences. And it is patently evident in our daily lives. What we do largely depends upon what we think, and what we think depends upon the language of thought.

The poet W.H. Auden held that "Language is the mother, not the handmaiden, of thought; words will tell you things you never thought or felt before." This is a common experience for most writers. As Cecil Day-Lewis, Poet Laureate of the United Kingdom, acknowledged: "I do not sit down at my desk to put into verse something that is already clear in my mind. If it were clear in my mind, I should have no incentive or need to write about it.... We do not write in order to be understood; we write in order to understand."[13] It is said that language expresses thought. In fact, thought is made possible by language. As the German philosopher Martin Heidegger (1889-1976) observes, "only when man speaks, does he think—not the other way around." Heidegger provocatively adds: "Man acts as though *he* were the shaper and master of language, while in fact *language* remains the master of man."[14]

Before we put our thoughts into words, as the saying goes, we really do not have much in the way of thought at all. Try it yourself: make the effort to form a thought without thinking words. Visual images are possible, of course, but complex thoughts are not. Sophisticated and sustained thinking is only possible through language, even when we are engaged in silent thought. Novelist E.M. Forster well captured this phenomenon when he asked: "How do I know what I think, until I see what I say?" Only when we give our thoughts linguistic form do we discover the full measure and content of our beliefs, opinions, judgments, and hopes.

Political theory employs critical thinking and practical judgment to develop political memes. This thinking and judgment is wholly beholden to symbolic language. And the memes developed—concepts, conventions, principles, rules and understandings that structure and transform social order and political life, which we call mores—are equally constructs of symbolic language. To argue that we should abide by certain laws, promulgate and protect certain rights, adopt certain principles and dedicate ourselves to certain ideals is to say that these mores—technological artifacts all—should constrain, impel and inspire us. As a normative enterprise, political theory employs conceptual tools to shape thought and behavior. We might say that theorists are in the business of persuading people to become tools of these tools.

Living in accordance with mores—laws, moral principles and ideals—is what distinguishes and elevates human life. But symbolic language and mores are artifacts, and most people do not want technological artifacts to control their lives. Indeed, people generally believe that technology is dangerous.

The belief that technology is dangerous is nothing new, as the myth of Prometheus testifies. The myth of Icarus is even more to the point, as it bespeaks the human tendency to *hubris*, or overweening pride. The ancient Greeks believed that when individuals displayed hubris, arrogating to themselves prerogatives that belonged to the Olympian gods, tragedy ensued. The myth of Icarus well illustrates this belief. Daedalus was a master craftsman, the most famous in all of Greece. To escape the island of Crete with his son, Icarus, he fashioned wings from feathers and wax. Father and son donned the plumed contraptions, and Daedalus warned Icarus not to fly too high. But the boy was filled with pride for his wizardly wings, and he ignored his father's prudent counsel. As Icarus approached the sun, his waxen wings melted, and the boy tumbled into the sea and drowned. Similar tales of technological hubris yielding tragic results are found in virtually all cultures. Dazzled by the power of their arts and crafts, humans are always biting off more than they can chew.

The tale of Frankenstein is perhaps the most famous modern example. The English author Mary Shelley (1797–1851) wrote her novel, *Frankenstein; or, The Modern Prometheus*, as industrialism was transforming the face of Europe. It tells the tale of a scientist, Victor Frankenstein, who constructs a man-like creature out of body parts employing newly discovered chemical processes. Upon bringing life to the formerly inanimate matter, the young scientist is horrified by the "monster" he has created, and flees. The abandoned creature, hideous to all who see him, is forced to survive by his wits. His anger at being brought to life and then abandoned is slaked by the blood of many victims, including the relatives and friends of Victor Frankenstein. Shelley's novel is a tale of technology out of control. Armed with the power of science, conscious life itself is created. But the creator does not know how to care for and control his creature, with tragic results.

The rise of industrial society was a fitting backdrop to Shelley's novel, as path-breaking scientific discoveries were ever-more frequent and coal-burning factories fouled nearby waterways, filled the air with acrid smoke, and transformed workers into their servile appendages. The Scottish philosopher Thomas Carlyle (1795–1881), Shelley's contemporary, wrote an essay on this "mechanical age," observing: "We war with rude Nature; and, by our restless engines, come off always victorious, and loaded with spoils." Carlyle's primary concern, however, was not the conquest and despoliation of nature. He was worried "how the mechanical genius of our time has diffused itself into quite other provinces. Not the external and physical alone is now managed by machinery, but the internal and spiritual also." The dominant "habit" of the times was the tendency to see the solution to every problem as a matter of efficient design and management. This orientation "regulates not only our modes of action alone, but our modes of thought and feeling." We have, Carlyle writes, "grown mechanical in head and heart, as well as in hand." Nowhere is this mechanical orientation more visible than in political life, Carlyle observes, pointing to the proliferation of committees, parties, institutions and constitutions. The fatal mistake of the age, Carlyle holds, is the widespread belief that human excellence and happiness can be achieved by proper design and efficient execution, by getting the machinery of government right.[15] The belief that there is a technological solution to every problem, Carlyle is saying, is dangerously misguided.

Across the Atlantic, Henry David Thoreau (1817-62) likewise worried about the mechanical age, which threatened the aesthetic and reflective life he sought in the woods surrounding Walden Pond. Life was being transformed into a harried existence wherein natural rhythms, wants and pleasures were replaced by the timetables and tensions of an age increasingly dominated by school calendars, train schedules, political campaigns, business plans and the endless making, selling, buying and consuming of goods and services. We now have telegraphs, Thoreau observes in *Walden*, but "nothing important to communicate." We are surrounded by sophisticated machines and devices, yet all these inventions are "but improved means to an unimproved end." And the endless bettering of technological means in the absence of higher ends was not even the worst of it. The greatest danger was that technology was turning human beings into means. Absent the leisure to pick the "finer fruits" of life, the man of the mechanical age "has no time to be any thing but a machine." Thoreau prophetically concludes with a lamentation: "But lo! men have become the tools of their tools."[16]

A century after Carlyle and Thoreau voiced their concerns about the mechanical age, the political economist John Kenneth Galbraith (1908-2006) addressed the power of the industrial state. He observed with foreboding that "we are becoming the servants in thought, as in action, of the machine we have created to serve us."[17] Our lives are indeed much impacted—and often seem constrained and constricted—by the technological artifacts created to serve us.

As we observe people on their smartphones wholly oblivious to their surroundings—heads cocked downwards, thumbs hurriedly pecking out text messages—we can well understand Carlyle's, Thoreau's and Galbraith's unease. A time traveler from an earlier age visiting a contemporary city might believe that the world had suddenly become populated by zombies who live in compulsive servitude to their hand-held devices. Indeed, a new word—*smombie*—has been coined to describe the zombie-like behavior of smart phone users. In response to the impact of these attention-hungry contraptions, other artifacts have been created to protect us. Laws now forbid texting while driving owing to the increased rates at which smartphone users cause traffic accidents, imperiling their own lives and the lives of bicyclists, pedestrians and other motorists. Some cities now have dedicated pedestrian lanes for people using smartphones, have embedded traffic signals in the pavement where smart phone users are more likely to see them, preventing their unwitting stepping out into traffic, and have erected prominent *smombie* warning signs. We have indeed become the tools of our tools—and it is dangerous.

## THE MIDAS TOUCH

The *smombie* phenomenon well illustrates McLuhan's observation that "All technology has the property of the Midas touch; whenever a society develops an extension of itself, all other functions of that society tend to be transmuted to accommodate that new form."[18]

Anything that the mythical King Midas touched turned into gold. Everything that contemporary technology touches—including its human operators—gets transformed into another part of the technological system. One might well view the smartphone as a very powerful technological meme that employs humans to reproduce itself, and colonizes human minds to this end.

Well before theories of memetic replication were developed, modern thinkers worried about the capacity of technology to transform human beings into cogs in its wheels. Max Weber maintained that we live in "an iron cage" of endless technological production. The modern order, he wrote, is

> bound to the technical and economic conditions of machine production which to-day determine the lives of all the individuals who are born into this mechanism, not only those directly concerned with economic acquisition, with irresistible force. Perhaps it will so determine them until the last ton of fossilized coal is burnt.[19]

Substitute "electronic and digital" for "machine" and "oil and natural gas" for "fossilized coal" in Weber's account, and his concerns map seamlessly onto the contemporary world. If renewable energy ever becomes truly clean and cheap, technological expansion may have broken free of one of its few remaining constraints.

For Heidegger, technology is indeed totalizing. It turns everything into what he called *standing-reserve*. In our technological age, Heidegger writes, "everywhere everything is ordered to stand by, to be immediately at hand, indeed to stand there just so that it may be on call for a further ordering."[20] Everything, everywhere—the earth, its natural resources and diverse organisms, and even people, understood as human resources—acquire the status of raw materials awaiting efficient integration into a boundless technological system. Heidegger worried that in the furious effort to gain mastery and control of the world, driven by the belief that the growth of technological power is an end in itself and defines human progress, we may become immune to much that makes life meaningful, including its profound mystery.

"Man has already begun to overwhelm the entire earth and its atmosphere, to arrogate to himself in forms of energy the concealed powers of nature, and to submit future history to the planning and ordering of a world government," Heidegger writes, adding that "This same defiant man is utterly at a loss simply to say what *is*; to say *what* this *is*—that a thing *is*."[21] Building on Aristotle's thought, Heidegger examined how technology was colonizing the diverse ways that humans can relate to each other and their world. Aristotle understood *techne* to be a specific form of knowledge that employs models, principles, or plans to *make* things. He contrasted *techne* with human capacities that allow us to know things, namely *episteme* (science) and *sophia* (philosophic wisdom). He also contrasted *techne* with *phronesis* or practical judgment, which allows us to live politically and act in concert. *Techne* is always instrumental, oriented to achieving a specific purpose. It does not constitute its own reward, as is the case with the pursuit of knowledge by *episteme*, the contemplative experience of *sophia*, and virtuous action grounded in *phronesis*.

For the person equipped only with a hammer, the saying goes, everything gets treated as a nail. For the technologically oriented person, the natural and social world gets treated as a storehouse of resources awaiting ever-improving plans for efficient exploitation. Plans are useful things: they focus attention and energy to achieve specific goals. We could not do without them. But every plan is also a constriction of perspective. Just as a theory focuses the vision of the theorist, so every plan creates a kind of tunnel vision for the planner. A technological frame of mind constricts thinking and behavior to its singular purposes.

There is an old Buddhist saying that when a pickpocket meets a wise man, he only sees pockets. Technological plans blind us to much of the world, including many of its most worthy features. Accordingly, the explosion of technological power that defines our times may be accompanied by the decline of philosophical, aesthetic and political capacities that allow us to bear witness to, express, and affirm the beauty and deep mystery of life and the meaning of being together with others.[22] The concern is that technology is in the driver's seat, and we are simply along for the ride. Perhaps more worrisome, the passengers are being radically transformed en route.

Consider a short essay written by a prominent cultural critic concerned about the impact of information technology. The critic warns that it will be "unfairly abused" by "unsuitable" people who have "no business with it." But the primary worry is not that this new form of IT will get into the wrong hands. The chief concern is that even those well suited for its use will suffer detrimental effects. People will "cease to use their memory and become forgetful." Their "internal resources" will diminish from lack of use. And as it will place a great quantity of information at people's fingertips, its users will "be thought very knowledgeable when they are for the most part quite ignorant." In short, this innovation will undermine key human capacities while allowing its users to feel much smarter and more skillful than they are. "And because they are filled with the conceit of wisdom instead of real wisdom," the critic concludes, "they will be a burden to society."

What innovation warrants such a harsh critique? Perhaps you guessed that the technology in question is the internet and that the critic was Nicholas Carr, whose article in the *Atlantic Monthly*, "Is Google Making us Stoopid?" produced a spate of soul searching among the world's IT-connected intellectuals. Subtitled "What the Internet is Doing to our Brains," Carr's essay, along with his subsequent books, asserts that "Googling" promotes distraction and forgetfulness, hampers concentration, creativity and compassion, gives the conceit of false wisdom, and diminishes judgment, reasoning capacities, and other forms of cognitive resourcefulness.[23] And this is to say nothing of how the search engine, and the internet more broadly, get abused by the wrong sort of people.

The internet is the most important innovation in the field of communication since the invention of the moveable type printing press by Johannes Gutenberg in the 1440s. This global grid of computer-based networks, a so-called "network of networks," and its World Wide Web, the vast and ever-expanding collection of documents, images and recordings connected through hyperlinks and URLs (universal resource locators) define the vast and ever-expanding realm of cyberspace. It is the twenty-first century's grand frontier. Indeed, more information is uploaded onto the World Wide Web each month than has been printed in all the books published since the dawn of civilization. The internet has been called "one of the most potent meme-replicating mediums ever invented," and the effort to control memetic production is considered "the geopolitical battle of our information age. Whoever has the memes has the power."[24] The power of the internet to replicate memes, influence thought, alter behavior, and impact the development of human faculties is vast and growing. But the internet is not the concern of our critic.

Perhaps you guessed that the harmful invention was *Wikipedia*, the online, open-source encyclopedia, which many a college professor has castigated for diminishing students' research skills, comparative fact checking, and critical inquiry. Or perhaps it was the smartphone, with its capacity to entertain, inform, schedule, navigate and provide sundry forms of "cognitive assistance" that deprive us of opportunities to employ, develop and strengthen our neural muscles?

These are also good guesses. But they, too, are wrong. The cultural critic in question was Plato. His jeremiad is found in the dialogue *Phaedrus*, where the philosopher assesses the pernicious effects of a bit of IT that reputedly emerged out of Egypt some years earlier: the written word.[25]

No doubt the invention of writing did encourage some forgetfulness. In ancient Greece, writing effectively replaced an oral tradition of cultural transmission that put a premium on memory, as exemplified in the rote learning by all educated Greeks of Homer's epic poems, the *Illiad* and *Odyssey*. These dramatic tales, transmitted across generations by word of mouth, heavily impacted Greek culture. But few today would agree with Plato that writing has made us stupid, or with Barnaby Rich, the seventeenth century Englishman, who warned that the growing "multitude of books" generated in his day by the recent invention of the printing press constituted "one of the great diseases of this age." A few decades later, Rich's dire opinion was seconded by the polymath Gottfried Wilhelm Leibniz, who maintained that the diminishing quality of writing brought about by the printing press would usher in a "return to barbarism."

To be sure, the number of books printed in the half century following the invention of the printing press rivaled the number of books hand-written by European scribes in the previous millennium. No doubt many of these printed books did not rise to the highest standards. But as the printed word found its way into more and more hands, the expansion of learning accelerated. Writing and printing did not make humanity lame-brained or barbarous. Indeed, the written and printed word much advanced our species, producing unprecedented levels of health, wealth and education. And many argue that the "interactive technologies" of the twenty-first century will further expand our horizons and may in fact "sharpen minds."[26]

Technology does have something akin to a Midas touch. It transforms both its objects and its agents. But the touch is not always golden. Neither is it always detrimental or irresistible. The Midas touch of technology might be understood in much the same way that Foucault conceived of power, keeping in mind that technological artifacts include not only machines and devices that constrain or control us, but also the mores and linguistic memes that stimulate our desires and shape our identities. We are not only the objects of technology, but one of its prime effects and its chief vehicle. The problem is not that every technological artifact is bad, but that all are dangerous. So the ethico-political choice to be made every day is to determine which is the main danger.[27] We cannot escape the reach of technology. But we can resist its most invidious forms.

Whether the most powerful, helpful or harmful technological artifacts of the future will be mores and linguistic memes or machines and electronic devices is an open question. Notwithstanding all his talk about iron cages, Max Weber believed that ideas constitute "effective forces in history." Ideas do not have a fully independent standing apart from the material conditions within which they develop. Employing a term coined by the German poet, novelist and playwright Johann Goethe (1749–1832), Weber speaks of an "elective affinity" between ideas and their coexisting forms of concrete economic and social relationships, which themselves stand upon a technological foundation. Our aim as theorists, Weber insists, should not be to "substitute for a one-sided materialistic an equally one-sided spiritualistic causal interpretation of culture and of history."[28] Instead, we should seek understanding of the relationship between ideas and the material conditions of life that generate and maintain them and that they, in turn, sustain and transform. The measure of a good theory of technology would be its capacity to help us navigate this complex terrain, and identify areas for creative resistance.

## THEORIES OF TECHNOLOGY

Political thinkers have been worried about the effects of technology for at least 2500 years. The reason is patent. As Leo Strauss observed, theorists as far back as Aristotle and Plato "demanded the strict moral-political supervision of inventions" because they realized that social and political change was inherently wedded to technological change.[29]

The printing press is a prominent example of this linkage. The first and the most widely printed documents that rolled off Gutenberg's press were "indulgences," which the Catholic church decreed would lessen for those who purchased them the time spent suffering in purgatory for their sins. In the half-century that followed Gutenberg's invention, hundreds of thousands of indulgences were printed and sold, helping Pope Leo X pay for the construction of St Peter's Basilica in Rome. In 1517, Martin Luther penned and printed his famous *Ninety-Five Theses*, a fiery denunciation of the practice of selling indulgences. Over the next few years, hundreds of editions of Luther's pamphlets rolled off the presses. In turn, Luther translated into vernacular German and printed the New Testament, and eventually the entire Bible, allowing the faithful to read scripture without the aid of priests. Luther was excommunicated by the Pope for his printed words. But the Protestant Reformation was unstoppable. A century of religious wars ensued in Europe, largely between Catholic and Protestant rulers. The nation-state system formed in the aftermath.

A century after the Peace of Westphalia had created a system of sovereign states, consolidating the political aftermath of the Protestant Reformation, the social theorists and historians of the Scottish Enlightenment explored the relationship between human technology and moral development. These theorists, including Adam Ferguson (1723–1816) and Adam Smith, maintained that the development of human arts and crafts was natural and proceeded in observable historical patterns. Accompanying the arts and crafts of each period was the development of corresponding "second natures," which the Scottish Enlightenment thinkers called "manners." Humankind, they believed, had four distinct phases of development—hunting, herding, farming and commerce. As these modes of subsistence evolved one into the other, so did law and other mores or manners.[30] For the thinkers of the Scottish Enlightenment, the progress of humankind was evident in the development of mores which corresponded to the material arts and crafts of each historical stage.

Karl Marx shared this progressive understanding of history. Ironically, given his trade as a writer, Marx did not highlight the power of the printed word to change history, and he mostly ignored the importance of language, ideologies and theories. Marx focused almost exclusively on material rather than moral development, arguing that technologies—material productive forces—were the chief drivers of history.[31]

Marx states that thoughts, moral values, religious beliefs and social relationships are all products of the *forces of production*, the material and social conditions that allow people to produce their means of subsistence. The forces of production include the *means of production*, that is, the raw materials and technology at hand, as well as the *mode of production*, also known as the relations of production, which refers to the social organization of labor. The mode of production changes over time, synchronized with the technological development of the means of production. With changes in technology come changes in economic relationships, and subsequently changes in the social and political values and beliefs that serve as ideological supports for these relationships.

At certain points in history, as technological innovation (means of production) develops, the economic structure (mode of production) fails to keep up. The values, beliefs and social relations that issue from the economic structure appear increasingly out of sync and unjust. When this occurs, a society becomes ripe for revolution. The revolution topples the old mode of production and institutes one better suited to the means

186

of production currently in place. In turn, the entire *superstructure* of cultural, political and legal relations is catapulted forward to become realigned with the *base* formed by the current level of technological and economic development.

The history of humankind, for Marx, may be described in terms of technological change and the economic relationships and social revolutions that follow therefrom. Thousands of years ago, when the means of production were based on primitive methods of agriculture, the mode of production was slavery. Slavery was deemed necessary to satisfy the demands of free men in a world where making ends meet was extraordinarily labor intensive. Improvements in agricultural methods during medieval times brought about relations of serfdom. Serfs owed allegiance and service to their lord and were tied to his lands, but they maintained certain hereditary rights and supported their families by their own labor. In turn, the development of spinning jennies and steam engines created the need for factory workers. Feudal social relations were abolished. Serfs left the land to work in cities. Wage labor, a money economy and capitalism developed.

Marx wrote that "In acquiring new productive forces men change their mode of production: and in changing their mode of production, in changing the way of earning their living, they change all their social relations. The handmill gives you society with the feudal lord; the steam-mill, society with the industrial capitalist."[32] The technologies employed to produce food, clothing, shelter and other goods determine the economic system, which in turn determines the political system. Marx's thesis that the exploitative world of capitalism would give way to an egalitarian future was based on his belief that technology had made the lives of workers so harsh and alienated as to foment a final revolution. In turn, technology would transform relative scarcity into material abundance, allowing the future communist society to satisfy the needs of all.

Max Horkeimer and Theodore Adorno, in their *Dialectic of Enlightenment* (1947), challenged Marx's technological determinism and utopian progressivism. They argued that the scientific and technological effort to gain mastery and control of nature, which largely defined the Enlightenment project, ineluctably leads to the mastery and control of human beings. Technology was not a force of liberation, but one of domination and repression. Their Frankfurt School colleague, Herbert Marcuse, originally accepted the Marxist thesis that technological development would allow the end of repressive forms of labor, as automation supplied basic needs and individuals used their leisure for more fulfilling activities. By the time he wrote *One Dimensional Man* (1964), however, Marcuse also believed that technological rationality was a vehicle for "repressive mastery."[33] And he asked whether nature too, not only human beings, required liberation from technology. The Promethean urge for mastery and control, Marcuse concluded, required exorcism such that human beings, along with other species sharing the planet, might fully experience their erotic and aesthetic potential.

Developing the work of the Frankfurt theorists, Jürgen Habermas investigated how the "lifeworld" was being colonized by instrumental rationality and the efficient pursuit of materially productive goals, leaving little room for communicative and interactive ways of being together. The lifeworld, in German *Lebenswelt*, is the realm of intersubjective experience: the socially, culturally and historically constituted world of meanings, beliefs and values. For Habermas, a one-dimensional, technological frame of mind that valorized strategic rationality was occluding other historically prominent expressions of human being, including the exercise of practical and political reason.[34] *Techne* was overwhelming *phronesis.*

Similar concerns were voiced by Jacques Ellul. In *The Technological Society* (1964), Ellul argued that the ever-expanding force of technology had "taken over all of man's activities, not just his productive activity."[35] For Ellul, technology is both a material and ideological force that threatens to homogenize the world under the mandate of efficient control. Technology strips human beings of their capacity for philosophical and political expression.

Not all political theorists see technology as totalizing and inescapable. For some, the challenge we face is developing the political means of selecting good technologies and preventing the use of bad ones. The Roman legal principle "What touches all should be approved by all" was voiced repeatedly in ancient and medieval times, and introduced the summons to parliament of Edward I, King of England, in 1295. Reflecting on this ancient political maxim, Mulford Sibley observes that "Now nothing touches all more directly than the introduction of new technology....[T]he most revolutionary changes of all, those involving technological innovation, are made in secret by corporate managers or boards of directors in response to the demand for immediate economic gain and with little or no consideration for the possible social impact or how it will affect the lives of future generations."[36] For Sibley, the task ahead is fundamentally a political one: to develop "the values, decision-making structure and will to distinguish between and among kinds of technology, rejecting some types and accepting others."[37] Likewise, Langdon Winner notes the centrality of technologies to our lives and underlines the "urgent need to think about them in a political light.... How can and should democratic citizenry participate in decision making about technology?"[38]

The urgency is patent, but the task is bedeviled by the possibility that our capacities for political thought and decision making, along with other cognitive and social faculties, are atrophying owing to our dependence on technology.[39] IT, including search engines, digital assistants (such as Siri, Alexa, Cortana and Google Assistant), and augmented reality (AR) devices potentially reduce the demand for and opportunities to exercise faculties such as memory, common sense, creativity, resourcefulness and face-to-face communication. Political theorists have a particularly important role to play in navigating these troubled waters. They bear the responsibility to employ the most powerful technology—symbolic language—to explore the comparative political risks, costs, and benefits of other technological artifacts, and to help foster the practical judgment needed to develop and deploy them selectively and prudentially.

We depend on technology to meet virtually every need. Acknowledging this dependence, Michael Kraft and Norman Vig observe that "Most people . . . cannot conceive of reverting to earlier life-styles or halting technological progress." Still, many fear that "technological change is out of control and now threatens to overwhelm traditional human relationships and values."[40] In recent years, both the dangers and benefits have grown markedly. People are ever more pleased with the benefits, as "the availability of material resources and technological sophisticated products and services" combine with and accelerate political and cultural transformations to yield a world of "broadening opportunities."[41] At the same time, there is reason to worry about the growing perils, as we become ever more enmeshed in and dependent upon powerful technological systems.

Consider the impact of IT on personal relationships. Social connection is crucial for human happiness and health. Thanks to social media—internet-based platforms that facilitate the creation and exchange of content employing mobile or web-based technologies—people are (digitally) more connected than ever. Facebook, launched in 2004, boasted over a billion users within a decade, and quickly doubled that number. YouTube experienced a similarly meteoric rise. In just over a decade from its 2005 founding, over a billion hours of YouTube were being watched every day. Other social media have also expanded rapidly, including Flickr, Google+, Instagram, LinkedIn, Pinterest, Reddit, Skype, Snapchat, Tumblr, Twitter, WhatsApp and platforms more prominent in the non-English speaking world such as LINE, QQ, Qzone, Sina Weibo, Viber and WeChat. These social media collectively have billions of users. While many platforms evidence short life spans, their aggregate impact is pervasive and enduring.

Over a quarter of the global population use social media. Youth are particularly dependent upon it, with young adults, on average, sending well over a hundred text messages a day and digital connections becoming more frequent than face-to-face socializing. This can produce an "ambient awareness" of information, events and people that is not available to the "unplugged" person.[42] And there are the positive benefits of "crowd-sourced" knowledge from social media. We have discovered the power of "collective intelligence" and the "wisdom of the crowd" as digitally connected people produce vast amounts of helpful information, comparative ratings, and collective judgment. With an eye to this phenomenon, it has been said that "the smartest person in the room is the room." [43] Today, the room contains billions.

At the same time, the decline in traditional social relationships is a troubling trend. Being digitally connected, with all the distractions it produces, can impede conversation and undermine social life. Indeed, a significant portion of smartphone users employ their devices purposefully to avoid social interaction. With young adults spending a third of their days online, rising digital connectivity may signal a decline in the human practice of and capacity for non-virtual social interaction. Online and virtual life can be enthralling. Indeed, people engaged in playing video games and participating in virtual worlds often derive greater satisfaction from their online activity than anything else they do in their lives. But the social and health effects of ever more alluring and powerful forms of IT are worrisome. People who spend much of their day online and multitasking across social media platforms—behavior particularly common among youth—demonstrate decreased cognitive control, are more likely to be distracted, have fewer non-virtual friends, suffer from greater levels of anxiety and depression, and have more difficulty concentrating and sleeping.[44] The impact of IT on people's personal lives is hard to exaggerate. The impact of IT on political life is no less troubling, and, at the same time, equally rife with opportunities.

## THE POLITICS OF INFORMATION TECHNOLOGY

Technological innovations have long been credited with the power to improve political life. The industrial factory, rural electrification, synthetic fertilizer, the automobile, telephone, radio, television and nuclear power were all celebrated in their times as democratizing forces.[45] Over the last half century, the technology most frequently deemed transformative of political life has been electronic media. President Barack Obama likely owed both his national campaigns' successes to their use of the internet, social media, and mobile-phone messaging to raise funds and mobilize volunteers and voters. Donald Trump's subsequent campaign took the exploitation of IT to a new level, using social media and the data it generated both to mobilize citizens likely to endorse him and to discourage turnout by those more likely to back his rival.[46] The 40 million tweets that circulated on November 8, 2016 made Twitter the largest source of breaking news on the US presidential election that day.

In 1967, Marshall McLuhan could already say that electronic media "has reconstituted dialogue on a global scale. Its message is Total Change, ending psychic, social, economic and political parochialism. The old civic, state and national groupings have become unworkable.... Too many people know too much about each other. Our new environment compels commitment and participation. We have become irrevocably involved with, and responsible for, each other."[47] The arrival of social media has vindicated much of McLuhan's vision. Some scholars call it "liberation technology," as it is frequently employed to mobilize protest and political participation, monitor electoral fraud, police abuses and other wrongdoings, scrutinize and hold governments accountable, and safeguard human rights and political freedoms.[48] The internet and social media have indeed created a digital global village, expanding our awareness of and sense of responsibility for planetary neighbors.

The political impact of IT is perhaps most vividly demonstrated in its deployment against oppression. So-called "smart mobs" mobilized by way of SMS text messaging or other social media have helped topple autocratic regimes. The ouster of Egypt's President Hosni Mubarak in 2011, after more than two weeks of popular protest, was much abetted by a Facebook page condemning police brutality. The page, "We Are All Khaled Said," depicted the mangled face of a young man who had been tortured and murdered by the Egyptian police during Mubarak's rule, as well as an earlier photo of Khaled Said in perfect health. It went viral, gaining half a million 'likes' before the Mubarak regime shut down the internet at the height of the protest. Reflecting on the event, Zeynep Tufecki observes that "perhaps for the first time in history, an internet user could click yes on an electronic invitation to a revolution. Hundreds of thousands did so.… The rest is history— a complex and still-unfinished one, with many ups and downs. But for Egypt, and for the rest of the world, things would never be the same again."[49] The so-called "Arab Spring" of 2010–12 demonstrated the political power of social media in over a dozen countries in North Africa and the Middle East that experienced widespread political demonstrations.

Around the globe, activists now utilize Facebook to initiate protests, Twitter to coordinate them, and YouTube to broadcast them. Even when IT does not help topple autocrats, it plays an ever-larger role in political life. For example, Ushahidi, a free and open-source digital platform, has been used in more than 160 countries to create maps of human rights violations, electoral fraud and malpractice, corruption and natural disaster damage. *Ushahidi* is a Swahili word that means *testimony*. Originally developed in Kenya to chart reports of postelection violence in 2008 employing SMS messaging, this "crisis-mapping" technology has been expanded to accommodate various social media platforms. By crowdsourcing data, Ushahidi has monitored elections in the US and many other nations, sped relief to victims of war and natural disasters, aided United Nations peacekeeping efforts, and mapped incidences of fraud, violence and sexual abuse. Other explicitly activist platforms include Change.org, Avaaz, Kiva, MoveOn, mySociety, and Upworthy, with aggregate memberships in the hundreds of millions.

Information technology is not only a force for liberation, however. It allows governments to monitor, surveil and repress citizen communication and assemblies, and to identify and punish dissenters. China has the largest number of internet users in the world, and the most powerful monitoring, filtering, censoring and controlling mechanisms. During the Arab Spring events, authorities specifically blocked the words "Egypt" and "Jasmine" from major Chinese search engines following the revolutionary activities in Egypt and the "Jasmine Revolution" in Tunisia that forced President Ben Ali to flee his country. In some authoritarian states, governments not only monitor, filter and censor information, they also employ online hackers to attack dissidents and post progovernment comments. Such media manipulation is not limited to the domestic politics of autocratic regimes. In the 2016 US election, Russian operatives used fake American identities on Facebook and Instagram to post and trend ideologically divisive images, stories and misinformation.[50] The apparent intent of Russia's authoritarian government in supporting these operatives was to influence the American election and undermine the democratic process.

191

The linkage of IT to authoritarian government is a pressing concern. Global philanthropist and financier George Soros has warned that giant companies such as Google and Facebook have become near monopolies. Were such IT platforms to form an alliance with authoritarian states, Soros warns, the level of surveillance and manipulation "may well result in a web of totalitarian control the likes of which not even Aldous Huxley or George Orwell could have imagined."[51] There is no doubt that IT can be, is, and will be deployed for politically unsavory ends, including authoritarianism. Failure to heed this threat, Evgeny Morozov warns, amounts to "cyber-utopianism."[52] It is a dangerous delusion. Politically speaking, information technology will always be a double-edged sword.

Cyberspace is a de facto public realm. But it is largely owned and operated by private businesses. Historically, IT has tended toward monopolies.[53] The power of today's largest IT corporations is abetted by the "network effect," wherein the more clients that employ a platform, the more useful that platform becomes to each user, increasing its appeal. The deployment of "analytics" also contributes to monopolistic power, as platforms with large user bases can measure, test and adapt their products in a quickly changing digital landscape to better exploit the marketplace.[54] Consequently, dominant platforms grow ever larger and fewer, while smaller platforms cannot gain a foothold or adapt quickly enough to survive. The network effect and analytics favor a small number of IT platforms in private hands that control the lion's share of cyberspace.

The increasing capacity of IT platforms to manipulate and control users is also a pressing concern. In 1971, Nobel Prize winning economist Herbert Simon presciently observed that in an "information-rich world," the most precious resource is attention, and the primary question is how "to allocate that attention efficiently among the overabundance of information sources that might consume it."[55] Most IT platforms are constructed to solicit and sustain their users' attention in order to increase revenues, which depend upon the frequency with which users are exposed to advertisements. Over fifty years ago, Jürgen Habermas drew attention to the "transformation of the public sphere into a medium of advertising," making it less a forum for citizen engagement and more a marketplace characterized by the manipulation of consumers. Such a "world fashioned by mass media," Habermas worried, would strip the public sphere of its most important function: critical exchange among citizens, including rational debate about public authority.[56] The rise of social media and its growing impact on the public sphere accentuates the importance of Habermas' concern.

Critics charge that online political activity, often labeled "clicktivism," represents "the digital degradation of political activism." The concern is that clicktivism replaces or "crowds out" traditional forms of political participation. Rather than engaging in and working to build personal relationships and sustainable organizations, people take the easy road of signing a few online petitions, "liking" an event or candidate, forwarding a Tweet to friends and followers, and perhaps giving a few dollars to a crowd-funded cause. As such, digital politics replaces sustained, face-to-face activism with isolated acts of watching alone, taking action alone, and, ironically, even sharing alone.

Social media content that induces mirth, awe, anxiety, and anger is more likely to be shared or forwarded. But we are not necessarily better informed, or more likely to engage in reasonable debate, when we are laughing, stupefied, fretting or fuming. Online "micro-donations" of time, ideological support, and money may amount to little more than "virtue signaling" that reaffirms one's ethical or political alignment with a like-minded tribe. It is the equivalent of a sugar rush: instant gratification with scant nutritional value. Real political engagement is more like eating your vegetables. In any case, most social media users do not appreciate or enjoy online political content. They find encounters with those of opposing political views stressful and frustrating and believe they have even less in common after engagement than before. Consequently, fewer than 1 in 10 social media users frequently address politics, while more than 4 out of 5 refrain from engaging in political discussion with online friends.[57]

Enthusiasts of digital politics, in contrast, observe that there is little evidence to suggest that online activities crowd out traditional political participation. Most people do not participate in politics off-line, either, so online activities may serve as a gateway, bringing otherwise uninvolved citizens, particularly youth, "up the ladder of engagement." Given the massive numbers of people involved in online activism, there can be significant worldly impacts. In turn, by "injecting the political into the everyday spaces and places of popular culture," hashtag activism and other forms of digital politics, which garner massive outpourings of support for causes such as violent racial discrimination or sexual abuse (e.g. #BlackLivesMatter and #MeToo), produce rapid cultural shifts regarding socio-political issues and attitudes that otherwise might remain suppressed. The undeniable fact is that digital politics is growing and constitutes the preferred and most prolific form of political participation in some countries and contexts, particularly for youth.[58]

IT has not only transformed the public sphere by impacting what goes on *around* us. IT modifies what goes on *in* us. Indeed, IT memes have effectively altered the neural processes and behavioral habits of half the world's population. Powerful IT platforms in pursuit of advertising revenues intentionally engineer addiction. Programmers have coined the term *brain hacking* to describe the methods used to form these addictive habits. Today, smartphone users are almost always attached to their devices, checking them for messages scores of times a day and employing them for multitasking across numerous platforms. Studies reveal that these activities alter brains and behavior.[59] Those deprived of their devices and internet access experience symptoms consistent with the effects of withdrawal from addictive drugs.

As people become ever more susceptible to the power of digital platforms and devices, the human capacity to exercise "freedom of mind" is threatened, with "far reaching political consequences." [60] Personal investment in political life may wane or evaporate as our attention is channeled into a cornucopia of addictive online exchanges, games, infotainment and shopping. When political issues do rise to the top of our news feeds, as "netizens" we may endorse or deride them merely by "clicking" a button, without engaging in critical thinking or addressing the demands of embodied action. While IT can clearly facilitate spontaneous endorsements and protests, it may simultaneously undermine the development of more enduring political relationships, alliances, organization and leadership. Smart mobs and "adhocracies" composed of fleeting cyberspace connections are not the best recipes for building and sustaining democratic institutions.[61] Yet we are prompted—perhaps the better word would be *engineered*—to believe that the solution to every problem is only a click away.

In turn, IT platforms may monitor, censor, or promote specific services, products, behavior and people in ways that are closed to public scrutiny. An experiment conducted during the 2010 US congressional election presented some Facebook users with an "I voted" button to click at the top of their news feed, while others also saw profile photographs of a few Facebook friends who had already clicked the "I voted" button. The impact was powerful: users who received the "social message" with their friends' photographs were over 2% more likely to vote, translating into 340,000 more votes cast.[62] That is a margin large enough to sway a national election. In this case, the experiment did not encourage support for a specific candidate. But the political capacity of IT platforms had been well demonstrated. This capacity is much enhanced when political campaigns use the "big data" such platforms generate to "micro-target" specific constituencies, at times dissuading voting through "dark" advertising. Facebook underwent scrutiny and criticism after the 2016 presidential election when it was discovered that data on over 80 million users were harvested by third parties without the users' consent to influence the election.[63]

The manipulation of citizens in cyberspace is perhaps most pronounced in the arena of "fake news." Social media and the internet are increasingly relied upon as sources of political information and misinformation. The abundance of misinformation in cyberspace is a product of the absence of traditional "gatekeepers," such as newspaper and magazine editors or television news program producers and anchors, who are responsible for ensuring news stories are vetted and fact-checked. During the 2016 presidential election, most US citizens were exposed to fake news stories from numerous IT platforms, and about half of those who recalled such stories believed them to be true. Importantly, people were much more likely to believe fake news that favored their preferred candidate.[64] In the three months prior to the election, patently fake election news stories generated more total engagement on Facebook than the combined top election stories produced by 19 major news outlets, including *The New York Times*, *The Washington Post*, *The Huffington Post*, and *NBC News*.[65]

In 1969, a tobacco industry executive wrote a memo entitled "Doubt Is Our Product." At the time, the tobacco industry was employing a small number of scientists to cast doubt on the scientifically established fact that smoking tobacco was addictive and dangerous to health. Decades later, the fossil fuel industry employed teams of scientists to cast doubt on the facts of climate change.[66] In both instances, sowing the seeds of doubt was aimed at protecting corporate profits. In 2018, Donald Trump sowed the seeds of doubt with charges that the mainstream media supplies "fake news." Here, again, doubt mongering was not aimed at cultivating citizens' capacity to think critically and make informed choices based on the best available evidence. It was designed to undermine belief that there are scientific and historical facts that citizens can and should collectively acknowledge, regardless of their partisan alignments. To the extent that citizens doubt the existence of non-partisan facts, political life is jeopardized.

Bernard Baruch, an advisor to Presidents Woodrow Wilson and Franklin D. Roosevelt who was appointed as US representative to the United Nations Atomic Energy Commission by President Harry Truman, stated: "On the question of principles, it is an inalienable right each of us has to express opinions on every policy animating this country, whether national or international. That is the highest function of those who live under a political democracy; of those who cherish the right of free speech. Every man has the right to an opinion but no man has a right to be wrong in his facts. Nor, above all, to persist in errors as to facts."[67] Baruch's words were paraphrased by Senator Daniel Patrick Moynihan, among others, who tersely remarked that "Everyone is entitled to his own opinion, but not to his own facts." Today many people, including politicians in the highest offices, make claim to their own facts.

Politicians can unabashedly deploy fabricated facts because citizens navigating cyberspace increasingly find themselves in a blinkered world of fake and personalized news.[68] Everyone is susceptible to the confirmation bias. People search for and predominantly perceive those bits of reality that confirm their beliefs and values. Challenging evidence tends to get ignored. The confirmation bias is a natural predisposition and its effects are widespread. The problem is that cyberspace has made it very easy to ensconce ourselves in self-reinforcing communities of the like-minded. In this blinkered realm, we hear, see and share only those facts—or fictions—that support our personal interests and ideologies.[69]

Just as high-school cliques homogenize the opinions of their young members, so electronic networks can reinforce and polarize the political ideologies of their users. The terms "echo-chamber" and "filter bubble" have been used to describe the experience of inhabiting a cyberspace world wherein one encounters only news and information that aligns with one's own dispositions, likes and dislikes, and previous online activities. Instead of being exposed to challenging and diverse opinions and data, as one might when reading a good newspaper, people online receive the "Daily Me." Their newsfeeds consist primarily of information, real or fabricated, that reinforces existing beliefs and predilections. Rather than serving as a shared public sphere, cyberspace can function as a mirror of one's own profile, a social media "selfie" composed of personal facts, friends, fictions and fixations.[70]

Fake news often falls into the realm of the absurd, and can easily be dismissed. Still, some fake news is quite believable, especially when it reinforces one's own ideological commitments. In turn, technologies for audio and video manipulation are improving rapidly, allowing broadcast video to be digitally altered with increasing sophistication. To make matters worse, fake news and misinformation are now circulated on social media by software applications that are automated. These "chatbots" can be programmed to post or tweet stories and opinions, mimicking human users. Networks of linked internet bots, called botnets, can follow and re-message each other, creating the illusion of opinions or events that are trending on social media. Campaigning politicians seeking digital support can purchase fake Twitter followers through agencies that create dummy accounts. Indeed, more than one in four Twitter accounts may be a bot, with large numbers of bots also engaged in blogging.[71] Bots clutter cyberspace and consume bandwidth, making it more cumbersome for people to communicate effectively. More ominously, they pass as real people, misrepresenting and reshaping the political landscape.[72]

Freedom of the press, it used to be said, belongs to those who own it. That has changed in an age of internet blogs, chatrooms and social media. Average citizens now have the virtually cost-free opportunity to communicate with large audiences. In many respects, however, the challenge citizens face is no longer how to access or widely disseminate information or opinions. The challenge is to discover and share useful and valid information with diverse citizens amidst a surplus of data, disinformation, automated trends, "click-bait" headlines designed to lure visitors onto fake news websites, and digitally manipulated videos.

Unlike newspapers, radio and television, social media and other forms of IT provide two-way or multiway forms of communication. Users are not only passive recipients of information but its creators, commentators and distributers. In such a world, citizens have a heightened responsibility, absent traditional gatekeepers, to verify stories, tweets and news before passing them along. Voltaire observed that if one can be made to believe absurdities, one can be made to commit injustices. The same relationship holds for fake news that spans the spectrum from the patently absurd, to the reasonable but demonstrably false, to the digitally manipulated and robotically trended. Democracy is an institutional arrangement that employs reasoned persuasion rather than force as a means of achieving collective order. But reasoned persuasion requires a shared foundation in reality. Whenever a common world of facts wanes, violence tends to wax. Nazism and Stalinism were cases in point, as the ideology, rampant propaganda and "big lies" employed by these regimes were coupled with appalling violence. Truth took a forced holiday, and the results were catastrophic. Absent a shared world of brute facts, brute force is never far behind.

The poet T.S. Eliot asked "Where is the wisdom we have lost in knowledge? Where is the knowledge we have lost in information?" Today we might add: Where is the information we have lost in cyberspace shams? Citizens who employ the internet and social media are not simply consumers of information. In an age of fake news and fabricated facts, they have become gatekeepers of truth and bear the corresponding responsibilities. Whether citizens are up to the task is yet to be decided.

## AUTOMATION AND ARTIFICIAL INTELLIGENCE

Robots might spare us much back-breaking, tiresome, repetitive, dangerous work. In turn, the efficiency of robots promises to stimulate the economy, producing more wealth and allowing more leisure. At the same time, robots and other forms of automation may cause unprecedented levels of unemployment. Perhaps, if governments institute Guaranteed Annual Incomes (GAIs), those who cannot find meaningful employment will be able to enjoy increased leisure while still managing to satisfy their basic needs. This is an option increasingly explored and advocated by scholars and politicians of all stripes. Conservatives believe a GAI may keep the economy growing while replacing inefficient and expensive entitlement programs and their bureaucracies with a single, simple, cost effective alternative. Liberals and socialists believe a GAI may provide the most effective and humane welfare net, ensuring basic needs with no loss of dignity, as its benefits would be received by all. Experimentation is certainly in order to determine if and how GAI programs might sustain strong economies while humanely addressing welfare needs in a world much disrupted by emerging technologies.

Even if a GAI proves to be effective, automation may have untoward social and psychological consequences. More leisure may not be as beneficial as we think. Most people believe their happiest moments are to be found in their free time. But research reveals that people experience greater happiness while they are working.[73] Taking on challenging tasks and engaging in meaningful work and interaction with colleagues produces a sense of fulfillment and connection, while leisure hours can be dogged by boredom and distraction.

Automation poses other ethical and political challenges. Self-driving vehicles, for example, must be programed to decide who will become the injured party in an unavoidable accident—the passenger(s) of the self-driving vehicle, the pedestrian on the nearby sidewalk, or the multiple children in the car driven by a distracted parent that has drifted out of its lane. Likewise, if autonomous weapon systems and drones are deployed by military and police forces, algorithms (automatic decision processes) will determine which targets will be engaged, disabled, or killed. How will these algorithms be developed to reflect ethical standards, and who will decide what these standards are? In turn, how will automation be politically regulated and deployed? Such ethical and political conundrums are deepened when private corporations are involved in the development and deployment of automated systems, as the source code for the automation algorithms are typically deemed proprietary and kept secret. Such source codes, and their biases, remain hidden from view and shielded from public oversight.

The problem goes well beyond automated weapon systems, drones and self-driving vehicles. Most IT platforms employ algorithms to determine the rankings and prominence of search results, advertised products and news feeds. Algorithms are also employed by government agencies and businesses for a wide array of purposes, such as determining which loan applications to approve, which schools children will attend, which applicants to select for job interviews, how employees will be evaluated, which medical procedures to follow, which inmates will be given parole, and in "predictive policing" to determine where officers patrol for crime.

An algorithm is a mathematical formula. As such, it sounds neutral and impartial. Often it is not. "Algorithmic discrimination" occurs when the formula employed by computer programs to produce useful data, rankings, or predictions demonstrates an unintentional but significant bias against specific individuals or groups, notwithstanding the presumed neutrality of the data being mined. The problem is that the data employed to construct an algorithm, unavoidably, is selectively chosen. It represents some subsection of the current state of the world. When the data employed demonstrates an inherent bias, the algorithms derived from the data are likely to be equally biased. Effectively, the status quo gets automated.

So, for example, life insurance agencies employing an algorithm but unaware of its specific effects might systematically charge more for black men than white men in the United States because black men, the data confirm, have a higher likelihood of early death. Likewise, banks employing algorithms might refuse loans to people with specific ZIP codes because clients living within those geographic areas have been more likely to default on their loans in the past. But is it fair for an individual to pay penalties and suffer hardships simply because of the color of his skin or the numbers in her ZIP code? Algorithms can transform accurate statistics into unjust policies. Most problematically, the algorithmic discrimination may remain hidden in the computer code so that neither agents nor victims become aware of the bias.

A political theory, while aimed at truth, can never fully escape the ideological biases of the theorist. Likewise, an algorithm, while aimed at predictive accuracy, can never fully escape the biases inherent in the data it utilizes. Complex algorithms and predictive models grounded in the mining of "big data" will increasingly be deployed to transform institutions, inform policy, and shape our personal lives. The problem is that predictive models are constructed, as Cathy O'Neil writes, "from the choices we make about which data to pay attention to—and which to leave out. Those choices . . . are fundamentally moral."[74] Future societies will be ever more beholden to algorithms and automation, and increasingly vexed by the moral and political challenges they present.

When algorithms are employed to supplement or replace human judgment, they should be open to public examination whenever possible. The mathematical formula and automated processes used to manage our personal and collective lives ought not achieve moral or political authority based on their inscrutability. However, as the "Internet of Things" grows—with tens of billions of digitally connected machines, appliances, vehicles, buildings, homes, computers, smart phones, and electronic devices (many embedded in human bodies)—massive amounts of information will be available for data mining and analytics.[75] Soon the Cloud may know us better than we know ourselves. Instances of algorithmic discrimination are likely to grow, as will opportunities for control and manipulation.

Some would suggest that we do away with automated forms of analysis, judgment and prediction altogether, putting people back in charge. That solution is unlikely, given technological trends. It also mistakenly assumes that if people were in charge, the problem of bias would disappear. We know better.

As history and social scientific research well demonstrate, all people, including experts in their respective fields, are inherently biased. People are also notoriously bad analysts and predictors. Their intuitions are often wrong, and their judgments suffer from the confirmation bias and other forms of self-deception. People frequently fool themselves, and others. To judge well, one must exercise critical thinking, remain open to and seek disconfirming facts, be wary of inherent biases, and regularly revise and reform one's assessments in light of the best available evidence.[76] That is not what most people do most of the time.

In any case, algorithmic predictions employing IT generated data can achieve benefits not otherwise attainable. In 2008, for example, Google outperformed the Centers for Disease Control and Prevention in predicting regional flu outbreaks by analyzing the geolocalities of its users' searches for flu symptoms. Such analytics may be even more accurate regarding issues that traditional surveys are unlikely to accurately gauge, such as attitudes and behaviors that people are reluctant to discuss openly.[77]

Adequately addressing the most pressing global challenges—climate change; food scarcity; resource depletion; pandemic disease; economic opportunity and equity in an increasingly automated world; and geopolitical instability, including failing states, civil and interstate conflict, and the accompanying refugee crises—requires digitally distributed data gathering, including crowdsourced "citizen science," big data analytics, and the coordination of human and artificial intelligence.[78] To foreswear these technological advances would amount to tackling the most daunting challenges of our times with one hand tied behind our backs.

Artificial intelligence, or AI, has already matched or surpassed human intelligence and competence in a growing number of arenas, including mathematical computation; games of strategy, such as chess and Go; language translation, reading and comprehension; medical diagnostics; various forms of complex pattern recognition, including facial identification; and driving vehicles. AI is even making strides in the arenas of creative writing, music composition and other forms of artistic endeavor.[79] If AI becomes proficient at computer programming, it may build ever better models of itself. This recursive self-improvement might lead to the development of superintelligence—also known as strong AI or Artificial General Intelligence. At that point, AI will match or surpass human intelligence and competence in all domains.

"The advent of strong AI is the most important transformation this century will see," computer scientist and inventor Ray Kurzweil predicts. "Indeed, it's comparable in importance to the advent of biology itself. It will mean that a creation of biology has finally mastered its own intelligence and discovered means to overcome its limitations."[80] Kurzweil maintains that superintelligence will be developed by mid-century if not sooner. Other experts in the field believe it may take longer, or will never occur. Still others hold that the future belongs not to AI per se, but to "centaur" or "cyborg" technology that blends human capacities with various forms of artificial intelligence.

The cyborg is a human being that has artificial (electronic or mechanical) implants or appendages. A centaur is a human being that operates interdependently with an external form of (typically, Cloud-based) artificial intelligence. The centaur demonstrates the benefits of Intelligence Augmentation (IA). While the centaur may have some embedded digital devices, its defining feature will be the synergetic power gained by blending human capacities and skills with artificial intelligence.

The ethics and politics of a world populated by centaurs, cyborgs, and other "posthumans" is difficult to conceive, let alone predict. Hans Jonas, a student of Heidegger, writes:

> All previous ethics... had these interconnected tacit premises in common: that the human condition, determined by the nature of man and the nature of things, was given once for all; that the human good on that basis was readily determinable; and that the range of human action and therefore responsibility was narrowly circumscribed. [T]hese premises no longer hold... Modern technology has introduced actions of such novel scale, objects, and consequences that the framework of former ethics can no longer contain them.... No previous ethics had to consider the global condition of human life and the far-off future, even existence, of the race. These now being an issue demands, in brief, a new conception of duties and rights, for which previous ethics and metaphysics provide not even the principles, let alone a ready doctrine.[81]

Jonas wrote these prescient words in 1984. They appear more apposite every day.

Bill Joy, the former chief scientist and co-founder of Sun Microsystems, addressed the most dangerous threats from technologies in the twenty-first century. In his provocatively titled cover story of the April 2000 edition of *Wired* magazine, "Why the Future

Doesn't Need Us," and in subsequent writings and interviews, Joy addressed the impact of robotics, genetic engineering, and nanotechnology. Such technologies may well cure diseases, extend our lives, eliminate back-breaking labor, end material poverty, and even heal the Earth, Joy admitted. But they may also produce self-replicating organisms that quickly get out of control, posing a greater danger to humankind than weapons of mass destruction.[82]

Technologies produce unintended consequences. When technologies are extremely powerful, the unintended consequences may be catastrophic. The danger of our creating "Frankenstein" monsters is for many the primary worry. But technological successes, not malfunctions, may produce the most frightful outcomes. The greatest danger may not be unintended consequences, but the equally irreversible impacts of intended consequences.

As assistive technologies become ever more sophisticated and powerful, some believe they will function like "guardian angels." Those who choose to go without them will feel "as handicapped relative to other humans as a human today who is deaf, blind, and mute."[83] We might realistically envision a world—perhaps in the not-too-distant future—where humans are successfully modified to increase, strengthen or add physical and mental attributes and abilities. Assume for the moment that these technologies deliver the goods, with no pernicious side effects. There are no Frankenstein monsters: just faster, stronger, smarter, healthier human beings. How could one argue against such success?

The political problem is that human enhancement might produce a caste system, with different opportunities, rights and privileges accorded to different kinds of persons depending upon their abilities. The decision simply to "opt out" of such technological enhancement may be unrealistic. Certainly, individuals may choose to live their lives with the bodies and minds that nature gave them. But consider the plight of parents. Assuming they have the resources to do so, would parents feel compelled to genetically modify their children, or give them cyborg enhancements after birth? Refusing such technological enhancements might condemn offspring to second or third-class citizenship. That may be too much of a burden for parents to bear. An enhancement arms race would develop, with each new generation displaying a marked improvement over its predecessor. Older siblings, no less than parents and grandparents, would quickly become economically, socially and politically disadvantaged if not defunct, the equivalent of an outdated operating system. It is impossible to see where a human enhancement arms race might end, but its trajectory is certainly troubled.

Will emerging technologies—including IT, artificial intelligence, robotics, nanotechnology, genetic engineering and synthetic biology—serve as guardian angels, or are they devils in disguise? Addressing genetic (germline) engineering and cyborg technologies, Bill McKibben observes that

[W]e stand precariously on the sharp ridge between the human past and the posthuman future, the moment when meaning might evaporate in a tangle of genes or chips. As we have seen, human meaning turns out to be fragile—we can either pile sandbags around it to keep it safe, or watch it wash away. And if it goes, it will take democracy with it. Forever.[84]

In a similar vein, Francis Fukuyama argues that genetically enhanced humans, not to mention cyborgs and superintelligent machines, will usher in a posthuman future where loss of belief in an essential human nature will lead to the loss of our "moral sense." That, in turn, will spell the demise of human rights and the end of democracy.[85]

With an eye to future politics, some insist that we should initiate the development of "person rights," as technological advances may soon present us with the challenge of recognizing and protecting genetically enhanced humans, centaurs, cyborgs, and potentially self-aware machines.[86] Indeed, growing numbers of "posthumanists" and "transhumanists" eagerly anticipate a post-Darwinian future where technology, rather than the blind forces of natural selection, will generate new forms of intelligent life that can blaze their own evolutionary paths. Whether the future merits such sanguine visions, or will more closely reflect dystopian nightmares, remains to be seen. One thing is clear: its political theory is yet to be written.

## The Technology of Theory

Technology has great benefits. Medicine protects us. Agriculture feeds us. Machines and bureaucracies satisfy sundry needs. Media allow us to connect and communicate. Educational and political institutions provide knowledge, security, freedom and justice. Without technology, we would find ourselves back in the Stone Age. Arguably, we would not even be fully human. To the extent that we understand symbolic language as a technological artifact, becoming fundamentally impacted by technology constitutes the defining feature of our species.

With Aristotle in mind, we can say that human beings are political animals in the sense that our full nature and potential developed and is manifested within collective life. With Darwin and more recent evolutionary science in mind, we can say that human being is the product of the interaction of genes and the memes, mores, mechanisms of governance and other technological artifacts, symbolic and physical, that our species crafted over the ages.

In 1941, Nazi bombers destroyed the British House of Commons. Two years later, Prime Minister Winston Churchill gave a speech to parliament demanding that the building be restored to its former condition, observing that "We shape our buildings, and afterwards our buildings shape us." The same might be said of all our technologies, including political artifacts. To become a "slave of the law," as Cicero advocates, or to "pay any price, bear any burden, meet any hardship, support any friend, oppose any foe to assure the survival and the success of liberty," as John F. Kennedy extolled, is to align ourselves with a principle and devote ourselves to an ideal. These mores both constrain and elevate us. Political theory deploys critical thinking and practical judgment to develop worthy mores—conceptual and normative artifacts that describe, explain, order and transform collective life. As strange as it may sound, political theorists are in the business of persuading people to become the tools of these tools.

The development and use of political artifacts to shape the souls of citizens received its first theorization with Plato. The tradition of political theory testifies to the historical development of such efforts. Recall Mary Wollstonecraft's argument, grounded in the thought of the Scottish Enlightenment, that if women were to gain the rights of men, they would also come to exhibit their fair share of the virtues. The political technology of constitutionally enshrined rights, Wollstonecraft was saying, would significantly and beneficially alter the character of citizens. Centuries later, as B.F. Skinner observed, the betterment of society by way of the design of rules, institutions and other political artifacts, though still in its infancy, had the potential to safeguard civilization and heal the planet. It is an unavoidable, interminable and dangerous undertaking.

We are *Homo fabricatus*. And we can be made better or worse by the technologies we develop, whether they are constructed of sentences, statutes, steel or silicon. Of course, the criteria for better and worse will always be much debated. To engage in that debate fruitfully, however, we must exercise critical thinking and practical judgment that is informed by evidence and open to difference. So it is safe to say that we should welcome technologies—educational, professional, social and political—that develop our capacities for critical thinking and practical judgment. We might also agree that technological artifacts—be they concepts or theories, constitutions or laws, institutions or processes, media or machines, algorithms or artificial intelligence—should facilitate the exercise of freedom, the pursuit of justice, the strengthening of democracy, and the advancement of knowledge, health and prosperity. We become worse when our tools cause our capacity for reasoning together in pursuit of these goods to atrophy.

Can we sustain liberty, reason, justice and democracy in the wake of accelerating technological innovation? Sustainability entails managing the scale and speed of change to conserve core values and relationships.[87] Whether we can employ ever more powerful and seductive forms of IT without undermining democratic institutions and our capacity for reason, ever more powerful means of human enhancement without threatening liberty and justice, and ever more powerful forms of AR, IA, and AI without undermining human prospects remains to be seen. Recalling Constant's concern, there may well be tools that are too heavy for the hands of humankind.

"The rise of the human neocortex," novelist Arthur Koestler observed, "is the only example of evolution providing a species with an organ which it does not know how to use."[88] Our technological innovations demonstrate this fact with terrifying force.

Wendell Berry, the agrarian man of letters, counsels us "to worry about the predomi-nance of the supposition, in a time of great technological power, that humans either know enough already, or can learn enough soon enough, to foresee and forestall any bad consequences of their use of that power."[89] Our Promethean ingenuity may prove too meager to foresee, avoid, or remedy its impacts. Upstream ingenuity will always exceed the ability to control downstream effects.[90]

Material technologies have world historic impacts. One might view the printing press, for instance, as facilitating the Protestant Reformation, and the subsequent formation of the nation-state system. But the ideas that were printed really made the difference: the indulgences issued by the Catholic Church, and Luther's 95 theses and other pamphlets that were published in opposition. Likewise, computers, smartphones, and data centers have made the internet and social media possible, with all their far-flung effects. But the ideas communicated through IT will have the biggest impact. Notwithstanding the crucial importance of material technology in shaping the path of history, for a symbolic species the most crucial artifacts are often conceptual.

Victor Hugo said that "there is one thing stronger than all the armies of the world: and that is an idea whose time has come." Ideas can be formidable forces. Yet ideas do not arrive in the world fully formed and poised to assume positions of authority. They are typically born as outcasts, see countless setbacks and revisions, and must be defended for long periods before their "time" finally arrives. Still, Hugo is right: ideas can become powerful agents of social and political change.

Political theories are sources of such transformative ideas. Like scientific theories, however, political theories are never actually proven to be true. At best, they survive all efforts to disprove them. The same fate awaits democratic practices, as John Dewey argued. Democracy is a lived experiment. The means of self-government and self-realization develop through ongoing efforts to solve social problems. Democracy stands or falls, Dewey insists, with the use of "intelligence to liberate and liberalize action . . . for the sake of possibilities not yet given."[91] At their best, democratic institutions, policies and practices are ethically laudable and practically feasible means of organizing collec-tive life that remain open to revision and replacement in the wake of deliberation and experimentation.

Advancing the democratic experiment entails the theoretical task of employing intelligence for the sake of possibilities not yet given. It entails the exercise of our capaci-ties as a symbolic species, employing linguistic tools to shape collective life. This is not to say that language and the ideas it allows can be reduced to a box of tools that we instru-mentally deploy.[92] In speech and writing many things get named and used for specific purposes. But some words—infinity, for example, or justice and freedom—both set us on a path to knowledge and bespeak the unknowable. Language can broaden and deepen our vision, shelter mystery, and prompt us to aspire to ideals. It allows us to reach for that which exceeds our grasp.

With regards to many technologies, including both concrete and conceptual forms, we do not so much use them as live through them. We think and act as the tools of our tools. That fact underlines the enduring, and arguably increasingly important, mandate for political theory. Political theorists bear the responsibility of exercising their own art and craft, their *techne*, to alert us to the dangers inherent to the life of *Homo fabricatus*, and to limn the ideals that reveal its potential.

## CONCLUSION

The most sophisticated, and potentially dangerous, forms of contemporary technology are grounded in science. They are based on scientific principles and informed by scientific insight. To understand the relationship of political theory to technology we must understand the relationship of political theory to science.

Science expands the boundaries of human knowledge, of what we know and can demonstrate that we know. A scientific theory lands just beyond the periphery of the known, and plants a flag. Experiments are then conducted to confirm and consolidate the newly discovered territory. As often as not, experimentation disconfirms the theory. The flag is extracted and theorists are encouraged to try again or to sail off in new directions. By this method—an exercise of premeditation and trial and error—science steadily expands the boundaries of the known. We are its beneficiaries, as our capacity to navigate what lies within those boundaries becomes ever more educated.

Philosophy, in contrast, explores the boundaries of human knowledge, and speculates on what lies beyond. It addresses how the unknown affects the known, or better said, how what we do not know can and should influence our navigations of the known world. This is especially true for the largely intangible realms of the human mind and human relationships within which political philosophy or political theory does most of its work. Here a little knowledge can be a dangerous thing if it is not leavened with a good dose of humility. In Socratic fashion, political theory serves up the humility.

As a product of the human capacity to straddle the boundaries of the known and unknown, the human condition becomes a quest for meaning. The pursuit of meaning is the part's effort to understand its relationship to the whole. Meaning is about mattering. It concerns purpose. Science has very little to say about meaning and purpose in human life. In this respect, political theory can never be replaced by science, as political life is rife with meaning but short on truth. Still, political theory should make good use of science. To well explore the impact of the unknown on our worldly navigations, political theorists must keep close track of what lies within the ever-expanding boundaries of knowledge.

Paradoxically, the scientific expansion of knowledge does not shrink the mandate of philosophically inclined disciplines like political theory. Science decreases ignorance. Yet in expanding the boundaries of the known, science simultaneously increases the extent of our contiguity to the unknown. Albert Einstein made the point graphically, observing that "As our circle of knowledge expands, so does the circumference of darkness surrounding it." Every expansion of the boundary of knowledge presents the opportunity to more deeply appreciate the extent of our ignorance. It also presents the opportunity to reassess how that ignorance should temper but not deter our efforts skillfully to navigate the world. Hannah Arendt said: "I believe it is very likely that men, if they ever should lose their ability to wonder and thus cease to ask unanswerable questions, also will lose the faculty of asking the answerable questions upon which every civilization is founded."[93] Political theory encourages ever more enlightened navigations of the world by asking questions that elude answers.

Technology undoubtedly will play a crucial role in finding solutions to dire global problems. But perhaps the most pressing problem we face is grappling with our relationship to technology. E.F. Schumacher observed that "man is far too clever to be able to survive without wisdom."[94] Information is organized data. Knowledge is useful information. And practical judgment, a kind of wisdom, is knowledge aware of its limitations. Can we organize the torrent of data we face each day and filter the burgeoning stream of information and misinformation to create useful knowledge? And can we cultivate critical thinking and practical judgment so we remain alert to the limits of our knowledge, and skillfully and ethically orient our ever-improving technological means toward improved ends?

Knowledge makes us clever. Critical thinking and practical judgment places our ingenuity in the context of our limitations, of the unknown and unknowable. Politically speaking, the most dangerous form of ignorance is not the mere absence of knowledge but the absence of awareness that we lack knowledge. The tendency to ignore our ignorance presents the greatest threat to soulcraft and statecraft, as Socrates already realized. There will always be important work for political theorists to do.

## REFERENCES

1   Langdon Winner, *Autonomous Technology* (Cambridge: MIT Press, 1977), 2.

2   Daniel Sarewitz, "Technology and Power," in *A Companion to the Philosophy of Technology*, eds J. Olsen, S. Pedersen and V. Hendricks (Chichester, UK: Wiley-Blackwell, 2009), 308–9.

3   Michael Kraft and Norman Vig, eds, *Technology and Politics* (Durham: Duke University Press, 1988), 307.

4   See Larry Hickman, *John Dewey's Pragmatic Technology* (Bloomington: Indiana University Press, 1990), xii–xiii.

5   Plato, *Laws* (7.803b), in *The Collected Dialogues of Plato*, eds Edith Hamilton and Huntington Cairns (Princeton: Princeton University Press, 1961), 1374.

6   Thomas Hobbes, *Leviathan*, ed. C.B. Macpherson (New York: Penguin, 1968), 81.

7   Jean-Jacques Rousseau, *The Social Contract*, trans. Maurice Cranston (New York: Penguin Books, 1968), 84.

8   See Lewis Mumford, *The Myth of the Machine: Technics and Human Development* (San Diego: Harcourt, Brace Jovanovich, 1967).

9   Hannah Arendt, *The Human Condition* (Chicago: University of Chicago Press), 139.

10   Kevin N. Laland, *Darwin's Unfinished Symphony: How Culture Made the Human Mind* (Princeton: Princeton University Press, 2017).

11   Terence W. Deacon, *The Symbolic Species: The Co-Evolution of Language and the Brain* (New York: W.W. Norton, 1997), 345.

12   Daniel C. Dennett, *Consciousness Explained* (Boston: Little, Brown and Company, 1991), 207.

13   Quoted in Clive Thompson, *Smarter Than You Think: How Technology is Changing Our Minds for the Better* (New York: Penguin, 2013), 51. And see Cecil Day Lewis, *The Poet's Task* (Oxford: Clarendon Press, 1951), 15.

14   Martin Heidegger, *What is Called Thinking*, trans. J. Gray (New York: Harper and Row, 1968), 16; Martin Heidegger, *Poetry, Language and Thought*, trans. A. Hofstadter (New York: Harper and Row, 1971), 146. And see Martin Heidegger, *Poetry, Language and Thought*, 132, 189; Martin Heidegger, *The Question of Being*, trans. W. Kluback and J. Wilde (New York: Twayne Publishers, 1958), 105.

15   Thomas Carlyle, "Signs of the Times," in *The Works of Thomas Carlyle*, ed. H. Traill (Cambridge: Cambridge University Press, 2010), 56–82.

16   Henry David Thoreau, *Walden and Civil Disobedience* (New York: W.W. Norton, 1966), 3, 25, 35.

17   John Kenneth Galbraith, *The New Industrial State* (New York: The New American Library, 1968), 19.

18   Marshall McLuhan, "The Playboy Interview: Marshall McLuhan," March 1969, *Playboy Magazine*. Accessed April 2018 at http://learningspaces.org/files/McLuhan_Playboy_Interview_1969.pdf

19   Max Weber, *The Protestant Ethic and the Spirit of Capitalism* (New York: Charles Scribner's Sons, 1958), 181.

20   Martin Heidegger, "The Question Concerning Technology," in *Basic Writings*, ed. David Farrel Krell (San Francisco: HarperCollins, 1993), 17, 332. And see Leslie Paul Thiele, *Timely Meditations: Martin Heidegger and Postmodern Politics* (Princeton: Princeton University Press, 1995).

21   Martin Heidegger, *Early Greek Thinking*, trans. D. Krell and F. Capuzzi (New York: Harper and Row, 1975), 57.

22   Martin Heidegger, *Existence and Being* (Washington: Regnery Gateway, 1949), 274–75.

23   Nicholas Carr, *The Shallows: What the Internet is Doing to Our Brains* (New York: Norton, 2011), 127, 140, 221. Nicholas Carr, *The Glass Cage: How Computers are Changing Us* (New York: W.W. Norton), 77.

24   Kalle Lasn, *Culture Jam* (New York: William Morrow and Company, 1999), 132, 123.

25   Plato, *Phaedrus*, trans. Walter Hamilton (New York: Penguin Books, 1973), 96–97.

26   Steven Johnson, *Everything Bad is Good for You: How Today's Popular Culture is Actually Making Us Smarter* (New York: Riverhead Books, 2006), 205.

27   See Michel Foucault, "On the Genealogy of Ethics: An Overview of Work in Progress," in Hubert L. Dreyfus and Paul Rabinow, *Michel Foucault: Beyond Structuralism and Hermeneutics*, 2nd edn (Chicago: University of Chicago Press, 1983), 232.

28   Max Weber, *The Protestant Ethic and the Spirit of Capitalism*, trans. Talcott Parsons (New York: Scribner's, 1958), 183.

29   Leo Strauss, *Thoughts on Machiavelli* (Glencoe, Ill.: Free Press, 1959), 298.

30   See Daniel I. O'Neill, *The Burke-Wollstonecraft Debate: Savagery, Civilization, and Democracy* (University Park, Penn.: Pennsylvania University Press, 2007), 1–49.

31   See G.A. Cohen, *Karl Marx's Theory of History* (Princeton: Princeton University Press, 1978), 29.

32   Karl Marx, *Selected Writings*, ed. David McLellan (Oxford: Oxford University Press, 1977), 202.

33   Herbert Marcuse, *One-Dimensional Man* (Boston: Beacon Press, 1964), 9, 12.

34   Jürgen Habermas, *Theory of Communicative Action*, vol. 1: *Reason and the Rationalization of Society*, and vol. 2: *Lifeworld and System: A Critique of Functionalist Reason*, trans. Thomas McCarthy (Boston: Beacon Press, 1984 and 1987).

35   Jacques Ellul, *The Technological Society* (New York: Vintage Books, 1964), 4.

36   Mulford Q. Sibley, *Nature and Civilization: Some Implications for Politics* (Itasca, Ill.: F.E. Peacock Publishers, 1977), 191–92.

37   Sibley, *Nature and Civilization*, 186, 193.

38   Langdon Winner, "Citizen Virtues in a Technological Order," in *Technology and the Politics of Knowledge*, eds Andrew Feenberg and Alastair Hannay (Bloomington: Indiana University Press, 1995), 67.

39   Leslie Paul Thiele, "Against our Better Judgment: Decision Making in an Age of Smart(er) Machines," in *The Political Economy of Robots: Prospects for Prosperity and Security in the Automated 21st Century*, ed. Ryan Kiggins (New York: Palgrave MacMillan, 2018), 183–209.

40   Kraft and Vig, *Technology and Politics*, 3–4.

41   Ronald Inglehart and Christian Welzel, *Modernization, Cultural Change, and Democracy: The Human Development Sequence* (Cambridge: Cambridge University Press, 2005), 3.

42   Thompson, *Smarter Than You Think*, 279.

43   David Weinberger, *Too Big to Know* (New York: Basic Books, 2011); Clay Shirkey, *Cognitive Surplus: How Technology Makes Consumers into Collaborators* (New York: Penguin, 2010); Howard Rheingold, *Smart Mobs: The Next Social Revolution* (New York: Perseus, 2003).

44   E. Castronova and G.G. Wagner, "Virtual Life Satisfaction," *Kyklos* 64 (2011): 313–28; Nicholas Kardaras, "Generation Z: Online and at Risk?" *Scientific American Mind*, Accessed, September 1, 2016. Accessed April 2018 at: www.scientificamerican.com/article/generation-z-online-and-at-risk/?WT.mc_id=send-to-friend; Sherry Turkle, *Reclaiming Conversation: The Power of Talk in a Digital Age* (New York: Penguin, 2015); Lee Rainie and Kathryn Zickuhr, "Americans' Views on Mobile Etiquette," Pew Research Center, August, 2015. Accessed April 2018 at: www.pewinternet.org/2015/08/26/americans-views-on-mobile-etiquette/; Kostadin Kushlev, Jason Proulx and Elizabeth W. Dunn, "Silence Your Phones: Smartphone Notifications Increase Inattention and Hyperactivity Symptoms," *Proceedings of the 2016 CHI Conference on Human Factors in Computing Systems*, 1011–20. Accessed April 2018 at: http://dl.acm.org/citation.cfm?doid=2858036.2858359. Kep Kee Loh and Ryota Kanai, "Higher Media Multi-Tasking Activity is Associated with Smaller Gray-Matter Density in the Anterior Cingulate Cortex," *PLOS One*, September 24, 2014. Accessed April 2018 at: https://doi.org/10.1371/journal.pone.0106698

45   Langdon Winner, *The Whale and the Reactor: A Search for Limits in an Age of High Technology* (Chicago: University of Chicago Press, 2014), 4, 20.

46   Joshua Greene and Sasha Issenberg, "Inside the Trump Bunker, With Days to Go," *Bloomberg Businessweek*, October 27, 2016.

47   Marshall McLuhan and Quentin Fiore, *The Medium is the Massage* (New York: Bantam Books, 1967), 8, 9, 16, 24.

48   Larry Diamond and Marc Plattner, *Liberation Technology: Social Media and the Struggle for Democracy* (Baltimore: Johns Hopkins University Press, 2012).

49   Zeynep Tufekci, *Twitter and Tear Gas: The Power and Fragility of Networked Protest* (New Haven: Yale University Press, 2017), 27.

50   Sheera Fenkel and Katie Benner, "To Create Rifts, Russians Liked Facebook Most," *New York Times*, February 18, 2018, A1.

51   George Soros, "Remarks delivered at the World Economic Forum, Davos Switzerland, January 25, 2018." Accessed April 2018 at: www.georgesoros.com/2018/01/25/remarks-delivered-at-the-world-economic-forum/

52   Evgeny Morozov, *The Net Delusion: The Dark Side of Internet Freedom* (New York: Public Affairs, 2011).

53   Tim Wu, *The Master Switch: The Rise and Fall of Information Empires* (New York: Alfred A. Knopf, 2010).

54   David Karpf, *Analytic Activism: Digital Listening and the New Political Strategy* (Oxford University Press, 2016), 60, 167.

55   Herbert A. Simon, "Designing Organizations for an Information- Rich World," in *Computers, Communication, and the Public Interest*, ed. Martin Greenberger (Baltimore, Md.: Johns Hopkins University Press, 1971), 40–41.

56   Jürgen Habermas, *The Structural Transformation of the Public Sphere* (Cambridge: MIT Press, 1989), 189, 171–72.

57   Joel Penney, *The Citizen Marketer: Promoting Political Opinion in the Social Media Age* (Oxford University Press, 2017), 152; Karpf, *Analytic Activism*, 60, 167; Maeve Duggan and Aaron Smith, "The Political Environment on Social Media," Pew Research Center: Internet and Technology, October 25, 2016. Accessed April 2018 at www.pewinternet.org/2016/10/25/the-political-environment-on-social-media/

58   Penney, *The Citizen Marketer* 7, 162–163; Helen Margetts, Peter John, Scott Hale and Taha Yasseri, *Political Turbulence: How Social Media Shape Collective Action* (Princeton: Princeton University Press, 2016), 51–52, 157, 199.

59   Loh and Kanai, "Higher Media Multi-Tasking Activity is Associated with Smaller Gray-Matter Density in the Anterior Cingulate Cortex."

60   Soros, "Remarks delivered at the World Economic Forum."

61   Tufekci, *Twitter and Tear Gas*, 76–77. See also Evgeny Morozov, *To Save Everything, Click Here: The Folly of Technological Solutionism* (New York: Public Affairs, 2013).

62   Robert Bond et al, "A 61-million-person experiment in social influence and political mobilization," *Nature* 489 (13 September 2012): 295–98.

63   Cecilia Kang and Seera Frenkel, "Facebook Says Cambridge Analytica Harvested Data of Up to 87 Million Users," *New York Times*, April 4, 2018. Accessed April 2018 at www.nytimes.com/2018/04/04/technology/mark-zuckerberg-testify-congress.html?emc=edit_na_20180404&nl=breaking-news&nlid=71023177ing-news&ref=cta

64   Hunt Allcott and Matthew Gentzkow, "Social Media and Fake News in the 2016 Election," *Journal of Economic Perspectives*, 31(2) (2017): 211–236.

65   Craig Silverman, "This Analysis Shows How Viral Fake Election News Stories Outperformed Real News On Facebook," November 16, 2016. Accessed April 2018 at: www.buzzfeed.com/craigsilverman/viral-fake-election-news-outperformed-real-news-on-facebook?utm_term=.iqwE8vxWE#.bhl5VkAK5

66   Naomi Oeskes and Eik Conway, *Merchants of Doubt* (New York: Bloomsbury, 2010). And see www.merchantsofdoubt.org/

67   "Lie Hints He May Enter Atomic Control Dispute," Toledo *Blade*, 9 October 1946, 2. Accessed April 2018 at: https://news.google.com/newspapers?id=AgokAAAAIBAJ&sjid=y_8DAAAAIBA-J&pg=5118,1400057&dq=wrong-in-his-facts&hl=en

68   Weinberger, *Too Big to Know*, 41.

69   Cass Sunstein, *#Republic: Divided Democracy in the Age of Social Media* (Princeton: Princeton University Press, 2017).

70   Eli Pariser, *The Filter Bubble* (New York: Penguin, 2011). And see Alexis C. Madrigal, "What Facebook did to American Democracy," *The Atlantic*, October 12, 2017. Accessed April 2018 at: www.theatlantic.com/technology/archive/2017/10/what-facebook-did/542502/

71   Penney, *The Citizen Marketer*, 113; Karpf, *Analytic Activism*, 40.

72    Philip N. Howard, *Pax Technica: How the Internet of Things May Set Us Free or Lock Us Up* (New Haven: Yale University Press, 2015), 209.

73    Carr, *The Glass Cage*, 15.

74    Cathy O'Neil, *Weapons of Math Destruction: How Big Data Increases Inequality and Threatens Democracy* (New York: Crown 2016), 218.

75    Howard, *Pax Technica*.

76    Philip E. Tetlock, *Expert Political Judgment* (Princeton: Princeton University Press, 2005); Leslie Paul Thiele, *The Heart of Judgment: Practical Wisdom, Neuroscience, and Narrative* (Cambridge: Cambridge University Press, 2006.

77    Seth Stephens-Davidowitz, *Everybody Lies: Big Data, New Data, and What the Internet Can Tell Us About Who We Really Are* (New York: Dey Street Books, 2017).

78    Philip Tetlock and Dan Gardner, *Superforecasting: The Art and Science of Prediction* (New York: Crown, 2015), 23; Pietro Michelucci and Janis L. Dickinson, "The Power of Crowds," *Science* 351 (2016): 32–33; and See iNaturalist, citSci.org and SciStarter.

79    Ray Kurzweil, *How to Create a Mind* (New York: Penguin, 2012), 116–17.

80    Ray Kurzweil, *The Singularity is Near: When Humans Transcend Biology* (New York: Viking, 2005), 296.

81    Hans Jonas, *The Imperative of Responsibility: In Search of an Ethics for the Technological Age* (Chicago: University of Chicago Press, 1984), 1, 6, 8.

82    Bill Joy, "Why the Future Doesn't Need Us: Our Most Powerful 21st Century Technologies—Robotics, Genetic Engineering, and Nanotech—are Threatening to Make Humans an Endangered Species," *Wired* (April 2000): 238–62; Bill Joy, "Act Now to Keep New Technologies Out of Destructive Hands," *New Perspectives Quarterly* 21 (4) (Summer 2000): 25–29.

83    Daniel Berleant, *The Human Race to the Future: What Could Happen – and What to Do* (Reno, Nevada: The Lifeboat Foundation, 2015), 61.

84    Bill McKibben, *Enough: Staying Human in an Engineered Age* (New York: Henry Holt, 2003), 198–99.

85    Francis Fukuyama, *Our Posthuman Future* (New York: Picador, 2002), 13, 83, 101.

86    James Hughes, *Citizen Cyborg: Why Democratic Societies Must Respond to the Redesigned Human of the Future* (Cambridge, Mass.: Westview Press, 2004).

87    Leslie Paul Thiele, *Sustainability*, 2nd edn (Cambridge: Polity Press, 2016).

88    Arthur Koestler, *The Ghost in the Machine* (New York: MacMillan, 1967), 312.

89    Wendell Berry, "The Way of Ignorance," in Bill Vitek and Wes Jackson, eds, *The Virtues of Ignorance: Complexity, Sustainability, and the Limits of Knowledge* (Lexington: University of Kentucky Press, 2008), 37.

90    See Leslie Paul Thiele, *Indra's Net and the Midas Touch: Living Sustainably in a Connected World* (Cambridge, Mass.: MIT Press, 2011).

91    John Dewey, *The Political Writings* (Indianapolis: Hackett, 1993), 7–8. See also John Dewey, *Human Nature and Conduct* (Mineola: Dover Publications: 2002); John Dewey, *The Public and its Problems* (Chicago: Gateway, 1946); and Axel Honneth, "Democracy as Reflexive Cooperation: John Dewey and the Theory of Democracy Today," *Political Theory* 266 (1998): 763–83.

92    Martin Heidegger, *The Piety of Thinking*, trans. J. Hart and J. Maraldo (Bloomington: Indiana University Press, 1976), 29, 222; *What is Called Thinking*, trans. J. Gray (New York: Harper and Row, 1968), 130; *On the Way to Language*, trans. P. Hertz (New York: Harper and Row, 1971), 90.

93    Hannah Arendt, *Thinking Without a Bannister* (New York: Schocken Books, 2018), 488.

94    E.F. Schumacher, *Small is Beautiful: Economics as if People Mattered* (New York: Harper and Row, 1973), 32.

# INDEX

aboriginal people 66, 106, 109–113; *see also* native people
accuracy 6–10, 198
activism 100, 191–193
Acton, Lord 76
Adams, Abigail 118
Adams, John Quincy 24
Adorno, Theodore 187
Aeschylus 174
affirmative action 65–66
African Americans 66, 106, 107, 114
agency: debates on human agency 84–85, 88–89, 97; political agency 3, 102
alienation *see* Marx, Karl
allegory of the cave 29
Althusser, Louis 87
*amour-propre* 148
analytics 192, 199
anarchism 26, 58, 60, 133; political thinkers on 42–43, 73, 75, 83, 96–97, 124, 147, 164
Anthony, Susan B. 119
Aquinas, Thomas 40, 160, 165–166
Arab Spring 191
Aragon, Ferdinand of 108
Arendt, Hannah 31, 68, 177, 206
aristocracy 62, 66–67, 75, 117, 150–151
Aristotle: on ethics and judgment 17, 162–166, 169; on knowledge 19, 29, 71, 80; on nurture 46–47; on political life 12, 20, 38, 52, 54, 75, 155, 160, 202; on rule 60, 62, 101, 116, 150; on technology 177, 182, 185
Artificial Intelligence (AI) 200
Ashcraft, Richard 21–22, 32
Auden, W.H. 179
Augustine of Hippo 40, 160
automation 187, 197–198

autonomy 12, 168; individual freedom and 54, 58, 84, 96–97, 99, 106, 122, 125; moral 18; and native Americans 112–113, 122
Aztec empire 109

Bacon, Francis 23–24, 27, 79, 80
Bakunin, Mikhail 58, 133
Barber, Benjamin 149
Baruch, Bernard 195
Baudrillard, Jean 88, 97
Beauvoir, Simone de 119, 124
Behaviorism 8, 98–100; *see also* social sciences
Benhabib, Seyla 115
Berlin, Isaiah 32, 142–143, 145, 148–150
Bill of Rights 53
Black Elk 113
Bonaparte, Napoleon 24
Bourdieu, Pierre 86–87
bourgeoisie 25, 132
Brown, Wendy 126
Burke, Edmund 141, 143

Calhoun, Craig 115
Calvin, John (Calvinism) 152
capitalism 26, 92, 132–133, 153, 187
Carlyle, A.J. 140
Carlyle, Thomas 180–181
Carr, Nicholas 183
checks and balances 76–77
Chodorow, Nancy 123
Christopher Columbus 108–110
Churchill, Winston 202
church-state, separation of 53–54, 127
Cicero 61, 142, 160, 163, 202
clicktivism 192
Coleridge 66

colonization 63, 113, 182, 187
commonwealth 24, 42, 55, 60, 147, 176
communism 25–26, 41, 127–128, 130, 132–133, 148, 187; compared with socialism 134, 136
communitarianism 84, 89, 149
Comte, Auguste 4, 133
Condorcet, Marquis de 81
Connolly, William 22, 88
consequentialism 162
Constant, Benjamin 76, 144, 203
constitutional rights 53, 64
cooperative activity 68
Copernicus, Nicolaus 78, 80
Cortés, Hernán 109–110
Crick, Bernard 52
Crook, George 112
cyber-utopianism 192
cyborg 200–202

Dahl, Robert 58
Daly, Mary 120, 121
Dawkins, Richard 50
Day-Lewis, Cecil 179
Deacon, Terrence 178
Declaration of Independence 105–106, 118
deconstruction 90, 93
deduction 79, 80
Deleuze, Gilles 88
demagogues 67, 82, 93, 99
democracy: in America 26, 66, 77, 94, 142, 195; in ancient Greece 62, 75, 101, 116–117, 140; liberal 26, 64, 66, 135; and rule 61, 67, 93, 135; strong 149; as statecraft and soulcraft 101, 102, 115
Dennet, Daniel 178
deontology 161–162, 167
Derrida, Jacques 88, 90
Descartes, René 81
despotism 43, 60–61, 76, 96, 149; and revolution 32, 42, 141
Destutt de Tracy, Antoine 23–25, 33
Dewey, John 115–116, 176, 204
dialectic 29, 73–75
Dicey, A.V. 144
digital politics 193
Dilthey, Wilhelm 14
discrimination 64–66, 193; see also affirmative action; algorithmic 198–199; reverse 65–66; sexual 116, 119, 120
DNA 44, 49
Downs, Anthony 153–154, 156
Dryzek, John 158
Du Bois, W.E.B. 107
Durkheim, Émile 85–87, 145

ecological 43, 52, 140, 151, 157–159
economic: equality 117, 135; freedom 54; oppression, power 66, 117, 135; rationality 151, 153–157, 159, 167; theory of politics 156
Edelman, Murray 92
education: discrimination in 114, 118; political 19, 64, 74, 149, 202–203; social 24, 40, 47, 64, 65, 84, 113, 126, 135, 185; in virtue 71–72
egalitarianism 114, 120, 135, 187
Einstein, Albert 79, 206
Eisenstein, Hester 124
Eliot, T.S. 197
elites 23, 37, 62, 64, 67, 68, 82, 92–95, 100, 133
Ellul, Jacques 188
Elshtain, Jean-Bethke 52
Enlightenment 81–82, 93, 101, 151, 186, 203
environmentalism 26, 43, 157–159
epistemology 17–19, 51–52; gendered 121, 123–124; ideological frameworks on 28, 87, 101
equality: formal 64, 120; of opportunity 64–65, 120, 125, 134, 149–150, 167; political 18, 66, 117, 119–120, 135; under the law 64–65, 120, 122, 149
equity 61, 122–123, 149, 163–164, 169, 199
Etzioni, Amitai 84
Euben, Roxanne 82

fake news 93, 194–197
false consciousness 25, 131, 146
Fanon, Frantz 63
feminism: 17, 43, 105, 116–126, 151, 168–169
Ferguson, Adam 186
Feuerbach, Ludwig 128, 131
Feynman, Richard 34
Firestone, Shulamith 120
Flanagan, Owen 126
Forster, E.M. 179
fore-conceptions 15
Foucault, Michel 88, 91, 93–98, 100–101; on reason 151; and technology 185
Fourier, François 127
France, Anatole 64, 95
Franklin, Benjamin 112, 195
free speech 142, 149, 195
freedom: economic 54; individual 54, 143, 149, 167; negative and positive 144–145; religious 53–54, 127
Friedan, Betty 119
Friedrich Engels 25–26, 127, 132
Fukuyama, Francis 26, 202
fusion of horizons 16, 169

Gadamer, Hans-Georg 15–16
Galbraith, John Kenneth 181

Galileo 42, 78–80
Gallie, W.B. 22
genes 37; and memes 178, 202; in nature and nurture 44–52
genocide 81, 111
Giddens, Anthony 87
Gilligan, Carol 121, 122–124
Goethe, Johann 185
Goldman, Emma 58
Gore, Al 157
government 40–42, 56, 105–106, 204, 112, 116, 119; definition of 20, 37, 176; and information technology 190–192, 197–198; machinery of 175, 177, 180; power and 57–61, 63, 65, 67, 76, 82–83, 92, 94, 133–134, 147, 160–161; protection from 53, 124, 144, 146
Gramsci, Antonio 92
Green, T.H. 142
Guaranteed Annual Incomes (GAIs) 197
Gutmann, Amy 154

Habermas, Jürgen 97, 156, 187, 192
habitus 86–87
Hammurabi 165
Harraway, Donna 169
Harrington, James 60–61, 76
Hegel, G.W.F. 25, 130–131, 140, 142
hegemony 92, 158
Heidegger, Martin 179, 182
Heilbroner, Robert 157
Henry, Patrick 140
hermeneutic 14–16
Hirschman, Albert O. 156–157
Hobbes, Thomas: 176–177; on human nature 42–43; on power and rule 57, 60, 83, 96; on social contract 125, 147
Holmes, Oliver Wendell 142
hominins 45, 48, 50, 178
*Homo: faber* 177–178; *fabricatus* 178, 203, 205; *politicus* 155; *sapiens* 44–45, 155
Horkeimer, Max 187
Hugo, Victor 204
humanism 80
Hume, David 155, 160
Huxley, Aldous 23, 192

Icarus 179–180
ideal types 10
idealism 24–25, 130–131, 133, 163
identity: 82, 89, 101, 131, 136, 157, 167; and difference 107, 109–110, 114–115; and gender 123 124, 126; and power 95, 97
Ideologues 24, 31
idols of the marketplace 23–24

independence: *see also Declaration of Independence*; of the individual 25, 58, 94, 122–123, 125, 131
individual consciousness 46, 52–53, 95
individualism: 82–84, 92, 95, 106–107; liberal 84; methodological 85, 88, 89; modernist 89, 90; *see also* structuralism
individuality 23, 38–39, 87–88; loss of 97, 110, 136
individuation 115
induction 79
information technology (IT) 176, 183, 191–192
institutions: cultural 47, 86; political 5, 12, 41, 53, 65, 76–78, 82, 95, 102, 202
Intelligence Augmentation (IA) 200, 203
interactionism 45, 49, 178, 202
Internet of Things 199
Iron Law of Oligarchy 9, 67
irony: definition of 3; and ideology 28–34; and postmodernism 91–93

Jackson, Andrew 112
James, William 33
Jameson, Frederic 88
Jefferson, Thomas 24; on liberty 18, 63, 105, 141, 149; and minorities 106–107, 112–113
Johnson, Andrew 112
Johnson, Samuel 148
Jonas, Hans 200
Joy, Bill 200–201
Judaism 108, 112–113, 127–128
justice: distributive 17, 166; *see also* equality (under the law); gender 120, 126, 168; impartial 122, 167–169; procedural 64–65, 122, 164; retributive 166; spheres of 166; substantive 65, 123, 164; spheres of 166
Justinian 165

Kant, Immanuel: on deontological justice 161, 163; on nature and nurture 41, 76–77, 87; on positive and negative liberty 142; on reason 151
Kate, Millett 116
Kelson, Hans 166
Kennedy, John F. 140, 203
Kepler, Johannes 80
King James of England 60
King, Martin Luther Jr. 63, 114
Koestler, Arthur 203
Kraft, Michael 189
Kurzweil, Ray 200
Kymlicka, Will 166

labor: division of 38, 87; Marx on 127, 129–132, 187–188; and property 144, 167–168; and women 117, 127
Laclau, Ernesto 135

language: as technology/tool 176–179, 186, 188, 199, 202; games 91; of politics 22

Las Casas, Bartolomé de 110

Lasswell, Harold 83–84

Leibniz, Gottfried Wilhelm 184

Lenin, Vladimir 25, 27–28

Lévi-Strauss, Claude 86–87

liberalism 84, 124–125, 135, 149

liberation technology 190

libertarians: positive 145–146, 148–149; negative 144–145, 148–149

liberty: civil 26 53, 58, 83; positive and negative 146–150; private 148; public 146

Lincoln, Abraham 55

Locke, John 24, 61, 83, 98, 142, 144

Louis XVI 141

Luther, Martin 185–186, 204

Lyotard, Jean-François 88–89

Macedo, Stephen 151

Machiavelli, Niccolò 15, 57, 61

machinery of government 174, 177, 180

MacIntyre, Alasdair 84, 115, 166

Macpherson, C.B. 43

Madison, James 41, 161

Mannheim, Karl 27

March, James 154

Marcuse, Herbert 187

Marx, Karl: on alienation and conflict 128–130, 132–136, 167, 187; on freedom and liberty 145 146, 149; on human nature 41–42; on ideology 24–28, 131–132, 134, 186; see also Marxism; see also production; on religion 127–128

Marxism: 25, 132, 143, 249, 167, 187; neo- 92, 135; orthodox 92; structural 87

mastery 152–153; over oneself 74, 145; over nature 81, 177, 182, 187

materialism 131–132, 134, 185

McKibben, Bill 201

McLuhan, Marshall 23, 177, 181, 190

memes 37, 49–51; as technological artifacts 176, 178–179, 184–185, 193, 202

metanarrative 89

methodologies 18

Michelet, Jules 81

Michels, Robert 9, 67

micro-donations 193

Midas touch 181–182, 185

Milbrath, Lester 159

Miliband, Ralph 135

Mill, John Stuart 8, 15, 118, 124, 143, 162

Mills, C. Wright 67

Mills, Charles 168

minorities 9, 65–67, 107, 114, 124, 166

modernism 78–82, 89, 92, 93, 98, 101; see also individualism (methodological); individualist 85; liberal 89; see also postmodernism; see also scholasticism

monarchy 60, 62, 75, 94, 143, 150–151

Montaigne, Michel de 162

Montesquieu, Baron de 61–62, 76, 142, 163

Montezuma 109

morality of care 122

morality of rights 122

More, Thomas 133

mores: cultural 120–123, 126, 143–144, 147; ecological 159; and genes 37, 46–52; of the Greeks 74; and postmodernists 89, 92, 97–99; as technological artifacts 176, 179, 185–186, 202–203

Morozov, Evgeny 192

Mosca, Gaetano 67

Mouffe, Chantal 135

Moynihan, Daniel Patrick 195

Mubarak, Hosni 190–191

Mumford, Lewis 177

Mussolini, Benito 175

Mutualists 58

Nagel, Thomas 62

native people 63, 107, 109–113

nature and nurture 39, 44–46, 49, 178; see also interactionism

Nazism 196

Newton, Isaac 9, 80

Nietzsche, Friedrich 31, 90

Niebuhr, Reinhold 77

normative theory 16–18, 20, 33, 151, 179, 203

Obama, Barack 190

Okin, Susan Moller 168

oligarchy 9, 62, 67, 75; see also iron law of oligarchy

original position 125, 168

Orr, David 158–159

Orwell, George 23, 192

otherness 98, 114, 116

padeia 71; see also education in virtue

Paine, Thomas 40–41, 117

Pareto, Vilfredo 67

parsimony 5–7, 9–10, 13, 33, 154

partiality 169

Pateman, Carole 121, 168

patriarchy 43, 117, 121, 124, 169

Patterson, Orlando 141

Peace of Westphalia 21, 43, 186

Pericles 71

perspectivism 90–91, 93

Pettit, Philip 12, 61, 76

philosopher king 19, 43, 62, 75–76, 150, 163–164; *see also* philosophy

philosophy: role of 32, 72–74, 77, 128, 205; *and see* political philosophy

Pinker, Steven 82

Plato 20, 30, 42, 62, 71, 74, 77, 80, 133, 146, 150, 154–155, 176–177, 185, 203; and

pluralism 53, 75, 135, 151, 163, 166

Plutarch 155

Poggi, Gianfranco 59

*poiesis* 155

*polis* 55, 117, 155

political: actors 68, 155; participation 66, 117, 149, 154, 190–193; parties 9, 68; philosophy 1, 4, 58, 205; technology 172, 206; theory 1–3, 11–12, 22–23

political animal 22, 39, 129, 202; Aristotle on 38, 52, 155, 177; and genetics 44, 49, 52

polity 61, 72–73, 75, 89, 150, 177

Pope, Alexander 163

Popper, Karl 34

populism 26, 67

posthumanist 202

postmodernism 85, 88–101, 135; *see also* modernism; *see also* structuralism (post)

power: over 56, 68, 143; with 68; of wealth 56, 59; of eloquence 56; of authority 56, 59; of prestige 56; of tradition 56; of coercion 56, 59; of might 56; elite 92

practical judgment 1, 20, 114–115; definition of 12, 164, 169; memes and mores 179, 203; and technology 182, 188, 206

*praxis* 155–156

privacy 53, 116

private property 54; Marx on 130, 134–135, 144–147

private realm 52–54, 116–117, 143

Procrustean 33, 108, 163

production: forces of 186; means of 131, 134, 186–187; mode of 186–187

progressivism 81, 187

proletariat 132, 133

Promethean 175, 178, 187, 204

Protestant Reformation 78, 153, 186, 204

Proudhon, Pierre-Joseph 58

prudence 60, 164

public: good 52–55, 60–62; realm 53, 116–118, 126, 148, 168, 192

race 44, 64, 86, 115; in history 109, 111–112; politics of identity and 124–125, 126

rationality: as action 153–154, 157; bounded 153, 155; communicative 151; ecological 158; economic 151, 153–157, 159, 167; feminist and

masculine 151; modern 82, 152; religious 152; strategic 188

Rawls, John 53, 125–126, 161–162, 168

reason 40–45, 49; *see also* dialectic; ecological, 151, 157; economic 151; and the philosopher 72 74; political 151, 154, 188; scholastic 154–155

Reign of Terror 23, 63

Renaissance 78, 80, 146

*res publica* 55

resistance 113, 146, 185; and individuals 59, 92; and power 60–61, 83, 92, 97, 100, 109–110

revolution: American 63, 105, 140; behavioral 99–100; Communist 25, 127, 128, 130–133; Copernican 79; French 8, 32, 58, 63, 117, 141, 143; Industrial 117; Jasmine 191; proletarian 25, 92; Scientific 78, 80–81

Rich, Barnaby 184

Rochefoucauld, François La 161

Roosevelt, Theodore 112

Rorty, Richard 88, 90–91

Roszak, Theodore 158

Rousseau, Jean-Jacques 106, 125, 143, 145–149, 177

Russell, Bertrand 56, 155

Sabine, George 22

Saint-Simon, Claude Henri de 8, 26

Sandel, Michael 4, 84

Santayana, George 21

Sarewitz, Daniel 175

Sartori, Giovanni 67

Saussure, Ferdinand de 90

scholasticism 24, 79–80, 101; medieval 154–155

Schumpeter, Joseph 156

science: of ideas 24; natural 8–10, 16, 54, 90; physical 8; scientific theory 7–11, 13; social 8–10, 12, 56, 88–90, 153

segregationists 63, 114

self: consciousness 38–39, 49; knowledge 16, 115; mastery 145

Shakespeare, William 46, 144

Shelley, Mary 180

Sheridan, Phil 112

Shklar, Judith 21

Sibley, Mulford 188

significance 6–7, 10, 18, 41

Simon, Herbert 155, 192

Skinner, B.F. 98–100, 203

Skinner, Quentin 21

slavery 38, 81; Marx on 187; in North America 106, 110–111, 114; Rousseau on 145, 146

smart mobs 190, 194

Smith, Adam 158, 186

smombie 181

social contract theory 106–107, 124, 125, 147, 168

social structures 84–88
social media 12, 50, 91; and fake news 196–197, 204; and political action 176, 189–194, 204
socialism 25–27, 105, 124, 127, 133–135, 197
Socrates 19, 67, 72–75, 115, 206; as ironist 28–32, 91; *see also* Socratic Method
Socratic method 51, 73; *see also* Dialectic; *see also* Socrates
Soros, George 192
soulcraft 71–72, 74, 102, 115, 206
souls: Aristotle on 150, 162; Plato on 40, 71–77, 160, 177; religion and 110, 128; Tocqueville on 94–95; soulcraft 71–72, 74, 102, 115, 206
sovereignty 20–21, 42–43, 60, 62–63, 83, 94, 96–97, 186; individual 144, 147
Spanish Inquisition 108
Spragens, Thomas 151
Stalinism 196
standing-reserve 182
Stanton, Elizabeth Cady 119
statecraft 71–72, 74, 102, 115, 206
Strauss, Leo 17–18, 29, 185
structuralism: 85–86, 88, 89–90; determinism 97; *see also* Marxism, *see also* poststructuralism 88
Supreme Court 114, 116
sustainability 158–159, 192, 203
symbolic: language 177–179, 188, 202; power 115; species 178, 204; tools 177–178, 202

*tabula rasa*
tautology 6–7
Tawney, R.H. 136, 159
Taylor, Harriet 118
*techne* 174, 177, 182, 188
technological artifact 52, 176–181, 185, 188, 202–203
Thompson, Dennis 154
Thoreau, Henry David 99, 181
Thrasymachus 29, 67, 161
Thucydides 43, 67
Tocqueville, Alexis de 94, 96, 111, 143
Todorov, Tzvetan 108–109
totalitarian 67, 133, 136, 192

traditionalism 78–80
transhumanist 202
trite 7
Trump, Donald 190, 195
Tufecki, Zeynep 191
tyranny 60, 62–63 75–77, 98, 120, 141, 148; tranny of the majority 94, 143

utilitarianism 162, 167

Vernant, Jean-Pierre 155
Vig, Norman 189
virtue signaling 193
Voltaire, Francois 79, 196
voting 54, 59, 156; and information technology 190, 194; voter turnout 66; and women 106, 117, 119

Waal, Frans de 48
Walzer, Michael 101, 166
war 5, 42, 48–49, 57, 60, 81, 96, 101, 147; Civil 114; Cold 175; *see also* colonization; Indian 112; Peloponnesian 43; Thirty Years 21; World War I 119; World War II 26, 119; *see also* revolutions
Warren, Earl 114
Washakie of the Shoshone 113
Washington, George 112
Weber, Max 10, 14, 27, 57–58
Winner, Langdon 188
Wittgenstein, Ludwig 32
Wolin, Sheldon 12, 115
Wollstonecraft, Mary 117, 203
women: genetics 46–48; political representation of 107, 119, 127; as political unequals 17, 65–66, 106, 116–118, 120, 125, 168, 150; religious inequality and morality 121–124, 203; as victims 126
women's suffrage movement 119

Young, Iris Marion 167, 169

*zoon politikon* 38–39, 177